OLD ENGLISH SHEEPDOGS

OLD ENGLISH SHEEPDOGS

Sylvia Woods &
Ray Owen

FABER AND FABER
LONDON BOSTON

First published in 1981
by Faber and Faber Limited
3 Queen Square London WC1N 3AU
Photoset by Granada Graphics, Mitcham
Printed in Great Britain by
Lowe & Brydone Ltd, Thetford
All rights reserved

British Library Cataloguing in Publication Data

Woods, Sylvia
  Old English sheepdogs.
  1. Old English sheep-dogs
  I. Title   II. Owen, Ray
  636.7′3   SF429.04

ISBN 0-571-11620-5

Contents

List of Plates

between pages 128 and 129

Acknowledgements

Our grateful thanks are due to many people for their help and encouragement while writing this book. In particular we should like to thank the Kennel Club for providing access to the Old English Sheepdog championship records and especially Mr J. Davies of the Awards Department for his help and co-operation, Messrs Sotheby and Co. for allowing us to search through their photographic records of old paintings and the British Library for making available so many otherwise unobtainable books. We wish to thank also Mrs Zoë Wyatt and Miss Judith Mackenzie who so kindly gave their time to talk about and demonstrate the art of spinning dog hair, Mr Peter Hughes for his advice on Chapter Five and Ray's wife Glenda for typing the manuscript and providing so many helpful suggestions as the book evolved. So far as photographs are concerned, we are grateful to Vic Keith who took most of them, to Percy Clegg for no. 3, to Don Holloway for nos. 6 and 21, and to the Bristol Associated Press and the BBC for permission to reproduce nos. 23 and 24 respectively.

Chapter 1

HISTORY AND CHARACTERISTICS
OF THE BREED

There have probably been sheepdogs for as long as man has herded sheep and that is a very long time indeed. Classical writers describe the ideal pastoral dog as one capable of both defending and herding, and as the Old English Sheepdog can so ably fulfil this dual role, it may be that the origin of the breed lies somewhere in selective breeding by shepherds. This probably took place over several centuries, resulting in a dog suited to our climate and terrain, strong and courageous enough to defend his charges yet adaptable enough to learn the herding techniques of the smaller dogs. So, although no definitive account exists of the ancestry of the Old English Sheepdog, it is likely that his present-day identity owes much to this search for a dual-purpose animal.

By the beginning of the nineteenth century, pastoral dogs still remained grouped, regardless of type, under the general heading of shepherd's or drover's dogs, but both written and pictorial descriptions were beginning to distinguish between the Highland Collie, other types of collies and the rough-coated sheep and cattle dogs, and it was the rough-coated dogs which, on the whole, tended to have docked tails. Richard Parkinson, whose *Treatise on Breeding and Management of Livestock* appeared in 1810, furnishes us with a description of a type of sheepdog which was appearing in increasing numbers, especially in the south, that more closely resembles the bobtail of

13

today. He writes '. . . there is one particular breed which seems naturally the best adapted [to droving] viz. a rough sort with a very long coat of soft hair, and distinguished by being without tails. Their colour is black or blue, with a white ring about the neck, a bald face and the belly and feet are white . . . the county of Dorset lays claim to this breed of dog and they are certainly to be found more generally in that county than in any other, but they are most frequently seen at Smithfield attending the London drovers. The hair of these dogs is a necessary protection against the severity of the weather as they have to lie by the fold side during many cold days while the shepherd is dressing the flock.' Parkinson himself bought 'two whelps of the rough Dorset kind' to work for him.

It is during the latter part of the nineteenth century that the rough-coated bobtail seems to have appeared in large enough numbers to draw attention to himself and to be distinguishable as a breed sufficiently unlike the other sheepdogs which were being used at the time, to warrant a special name. So he began to be called 'the sheepdog' to distinguish him from 'the collie' and then one finds he is called 'the English sheepdog' (possibly because the collies at the time were often called, correctly or incorrectly, Highland Collies). A little later, at the turn of the century, he is granted his full title of Old English Sheepdog. Dean's *Penny Guide Book on Dogs*, written by Dr Gordon Stables in 1909, contains illustrations of dogs. The 'sheepdog' picture is of an Old English Sheepdog, while two drawings of 'collies' show a Border Collie and the rough-haired 'Lassie' type. By 1914, W. D. & H. O. Wills Tobacco Company of Bristol had issued a cigarette card of an Old English Sheepdog. A little earlier, the 1903 edition of *Our Friend the Dog*, also by Dr Stables, had included a chapter on the Old English Sheepdog which was not in the earlier editions of the book published in 1877 and 1884. The 1903 edition had been updated to include 'an appendix of the latest breeds'. The book has, besides a textual description, two illustrations of the Old English Sheepdog. The picture in the introductory chapter does not look very much like a member of the breed, with its dark coat and Bearded Collie

14

head, but the illustration placed immediately above the written description is just like the Old English Sheepdog as we know it today.

While Parkinson suggests Dorset as the county of origin of these dogs, other authorities cite Oxfordshire, Wiltshire, Berkshire, Hertfordshire and Sussex. There were, in fact, so many bobtails working in Sussex that they earned for themselves at one time the name of the Old English or Sussex Sheepdog, and Adelaide Gossett devotes a whole chapter to the breed under this name in her *Shepherds of Britain*, published in 1911. These dogs are described as being 'shaggy, with a great deal of woolly hair over the eyes as in the face of the poodle, bluish-grey and white in colour, with stumpy tails and very intelligent'. The text is illustrated with a picture of Bob, a Sussex Sheepdog belonging to shepherd Dick Flint of Blatchington, which is easily recognizable as an Old English Sheepdog. The same book contains a chapter on 'The Shepherd and his Dog', contributed by Walter Baxendale. He distinguishes three types of shepherd's dogs: the rough-coated collie, the smooth-coated collie and the Old English Sheepdog. He remarks that these three breeds are being given classes at shows and that a fourth type, the Shetland Sheepdog, is also being given a few classes.

Although most of the evidence seems to show that the breed beginning to be known as the Old English Sheepdog was mainly confined to the south, there were members of the breed to be found in the north as well. Adelaide Gossett quotes a Scottish friend as writing in a letter, 'You have a very beautiful old breed of sheepdog in Sussex. I have seen them in the north where they are always called Sussex Sheepdogs.' There is also a story told by Dr Edwardes-Ker, an early breeder of the Old English Sheepdog, of how one of these dogs, purchased in Dumfries and sent down south with a cattle drover, ran away after a fortnight, back to his former owners. This link with Dumfries recalls the Gainsborough portrait of the Third Duke of Buccleugh, painted in 1771, where the Duke has his arms clasped about what appears to be an Old English Sheepdog. It is considered by many people to be the oldest known portrait of the breed. The Duke of Buccleugh's residence, where the portrait was painted, is Drumlanrig Castle, some twenty miles from the town of Dumfries.

Reading through these various accounts of the breed, and studying the accompanying illustrations, one begins to suspect that even in the early years of the twentieth century, there were still several versions of the Old English Sheepdog. Certainly, at the very earliest shows, that is from 1873, when three members of the breed were first exhibited in Birmingham, there were several varieties of sheepdog which might, more or less, be classed as Old English.

Among them was one which stood out as particularly attractive and typical. He had a long, rough, blue-merle coat, smallish ears hanging close to the side of his head which was white or white and grey with long, shaggy hair and he had a bobbed tail. In 1888, in order to perfect and perpetuate this type, Mr William G. Weager and a band of enthusiastic breeders founded the Old English Sheepdog Club and earned for themselves the following comment from Rawdon Lee in his *History of the Collie or Sheepdog* published two years later in 1890: 'As a fact, the Collie Club refuses to acknowledge him [the bobtail] so he is left to the tender mercies of a few enthusiastic admirers who formed a special club of their own to promote and foster their fancy and it will be the fault of the public rather than of themselves if the bobtailed sheepdog does not blossom into a fashionable beauty.' Rawdon Lee thought that it would not, but the subsequent history of the breed has proved how wrong he was.

One of the first tasks of the newly founded club was to establish a Standard which would lay down rules about what the breed was to look like for all time. As Aubrey Hopwood remarks in his *Old English Sheepdog* of 1905, this was a formidable task because 'there were about as many different types of bobtail as there were members of the club and each member stood staunchly by his own.' However, between them they evolved a standard and set out to breed all future bobtails to that conformation. Thanks to the devoted work of these early breeders, the Old English Sheepdog emerged with the desirable qualities fixed in and the less desirable attributes bred out, and breeders and owners of today's dogs owe them a tremendous debt of gratitude.

As the original Breed Standard differs in some respects from the present one, the earlier one is set out here as a matter of interest.

THE 1888 BREED STANDARD

Skull	Capacious and rather squarely formed, giving plenty of room for brain power. The parts over the eyes should be well-arched and the whole well covered with hair as defined in 'coat'.
Jaw	Should be fairly long and square. The 'stop' should be defined but not to a great extent.
Eyes	These, of course, vary in different colours of dogs. In the dark blue shades they should be dark brown. In the lighter colours, they will be found to follow them and become paler in shade, while where white predominates, a wall or marble eye may be considered very typical.
Nose	Always black in colour, fairly large and capacious.
Teeth	Strong and firm and should be evenly placed in the jaw. Working dogs often have their incisors broken off. [See Chapter Eleven, p. 202.] This is in no way detrimental.
Ears	Medium sized and carried close to the head, coated with hair of moderate length.
Legs	The forelegs should be straight and possess plenty of bone. They should remove the body a medium height off the ground, without approaching legginess. They should be well-coated all round.

Feet   Moderately large; round; toes well-arched and pads capacious and hard.

Tail   This is a most important point in the Old English Sheepdog. Without a doubt many dogs are bred without the slightest approach to a caudal appendage, while on the other hand, some in the litters will be found with half, three-quarter and whole-length tails. The breeding of those without tails should be encouraged and persevered with and be given preference to in judging providing the dogs are good elsewhere. A tail of any length takes away the appearance and the corkiness of the dog. A docked dog can generally be detected by the bluntness at the end of the stump.

Neck and Shoulders   The neck should be fairly long, arched and graceful and well-coated with hair. The shoulders should be set on slopingly and the dog generally to be found to stand lower at the shoulders than on the hind quarters.

Body   Rather short and very compact. The ribs should be well sprung, and brisket deep and capacious. The loin should be very stout and to a certain extent arched, while the hind quarters should be bulky, the hams densely covered with coat, very often of a softer and more woolly description than is to be found on other parts of the body.

Coat   Profuse and of good texture i.e. fairly hard and strong. There should also be a double or under coat.

Colour   Varies, but preference should be given to dark blue, light or pigeon blue and steel grey dogs. The colours are generally intermixed with white, which imparts to the dog a more attractive appearance. White collars, legs, chest and face should be encouraged.

Height   Fair stand and measurement of the shoulder from twenty inches upwards. The bitches, of course, smaller than the dogs. Great height is not to be encouraged, for it takes away from the corkiness and cobbiness of the dog.

General
Appearance He is a strong, compact looking dog, profusely coated all over. He generally gallops with his head down, having a peculiar springing style of movement, and his whole make and shape of body should strike one as being very much after the style of a bear. An animal which people not conversant with the breed will generally quote as an analogy.

The scale of points by which the dog should be judged was set out in the following manner:

Skull	10	Legs (if coated)	10
Jaw	5	Tail (undocked)	10
Eyes	5	Neck and shoulders	10
Nose	5	Body, loin, hind quarters	10
Colour	10	Coat	10
Teeth	5	Marking	5
Ears	5		
		Total	100

Not all of those interested in the breed were in full agreement over the Standard. Some considered that docked tails were neater than the short stumps the undocked dogs were born with and wondered what should be done about the majority of the members of each litter which were born *with* a tail. The question of size was also controversial; some considered it to be far too small, for many of the good working dogs were much larger. Dr Edwardes-Ker, a founder member of the club and one of the most enthusiastic and optimistic of breeders, was particularly outspoken: 'Are they trying to breed whippets?' he demanded.

Dr Edwardes-Ker was convinced that the breed was one of very ancient origin and that, provided there was English

Sheepdog blood somewhere in the strain, a perfect specimen would from time to time turn up. He writes as no breeder would dare to do today, and claims that he '. . . owned first-class sheepdogs whose parentage would make one's hair stand on end with amazement at the fearful incongruity of its component parts'. He describes liaisons between animals which had shown no sign of sheepdog blood, resulting in a pup with jet-black fur and white markings who, 'in a few weeks, chameleon-like, assumes the silvery blue livery of his ancient British ancestors and makes his bow to the public as a pigeon blue and white English sheepdog, "breeder and pedigree unknown".'

This search for the elusive pigeon-blue coat obsessed Dr Edwardes-Ker, but to his chagrin, after a long search he only managed to produce blue-grizzle dogs who became smaller with each succeeding generation. In desperation, he mated his elderly bitch, Dame Margery, to Jockey, a large bobtailed dog with a thick, but smooth coat of yellow sable, in hopes of improving size. To his great surprise, one of Dame Margery's two pups had a coat which turned into the prized pigeon blue. This puppy was named Sir Caradoc and sired the prize-winning Sir Cavendish. Dame Margery had been bought at Norwich Market for half a crown, and this method of obtaining dogs was typical of the time, when breeders would keep their eyes open for likely specimens among the Smithfield dogs and other working dogs which they would purchase for a few shillings. The sire of another famous dog was obtained in this way; this was Bob, a huge grizzled dun-coloured animal, standing twenty-five inches at the shoulder, who was bought from a local shepherd. Bob sired Sir Guy, a fine Old English Sheepdog who was the first champion to be made up under Kennel Club rules. One of the most famous dogs of these early days, Wall-eyed Bob owned by Mrs Fare-Fosse, is said to have changed hands at a pub for a sovereign.

The early breeders watched each other's efforts with interest and were free in their criticism. Dr Edwardes-Ker describes Watchman, a fellow breeder's dog, as a beautiful animal to look at, but not a good specimen of a bobtail with his coat worn in ringlets and his ears 'as big as a blacksmith's apron'. In his own highly descriptive terms, he tells his readers what a bobtail's coat *should* look like. His hair should be like that 'on a clodhopping countryman's head . . . no curl, but the sort of head you could wipe your boots on.' This is hardly the language of the official Breed Standard, but it is clear what he meant.

These early champions and other outstanding dogs had a much longer show career than the dogs of today and they also won an outstanding number of awards. The breed was still in its early stages of development and there were not so many good dogs around as there are now, but the good ones had the reputation for being fine specimens of great character and proved an excellent foundation for the generations of bobtails who have followed them. Ch. Sir Cavendish, born on 29 May 1887, sired by Sir Caradoc out of Dame Ruth, bred by Dr Edwardes-Ker and owned by Dr Lock, did very well in the years 1888 to 1894. He won at Birmingham in 1888 and at Gloucester, Cardiff, Brighton and Crystal Palace in 1890. In the following year he won firsts at Crufts, Liverpool, Bath, Manchester, Birmingham, Gloucester and Crystal Palace. In 1892 he won again at Crufts, Bath, Leeds, Manchester, Crystal Palace, Leeds and the Kennel Club.

In 1893 and 1894 he took first prizes at Birmingham, Preston and Portsmouth. There was also Ch. Watchboy, born in July 1890, sired by Stracathro Bouncing Bob out of Nellie II, bred by Mr R. Abbot. He won over twelve firsts and four CCs and was the ancestor of many later prize-winning dogs and bitches. Harkaway, born in 1891, sired by Grizzle Bob out of Rachel, bred by Mr J. Thomas, was another well-known winner of his day and proved to be a very good stud dog. Aubrey Hopwood recalls him particularly for his exceptionally good coat which he passed on to succeeding generations of bobtails.

Ch. Victor Cavendish, born in 1879, sired by Young Watch out of Grey Queen, was bred by Messrs Thickett and Shaw. His maternal grandsire was Sir Cavendish. He did exceptionally well, winning forty-two firsts and twenty-five special prizes at twenty-eight shows, and he won the Old English

Sheepdog Challenge Cup three times. Photographs of this great prizewinner show that he was mismarked on his rump, where he had a noticeable white area. Mrs Fare-Fosse bred Ch. Rough Weather who was born in 1900, sired by Sir James out of Daphne. He distinguished himself by winning 150 first and special prizes. Ch. Dairymaid was one of the best bitches in her day. Owned and bred by Mr Weager, she died young, but in her four years of life she was virtually unbeatable, winning major awards at Crufts, Birmingham and the Kennel Club in 1892 and 1893. Ch. Lady Scaramouche, born in 1893, sired by Ch. Watchboy out of Lady Cavendish and bred by Dr Lock, won many CCs during her show career which spanned the years 1895 to 1901.

No one is sure of the parentage of Dame Barbara who was owned by Sir Humphrey Trafford, president of the Old English Sheepdog Club. She won CCs at Birmingham and Crystal Palace in 1898 and in Liverpool in 1899. Another outstanding bitch was Ch. Fairweather, born in 1898, sired by Sir James out of Birthday and bred by Mrs Fare-Fosse. In 1899 at Crufts as a nine-month-old, she won every prize for which she was eligible, gaining a CC and eleven special prizes. In her show career, she won literally hundreds of prizes and cups, and also found time to produce four litters of puppies. While this outstanding bitch was having such phenomenal success as a puppy, another outstanding champion-to-be was born. This was Ch. Bouncing Lass sired by Young Watch out of Peggy Primrose. She was bred by Mr Butterworth and owned first of all by Mr C. W. Macbeth. After winning her first three CCs, she was bought by Mr W. S. Tilley and his brother and went on to win more. After the Tilley brothers took her to America and sold her there she took the Vanderbilt Cup in New York in 1903 and 1904 and contributed much to the popularity of the breed on the other side of the Atlantic.

These were some of the dogs and their owners who are looked upon as the pioneers of the breed, and it may be said by some that the Breed Standard laid down by the committee of the Old English Sheepdog Club a few years after its foundation in 1888 has remained virtually unchanged since that time. On the other hand, many today are only too aware that among the Standards of the Working Group, of which the bobtail is a member, the one set out for the Old English Sheepdog is among the shortest and least detailed. While the Standard for the Boxer, a relative newcomer to the Working Group, commands three pages of closely defined directions, the bobtail's Standard is covered by three-quarters of a page. The Standard gives no specific guidance as to weight and height and this omission has allowed variations to creep in. On the whole, the breed appears to be getting smaller, and some fear that if the trend continues, the Old English Sheepdog will no longer be looked upon as a large breed. Nor is the Standard clear about the vexed question of white markings on the body. A white flash on the grey-blue body coat means for most judges and breeders that the dog is mismarked, but there is no official recognition of this in the Breed Standard. There are other ambiguities: for example, how long is 'fairly long' as applied to the jaw, and how 'moderately coated' should bobtails' ears be? A newcomer to the breed is always advised to visit the show rings to see what a good specimen of the breed looks like, and this is sensible, practical advice, but with a Breed Standard which is lacking in so many clear directives, differences begin to appear in the ring and it is very confusing for the novice and even the experienced breeder to steer a course through all the slight, but increasingly significant differences in conformation which show in the breed.

There has been at least one welcome change in the updated Breed Standard of 1978. Previously, the colour had been described as 'Any shade of grey, grizzle, blue or merle, with or without white markings or in reverse', which meant that a dog with a white body and grey head could be admitted into the show ring. In fact this never happened, because tradition (not the Standard) decreed that this was unacceptable. The 1978 Standard omits the words '. . . or in reverse'.

THE KENNEL CLUB STANDARD OF THE OLD
ENGLISH SHEEPDOG, 1978

General
appearance   A strong, compact-looking dog of great sym-
metry; absolutely free of legginess; profusely
coated all over; very elastic in a gallop but in
walking or trotting has a characteristic ambling or
pacing movement; and his bark should be loud,
with a peculiar 'pot-casse' ring in it. All round he
is a thick set, muscular, able-bodied dog, with a
most intelligent expression, free of all Poodle or
Deerhound character.

Head and
skull   Skull capacious and rather squarely formed,
giving plenty of room for brain power. The parts
over the eyes should be well arched and the whole
covered with hair. Jaws fairly long, strong, square
and truncated; the stop should be defined to avoid
a Deerhound face. Nose always black, large and
capacious.

Eyes   Dark or wall eyes are to be preferred.

Ears   Small and carried flat to side of head, coated
moderately.

Mouth   Teeth strong and large, evenly placed and level.

Neck   The neck should be fairly long, arched gracefully
and well-coated with hair.

Forequarters The forelegs should be dead straight, with plenty
of bone, holding the body well from the ground,
without approaching legginess; well-coated all
round. The shoulders sloping and narrow at the
points, the dog standing lower at the shoulders
than at the loin.

Body   Rather short and very compact, ribs well sprung
and brisket deep and capacious. The loin should
be very stout and gently arched.

Hindquarters The hindquarters should be round and muscular,

	hocks well let down and the hams densely coated with a thick, long jacket in excess of that of any part of the body.
Feet	Small, round; toes well arched, and pads thick and round.
Tail	Puppies requiring docking should have the operation performed within a week from birth, preferably within four days.
Coat	Profuse, and of good hard texture; not straight, but shaggy and free from curl. The undercoat should be a waterproof pile when not removed by grooming.
Colour	Any shade of grey, grizzle, blue or blue merle, with or without white markings; any shade of brown or sable to be considered distinctly objectionable and not to be encouraged.
Weight and size	Twenty-two inches and upwards for dogs, slightly less for bitches. Type, symmetry and character of the greatest importance, and on no account to be sacrificed to size alone.
Faults	A long, narrow head.

Note — Male animals should have two apparently normal testicles fully descended into the scrotum.

SCALE OF POINTS as laid down by the O.E.S. Club in an advisory capacity.

Head	5	Jaw	10
Eyes	5	Nose	5
Colour	10	Teeth	5
Ears	5	Legs	10
Body, loins and hind-quarters	20	Neck and shoulders	10
		Coat	15
		Total	100

A Closer Look at the Breed Standard

From the judge's point of view, the sheepdog's head is worth over one third of the maximum possible points he can award the dog. It is therefore a feature of some importance. The Standard specifically notes that the skull should be 'squarely formed', any tendency towards a long, narrow head is quite out of character and falls short of the typical large, shaggy head of the bobtail. The jaw must be fairly long and square and the stop, that is the part of the face where the muzzle begins to jut out from the forehead just below the eyeline, well defined. In other words, the forehead should not slope as with the greyhound type of face; on the other hand, neither should the muzzle stick out from a rounded forehead like a poodle's. In show ring bobtails, the head hair is very long and the eyes cannot be seen, but their colour is a matter of importance. Very dark brown are to be preferred, although the 'wall eye', which resembles a china-blue pearl button, is also correct. All those light browns to yellow, waspy colours are most objectionable. Wishing to preserve the merle coat, the early breeders devoted themselves to breeding out the brown coats (which are seen as correct and acceptable in the Old English Sheepdog's close relative, the Bearded Collie) and it was found that the lighter shades of brown eye colour related to light brown coats, while the darkest grey and blue coats had a corresponding dark brown eye colour. But now that the brown and fawn coats are almost bred out of the Old English Sheepdog, the resulting matings of greys to blues of all colours has produced eye colour of equal variance; although all the genes are present to give many eye colours, only dark brown or blue is considered correct. Eye rim pigmentation is not asked for in the Standard, but nothing sets off a good eye better than a dark ring separating the white of the eye from the white coat on the head.

The ears should have a moderate coating of hair and be carried flat to the sides of the head, so that they are virtually indistinguishable among the mass of face and head hair. Although the Breed Standard calls for 'small ears', the term is relative because a tiny ear would look as ridiculously out of proportion as a large, spaniel-type ear. The ear flap, or leather, as it is called, should be placed neither too high nor too low down on the side of the head but in a position where it will not affect the balance of the chrysanthemum-shaped head as it sits atop the neck, nor be damaged when the dog is at work. Although the ears generally lie flat, a young dog, while teething, will tend to have fly-away ears, but these settle down when teething troubles are over. There is nothing so charming as a bobtail 'using' his ears when encountering a strange noise, while at the same time tilting his head from side to side.

On the sheepdog's face, all that should show, apart from the hair, is the huge, usually moist, black nose. The small, button-like noses one often encounters on pretty bitches are quite wrong and can be blamed on the incorrect truncation of the muzzle behind. The length of pink tongue which usually protrudes immediately beneath the nose is an entirely endearing quality, but one which is, of course, irrelevant to the Breed Standard.

Some judges, while putting great emphasis on the dog's teeth, in fact examine only the incisors. The adult bobtail should have forty-two teeth. The lower jaw has six incisors, two canines, eight premolars and six molars, and the upper jaw has six incisors, two cannines, eight premolars and four molars. The Standard is ambiguous on the subject of teeth, which gives rise to many an argument. The bite most favoured by judges is that of a 'tight scissor', with the upper set of teeth overlapping the lower. The 'level' referred to in the Standard surely means that the teeth are upright in the gums in a level plane—not, as is commonly seen, with the middle two bottom incisors leaning out or stepped forward. The two main faults to be found in this area are the undershot jaw where the lower set of teeth project beyond the upper set, and the overshot jaw where the upper set project well over and beyond the lower teeth.

The ideal bobtail leg has strong, flat bone; it should be heavy enough to carry the body above it and, with 'balance' in mind, should be proportional to the size and sex of the dog. The dog should not appear leggy by reason of extra long fore-feet, and his legs should be well-coated all round with hair. The pasterns should be strong, the feet small with thick-skinned, compact, round pads and well-arched toes. The idea of a bobtail with small feet may sound incongruous to those who do not know the breed, but in point of fact, he should stand well-poised on legs and feet which should not splay out—a condition commonly known in the breed as 'Queen Anne legs'. The feet owe their large appearance to the amount of hair hanging over them, not to bone structure or over-large pads. Pads should not be cracked, and any excess hair between the pads should be carefully cut away. This will help in forming a good, tight foot. The line from shoulder to toe as the dog faces you should be absolutely straight.

The hindquarters should be rounded and muscular with hocks well let down—which really means short. As the Breed Standard notes, the hams should be more densely coated than any other part of the body. The back view of the dog gives a bear-like impression, and the fall of hair from the hocks should bring to mind the feet of a shire horse. The hind legs should appear straight when viewed from behind, and stand apart yet parallel to each other. Unfortunately cow hocks are seen all too often in the show ring. Proper grooming will enhance the correct characteristics of the hindquarters to best advantage.

The neck and shoulders are important items, as the points system indicates. The neck should be reasonably long; this is understandable in a breed which is traditionally a working one. No sheepdog with a short neck can see over the backs of sheep or over the tops of long grass and tussocks if he is lying guarding his charges. A decent length of neck flowing into shoulders which are sloping and inclined to narrowness at the points (which should have only a finger's width between them), results in a perfectly balanced reaching movement, whereas an upright shoulder blade or a heavy coarse shoulder makes the dog in motion look as though he is ploughing through a sea of porridge, and results in elbows that stick out and legs that are not set on properly. A good specimen of the breed does not have an enormous expanse of chest; this would lead to poor stance and impede his natural movement.

The Old English Sheepdog is not a long-bodied dog. He should be short and compact and slightly 'cobby'. The brisket (i.e. the part of the dog from his back behind his shoulders down to his thorax behind the front legs) should be deep and his ribs well-sprung. He should also possess strong loins. He should be slightly lower at the shoulder than at the rump; this is known as the 'rise'. A good rib cage allows for plenty of breathing room, necessary in the working sheepdog, while muscular hindquarters and loins give the dog strength and agility. The long narrow bodies with flat sides which one sometimes sees are out of proportion. They would not fit into the square box formed by a line dropped from the point of the shoulder to the ground, which is equal in length to a line drawn from the point of the shoulder to the rear end.

Tail docking should take place about four days after birth on the normal puppy. The operation may be deferred for a day or two on weaker puppies, but all puppies must be docked before they are seven days old. The tails should be cut right off so that no portion remains. Puppies born without tails are extremely rare; in fact we have only ever heard of one case.

The bobtail should have a double coat; the undercoat soft and waterproof and the overcoat or guard hairs of a good hard texture. They should not be straight, but they should not be kinked or curly either, merely shaggy. Technically, one demands a good 'break' in an Old English Sheepdog's outer coat. This might best be described as slightly wavy, with a natural bounce, but definitely not curled or crimped. One must consider the quality, texture and condition when assessing the bobtail's jacket. The profuse coat should be groomed in such a way that the dog does not appear fat. The undercoat is too often completely removed, which means that the outer coat has no support and either lies flat or blowing in the wind. Rarely does one find hard texture and profuseness on the same dog. A crisp coat presents the exhibitor with problems because of the way the ends continually crack off. The softer-coated varieties, on the other hand, can be seen parading with coats almost touching the ground. The original purpose of the undercoat was not only to keep off the elements, but also to protect the animal from the teeth and claws of marauding bears and wolves while he acted as protector of his flock. The less undercoat is removed, the less the coat tends to mat. When a judge parts the outer guard hairs, he is invariably looking, not for insects, but for the cotton-wool undercoat beneath.

Condition nowadays appears to have been handed over almost exclusively to the chemist and herbalist, and the bewildering choice of powders, pills and potions awaiting the exhibitor at a show is enough to make his head reel; he has to be strong-minded indeed to steer his way through all the advertisers' enticing promises. Many of these commercial products are helpful; it is the choice and range which confuse. But availability of all these medicaments means that patchy coats of varying length, wispy, dry or greasy hair and discoloured, poorly brushed coats should be things of the past, although even show-conditioned coats are of course subject to the weather, the seasons and the age and physical condition of the animal. A bobtail in peak condition and on top of his form is one of the most heartening and endearing sights in the dog world, and all owners should try to keep him this way.

Chapter 2

BUYING YOUR DOG

Before buying an Old English Sheepdog you must ask yourself seriously whether you have the right sort of home to offer a dog which, however small and attractive at eight weeks, is going to become an extremely large, shaggy addition to the household in a very few months. Like Topsy, he will grow, and continue to grow. You must be prepared to cope with huge paws which always seem larger when they are wet and dirty, and of course he has four feet compared with your two. He will grow a coat which requires regular grooming to prevent it from becoming tangled and matted, and his large frame will require a proportionally substantial diet. He will also need plenty of exercise and, if possible, free access to a garden or at least a yard, which means that a flat is not really a suitable home for him. If, after reading this, you are still determined to go ahead and buy your puppy, you are probably the right sort of owner for this very attractive breed.

THE CHOICE OF DOG OR BITCH

If you are hoping, or definitely planning to breed, the choice is already made for you. If you are merely looking for a family pet, the choice is not so clear-cut. Many people will tell you that a bitch is more affectionate and less inclined to roam than a dog. In fact, any well-trained dog should stay with his owner, or if running on ahead during exercise, come back at call. However,

31

there are dogs of any breed who are adventurous—or amorous
—and who will find a way out of the best-fenced garden, or take
off in the middle of a walk. As Cowper said of his spaniel Beau:

> You cried 'Forbear'—but in my breast
> A mightier cried 'Proceed'—
> 'Twas Nature, sir, whose strong behest
> Impelled me to the deed.

Beau was killing birds, but he might equally as well have been
chasing a lady friend. A bitch is perhaps less likely to wander
from home or to take to her heels during a country walk, and if
you decide to buy a dog, it might be worth your while to take him
to training classes when he is old enough. If you are buying a
bitch, you must remember that from the age of about ten months
she will regularly come into season for three weeks, twice a year
at six-monthly intervals. During the time that she is in season,
she must be kept away from all male dogs, unless you intend to
mate her. Some owners get around this difficulty by having the
bitch spayed, but this cannot be done if you intend to show
her under Kennel Club rules, unless she has progeny registered
at the Kennel Club.

Some people make out that looking after a bitch during the
time she is in season is a very tedious chore, but we have several
bitches, and find that with a reasonably-sized garden and
vigilant eye, we manage very well. We have also discovered, as
have many other owners, that bitches seem to adapt themselves
to each other and eventually all come into season together; this
is very convenient for the pet owner, but not, of course, nearly
so satisfactory for the breeder. Really, the choice of dog or bitch
is yours alone. Dogs tend to be slightly larger and heavier than
bitches, but if you have no particular preference, the best thing
to do is to wait until you see the litter and just pick the pup you
like best, regardless of sex. If you begin with a bitch, you must
face the fact that if you decide to buy a dog later on, you will
have to resolve the problem of housing and exercising facilities
when the bitch is in season.

PREPARING FOR THE PUPPY'S ARRIVAL

Before setting out to bring a puppy home, you must make your preparations for receiving him into the house. Details on kennelling quarters will be found in Chapter Four, together with more advice about dogs in the house. For the moment we are just considering your puppy's basic requirements on his arrival. He will need some place which he can consider his own during the day and where he can sleep undisturbed each night. With the larger breeds, commercially produced beds are rarely large enough for the fully-grown dog to stretch out on. The Old English Sheepdog generally does better on an old folded sleeping bag or something similar, covered with a blanket. Make sure of course that it is not in a direct line of draught. A bed similar to a kennel bed is ideal, and a large wooden platform some four inches high, three feet wide and five feet in length will allow a fully grown adult to lie comfortably; bedding placed on top of this will allow him further luxury, although bobtails actually spend much of their time seeking a cool surface to lie on and will frequently desert their bed for vinyl tiles or concrete.

An eight-week-old puppy needs the security of a more enclosed space. His bed could be made up in a corner, so that he has the protection of two walls, or you might prefer to make a bed for him in a large cardboard box with a hole cut out in one of the sides. The Old English Sheepdog does not like to curl up in a basket, so it is not worth buying one before you get your puppy, for he is more likely to cut his teeth on it than to lie in it. It is not necessary to spend a lot of money on your dog's bed in order to provide him with a suitable one. An expensive dog rug from a pet shop will probably be chewed and dragged through the garden, and it is more economical to use an old piece of clean blanket cut down to size. Many families who have taken to sleeping under continental quilts may have several spare blankets tucked away, which can be used for this purpose.

Feeding equipment also needs to be purchased in advance, and when buying a feeding bowl, avoid the deep, narrow ones especially designed for spaniels. You want something your dog can get his large, square head into. Pottery bowls tend to keep fresh water cool and they have the added advantage of being heavy and difficult for a playful puppy to knock over. Large washing up bowls made of light alloy make ideal feeding bowls and will last a lifetime. They can be scrubbed and washed with boiling water and will never crack. Plastic bowls on the other hand, make chewy toys, although plastic buckets, dropped into a fixed ring in the kennel are very serviceable.

Have some basic grooming equipment ready at home; use a brush with bristles set well apart and never choose a wire brush, whatever the pet shops tell you; the wire teeth or bristles never penetrate the outer coat and consequently, the whole coat from the skin outwards to the tip of the guard hairs is never properly groomed and quickly becomes matted.

You will be tempted to buy a collar and lead as soon as you have decided to buy your puppy, but it is really a better idea to wait until you have him home. Puppies' necks are surprisingly large and you may well find, if you are unused to the breed, that the collar you have bought is too small. If you are having a name disc engraved, give your own address and telephone number, but do *not* put the dog's name on the disc. Experience has shown that unscrupulous finders can, and do, make out that the dog is their own by demonstrating that the dog answers to his name when called.

FINDING A BREEDER

A major problem facing anyone new to the breed is knowing where to find a puppy. You should certainly go to a reputable breeder rather than looking for your puppy in a pet shop or departmental store, where you would be extremely unlikely to find a good one; avoid, too, those kennels which advertise puppies of all breeds. Breeders who care about the welfare of their stock and about keeping up high standards do not sell their puppies to the multi-breed trader. The Kennel Club, the Old English Sheepdog Club or any of the regional Old English

Sheepdog Clubs (all of whose addresses are in the Appendix), will provide you with a list of breeders in or near your area.

It is always a good idea, if you can manage it, to attend one or two major dog shows. Go to the ringside and watch all the classes for the breed, and you will see some of the best examples of the sort of dog you want to own. Buy a show catalogue and mark down any dog you particularly like the look of. The owner's name and address will be in the catalogue. During the show, you may find that some of the owners at the benches with their dogs will have time to talk to you, but remember that they are all anxious to get their dogs ready for the judge's opinion, and it is certainly not a kindness to talk to them when they are concentrating all their efforts towards grooming and preparing their dogs for entry into the ring. However, most exhibitors will find time to deal with an inquiry at some point during a show, which is, after all, his or her shop window, and the genuine prospective buyer is always welcome. If, for any reason, you fail to contact the breeder of your choice at the show, a telephone call making an appointment to visit the kennels is the best way of introducing yourself.

CHOOSING YOUR PUPPY

If the puppies have been born at the kennels, you will have a chance to see their mother but probably not the father. Stud dogs are very carefully selected for individual bitches so that the resulting litter inherits the sort of traits characteristic of the best of bobtails. This means that even if the kennels has its own stud dog, he will not be used for all the bitches in the kennels. As a newcomer to the breed you will hardly be in a position to discuss genealogies, but you might make some inquiries about a certain hereditary disease to which many large breeds, including the Old English Sheepdog, are prone. This is hip dysplasia (more fully discussed in Chapter Five). For some years breeders have been making great efforts to avoid producing puppies with this particular weakness; before mating a bitch or offering a stud dog they will have had them X-rayed and will use only stock free of hip dysplasia for breeding purposes. Another disease which appears to be inherited is entropion, which is an inward-growing eyelid. This condition can be remedied by an operation, but reputable breeders would not breed from stock known to have this condition or who carry it genetically.

Having disposed of the problem of these two diseases — and most breeders will be able to assure you at once that their stock is free of them — you can really get down to the business of picking out your puppy. This is not easy, because a litter of Old English Sheepdog puppies is one of the most engaging sights in the world, and you will want to buy the lot. However, take a look at their mother, and this immediate reminder of the size of the end product will quickly return you to your senses.

As a first-time owner, you may not realize that while you are trying to sum up the breeder's stock, he or she is likewise summing you up and assessing the type of home you will be able to provide for the puppy. There may be eight puppies in the litter, but there could be about twenty prospective owners, and the breeder has to fit the right puppy to the right owner as far as possible. Help the breeder as well as yourself by stating, as precisely as you can, the sort of puppy you want and what you want it for. Do you have a preference for a dog or a bitch? Are you wanting a family pet, or are you looking for an animal with show potential? Are you going to set up your own kennel with a view to breeding show dogs? The answers to these sorts of question will help sort out the puppies which would be suitable for you from those which aren't.

Obviously, it is no good taking a puppy which, for one reason or another, does not appeal to you. The two of you are going to be together for the next eleven or twelve years and you want it to be a happy partnership. Some people tend to choose the liveliest puppy, the one who rushes up and follows them wherever they go. This may be a sign of immediate rapport which heralds a happy time in the years to come, but remember that puppies sleep as much as eighteen hours a day, their energy going more into growth than physical activity during these early months, so if your visit coincides with the puppies' after dinner nap, don't be surprised if they are not as active as you expect them to be.

If you have children, take them along with you when buying a puppy; this will not only enable them to see the mother, but will also give them a chance to receive a short course of instruction from the breeder on puppy care and handling of puppies which will make much more impact than if they hear it second-hand from their parents.

You are sure to notice a difference in the markings of the puppies in the litter, and this may influence your choice. When you see them at eight weeks old, they will be black and white, bearing little resemblance to the fully-grown shaggy grey and white dog. Strictly speaking, that black colour is called 'blue', and if you look at the skin pigmentation beneath the black hair you will see why; it is a bluish-grey, whereas beneath the white hair the skin is pinkish white. Whatever hair is white on the puppy remains white in adulthood. The blue hair will turn grey — light grey at first, darkening up later as he matures. Try, then, to see the puppies as adults. Do you like the one with the all white head? Or would you prefer a pair of grey ears? Or perhaps one grey ear with a splash of grey over the eye? While many show dogs have a completely white head, this is not necessary to conform to the Breed Standard, and many show dogs do indeed have attractive grey markings on the head. A white neck is an asset as it prevents the dog's body from looking too long instead of 'cobby' and compact — it also has the effect of visually lengthening the neck, which is desirable in a show dog. White fronts, underparts, front legs and feet and white on the lower hind legs are all acceptable markings and are very attractive. The only markings which is found unacceptable by most judges in the show ring is an area of white (a flash) on the back or the sides. If you are proposing to breed from your puppy, dark markings on the head will help towards producing offspring without these flashes on the body.

It will become apparent at the puppy stage, before the coat has begun to grow, whether any of the litter has a 'wall eye', that is a blue eye (the other being the usual dark brown). This is not a fault in the Old English Sheepdog and some people like the odd eyes, although the long fall of hair hides them in the adult dog. Occasionally, a puppy will have a pair of blue eyes. Again, this does not count as a fault in the show ring. Apart from wall eyes, the dog's eye colouring should be dark brown. (If you want to show your dog, avoid light brown ones.) A dark pigmentation around a dark brown eye is considered an asset. It is not always apparent in a puppy, but if some of the skin immediately surrounding the eye is dark, or you can see little dark specks on the eye rim, you may find that it spreads all round the eye as the dog matures.

Some of the puppies in the litter may have 'butterfly' noses, that is, noses with large or small areas which are pink instead of black. The nose will blacken as the dog grows older. We have never known a dog whose nose did not eventually grow completely black.

Look inside the puppy's mouth and make sure that the milk teeth are all there and that the gums are healthy. If there are signs of dark pigmentation on the roof of the mouth, this is quite normal, many adult dogs have very dark upper palates. When looking for a puppy with show potential, the future conformation of the mouth is the hardest thing to be clear about, for no breeder can foretell with absolute certainty how the puppy's mouth is going to develop. The bite to choose in an eight-week-old puppy, where the jaw is still to grow on, is the one where you could get the width of a tooth between the upper and lower sets when the mouth is closed. In other words, where the puppy's jaw is overshot by the width of one tooth, there is the likelihood of a good adult mouth developing the correct bite required by the Standard. This rule is not, however infallible. An apparently good mouth in a puppy can alter radically when he gets his adult teeth, and many a promising show career has ended prematurely because of this. If you are not interested in showing your dog, the position of the teeth is not as important, so long as it does not impair the dog's ability to eat.

The puppy's head should be large and square, with a

complete absence of any deerhound narrowness of jaws or forehead, and his ears should lie neatly at each side, not sticking out, or being placed too high. Look inside the puppy's ears to see that they are clean and free of wax or other discharge.

Check that the tail has been properly docked, that is, close against the body. An Old English Sheepdog should have no suspicion of a stump. When he is pleased, he wags his bottom. One hears increasingly of puppies who come into the show ring and have to be re-docked at a later date because the vet who performed the original operation left too much of a stump. This necessitates an operation under anaesthetic and requires a lengthy convalescence, leaving the pup with a sore rear end for quite a few days.

The whole body should be firm and stocky, and it should be narrower at the shoulders and higher and larger at the back. Look at the puppy from the back view to make sure that his legs are not placed too close together and that they are straight without any suspicion of a 'cow hock' look (i.e. knock kneed, with hocks swinging in to meet each other). His back legs from the side view should have some angulation, that is, the hocks should be low down on the legs rather than high up, with a correspondingly short length of pastern with the stifle sweeping round to join the hock, not straight as is seen too often.

When you pick the puppy up, his body should feel well-covered, with a sturdy bone structure, and there should be an absence of pot-belly, which, if it exists, is a possible sign of worms. You ought anyway to ask the breeder whether the puppies have been wormed. They usually are as a matter of course, but if this has not been done, you must do it. You will find the PRO Dogs Worming Chart for Breeders an invaluable guide for worming your puppy. Worms kill more puppies than many people realize and are certainly more to blame for poor starts in life than almost any other factor. In the absence of the chart or other specific professional advice, consult your vet about the dosage rather than relying on a proprietary brand. Some brands are very good, but others are either ineffective or too strong.

It is possible that when you hold your puppy, you will be aware of a soft lump in his middle, in the region of the navel. This indicates an umbilical hernia which is not a serious cause for alarm. It can be pushed gently back into place but it will slip out again. If it does become very large, it can be operated on; however, this is not usually necessary, although your vet will advise you to have it stitched up if your puppy is a bitch, before she starts a family. Before buying your puppy, run your hand through his coat to make sure that the skin is clean and healthy and free from scabs and scurf and that the coat itself is free from lice or fleas.

This sounds a formidable check list, but a litter from a reputable breeder will invariably be sound, and he or she will be the first to point out any deficiencies and discuss them with you.

INOCULATION

When you visit the litter to make your choice, the puppies should be anything from eight weeks to twelve weeks old. A puppy of less than eight weeks is too young to leave the litter. Nor can it have the full inoculation against distemper and hardpad, hepatitis and the two forms of leptospirosis until it is twelve weeks old. These inoculations will be your responsibility and your vet will do them for you, and this will mean two visits, with a fortnight's interval. Until the inoculations are completed, and for a week afterwards, the puppy should not be taken into the street or other public places. If you have to take the puppy out before this time, he will have to be carried and he will feel very heavy after the first few yards. Give your arms a rest by placing him on top of a wall, or any place untouched by dogs or human feet — the bonnet of a car is another useful resting ground, although the owner might not agree.

After the inoculations, the vet will give you a certificate in the dog's name with details of the date and dosage received and another date, usually eighteen months ahead, when the dog should have its booster dose. Each time the booster is given, the vet fills in details of the dosage and the next date for a visit, so if you move to another area, you can take the inoculation document with you when you visit your new vet and he can see just what is required.

PAPERWORK

You will not need a dog licence until the puppy is six months old. Then you are required by law to have one unless you are using him as a working dog with animals. Guide dogs for the blind are also exempt. Your local Post Office will issue you with the licence.

There are papers which you will have to deal with as soon as you have bought your puppy. These are his registration documents. It is likely that the puppies will already have been registered with the Kennel Club in their breeder's name. If so, you may have to wait some time for the documents as the Kennel Club is currently introducing computerization for all their canine records and until all the paperwork is transferred on to tape, delays will occur. You will be given a Kennel Club transfer form which you must fill in and send off to Clarges Street together with the current transfer fee so that ownership can be in your name. This is very important if you intend to show your dog under Kennel Club regulations and also if you are buying a bitch and want to breed from her.

You will also be handed a pedigree certificate by the breeder setting out the names and Kennel Club registration numbers of the puppy's parents, grandparents and great grandparents and, in some cases, great-great-grandparents. When you come to know more about the breed, particularly if you visit shows and read the weekly dog papers, this certificate will become of increasing interest to you as you recognize the various dogs from different kennels who appear among your own dog's ancestors. It is also important later to be able to refer to it when seeking advice about choosing a mate for your dog or bitch, although most breeders know their stock so well that they can reel off genealogies while you are still taking the certificate out of its envelope.

Some breeders insure their puppies with one of the specialist livestock companies, and you will be well advised to continue the cover when the one month cover note you receive on purchasing the puppy expires. Particulars of the coverage vary from company to company but generally include death by accident from any cause, death by illness or disease, loss by stealing or straying, veterinary fees and loss of value. With the sum insured being up to £200 and the premium being 3p for each £1 (sterling) value, it is a wise investment. Another added bonus a good breeder will provide is to include in the purchase price enrolment into one of the Old English Sheepdog Clubs. This will keep you in touch with the breed and any activities that are happening in your region.

TAKING YOUR PUPPY HOME

You have now to get your puppy home, and this generally involves a car journey. However near you may live to the kennels, a car is pretty well essential as not only is an Old English Sheepdog puppy very heavy to hold, but he will not be able to walk with a collar and lead until the inoculations have been completed, quite apart from the fact that, without training, a puppy does not walk easily when tethered from the neck. Your puppy may travel best on the floor of the car. It is hard to be sure why this is, because there seems to be more vibration and road noise down there, but the fact remains that often a puppy who is restless on a car seat will settle quickly on the floor beneath the seat, if he can fit himself in. Possibly the security of being beneath something appeals to him. Car sickness is something young dogs are prone to, although they usually grow out of it, so drive as gently as you can and have an old piece of towelling and some newspapers in the car. If your puppy should be sick on his first journey, don't scold him; he can't help it. Leaving the security of the litter, being handled by a stranger

42

and then being taken off, alone, in a car, must be a very traumatic experience, and he needs all your sympathy and forbearance at this time. It is not advisable to give a sedative tablet to a young puppy when travelling, because he will spend his time trying to fight off the effects of the drug and this, coupled with the terrors of the journey, makes things doubly hard for him.

SETTLING IN

You will already have prepared the puppy's quarters, so introduce him to his bed as soon as you get home. He may not stay in it, preferring to have a wander round and do a little exploring, but encourage him to find his way back to his bed and put him into it if he lies down and wants to rest, and it will very quickly dawn on him that this is his own special place. It will further add to his sense of security if you can put the bed under a table, or at least in a corner — not so far away that he feels isolated but just sufficiently apart for him to feel he will not be disturbed if he wants to relax and close his eyes. Dogs seem to like having some sort of roof above them, especially when they are new to a place.

CHILDREN AND THE NEW PUPPY

Don't let other members of the family disturb your puppy too much on his first day. Give him a chance to get used to his new surroundings. If there are children in the family, they will generally be very enthusiastic about the new arrival and it may be necessary to curb this enthusiasm a little. Because the Old English Sheepdog puppy is heavy, children should not be allowed to carry him about. They can be inadvertently rough in their handling, and they may well squeeze him too hard or drop him. They may damage themselves by carrying too heavy a weight and they will certainly almost always damage a young puppy who always has a soft spot on the head where the bony plates forming the skull have not quite knitted together, and needs to be treated with great care. So make a rule that children do not pick the puppy up, but let them stroke him gently while sitting near to him. An adult should pick the puppy up with both hands — one under the chest and the other round the rear end. When placing the puppy back on the floor, make sure that all four feet touch the ground together, and that the floor surface gives a good grip. Linoleum, tiles and polished wood do not afford a puppy enough stability. Explain your actions to the children and do not allow loud games and noise near the puppy's quarters. The common-sense rules which govern the safety of children in the house apply equally to the puppy — beware of stairs; switch off electrical appliances at the wall-point; avoid trailing electric cables (they are the first things a puppy will chew); kitchen cupboards need catches that are dog- and child-proof; keep medicines, cleansing agents, rat poison, slug bait and other similar potential dangers locked up. With temptation out of reach, and with sensible training, your bobtail puppy, before long, will be herding children instead of sheep.

YOUR PUPPY'S FIRST NIGHT

A big decision that has to be made is where the puppy is to sleep. Like most dog owners, you may want him to sleep downstairs, so begin as you mean to go on, but be prepared for the puppy to object vocally for a night or two. He will cry or howl because he is lonely. If you call out to him or talk to him, do it from outside the room he is in, or he will associate howling with your coming through the door to make a fuss of him and you will have started a great deal of trouble for yourself. A rubber hot water bottle with a blanket or towel wrapped around it will help to fill the empty part of his bed and provide something warm and soft to sleep against — a substitute for the brothers and sisters he has left behind. Before very long, you will find that he accepts his sleeping quarters and you can dispense with the hot water bottle. If there is another dog in the family, the problem of sleeping downstairs is not so acute because the puppy has the company of the older dog. Of course, if you can't trust the older dog with the puppy, separate them at night and also when you cannot be with them during the day, until the older one has accepted the newcomer. A bigger threat probably comes from the established family cat who is far more likely to establish his territorial rights than another dog. Whatever other pets you have at the time of the new puppy's arrival, be sure to make an extra fuss of them, so that they do not become jealous. This way, cats and dogs will more readily accept the new bobtail.

FEEDING YOUR PUPPY

Before taking your puppy home from the kennels, ask the breeder to give you a diet sheet or at least some indication of the type of food the puppy has been used to, because an abrupt change of diet can cause stomach upsets. Details of feeding an older dog are given in Chapter Four, but an indication of the sort of food the very young puppy should have is given here. He has a great deal of growing to do in the weeks and months ahead, and it is essential that he has plenty of the right kind of food to encourage good growth and a sturdy frame.

At eight weeks he should be having four or five meals a day. Let your puppy tell you by his own reactions whether he likes the food and how much he wants. If food is left in his bowl, cut down the quantity at the next meal-time, and if there are still left-overs, cut down from five to four meals a day. A fussy eater might be missing the competition of his litter mates, and breeders always run on two puppies together for just this reason. If your puppy is an 'only child', feed the cat, if you have one, at the same time, but make sure that the puppy doesn't steal the cat's food and vice-versa. Lack of appetite may indicate the presence of worms and it is always advisable to worm regularly.

Your puppy's early morning feed, given after he has been outside first thing, should consist of half a pint of milk with one teaspoonful of glucose mixed into it, served with some cereal. Weetabix or Farex baby food are both good for the puppy and complete puppy cereals, obtainable from most pet shops, are great body builders. By lunch-time, your puppy will be ready for his first meat meal of the day. Mix six ounces of minced or finely diced meat, or tinned puppy meat, with puppy meal which has been soaked in hot water or gravy for about a quarter of an hour previously. At tea-time, give the puppy some milk pudding like rice or semolina with egg. The evening meal should be the same as the mid-morning meal, with the addition of vitamin tablets; instructions on the box will tell you how many to give. Before you go to bed at night, you can give your puppy another cereal meal similar to his early morning one.

You will have noticed that the non-meat meals involve milk, but too much of this will make the puppy's bowel movements very loose. It is a good idea to water down all milk 50-50 for the first week, and also to feed only white meat, scrambled eggs and boiled rice for the first seven days in order to help the puppy's digestion adjust to the change in environment. Even a change in water can cause a digestive upset.

Never let the puppy dictate to you; if you pander to all his fancies, it won't be long before he has you buying the best steak. Ring the changes by all means, giving fish, rabbit and chicken (but mind the bones). Your own left over vegetables will also be demolished by his voracious appetite if you feed them with his meat meals. Give him enough, but don't overfeed. Puppies' bones are soft and many a beautiful conformation has been ruined by puppy fat pushing out shoulder placements, and I strongly believe that fat puppies never get a good hip dysplasia X-ray plate.

TOYS AND PLAY

The puppy's life consists of eating, resting and playing. During the periods of play, he will need some toys and if you do not provide them, he will find his own — dirt, stones or your prize

46

plants from the garden, Ordnance Survey maps and chunks of upholstery from the car, wooden spoons from the kitchen, full spools of cotton from the work box, to say nothing of cardigans and sweaters — on or off the body of the person who owns them. Pet shops sell a wide variety of balls, dog chews, rubber bones and other play things, in fact you will probably not know what to choose and it is worth remembering that puppies are often happier with an old piece of rag or an ancient shoe or glove than the expensive contents of the local pet shops. But remember, a puppy will not be able to differentiate between an old slipper and your new pair, so let him know what he can and can't have.

While playing with your puppy take care not to have too fierce a game of tug of war with him as it might damage his teeth, or the new ones coming through, when he is a little bit older. Playing with a puppy is a good way for the two of you to get to know each other and will help the puppy to identify with you as his owner. While no serious training should be contemplated in the first few weeks you have your puppy home, you can turn some activities into a sort of educational play, where he learns the meaning of 'No' and 'Good boy' (or girl) and you can, as he grows older, use the command words 'sit' and 'come' when it is appropriate. The puppy likes to play and to please and the early parts of his training should be an extension of his periods of play with you. If the puppy plays on his own in a yard or garden, make regular checks to see that all is well. Above all, respect the growing puppy's need to rest. When he had had enough play, he will stop and flop right out and go to sleep. Teach children to refrain from teasing him into more play when he has stopped of his own accord to recharge his batteries.

THE ALTERNATIVE TO HAVING A PUPPY:
THE OLD ENGLISH SHEEPDOG RESCUE SCHEME

It could be that, instead of having a puppy, you may be interested in giving a good home to a dog or bitch which has had an unhappy start in life or whose owner has died or is too ill to care for a dog any more. Unfortunately, the breed is one which sometimes attracts the wrong kind of owner, people who want the dog for its size and looks but who are not prepared to undertake the feeding, grooming and care a bobtail requires. So it has been found necessary to set up the Old English Sheepdog Rescue Scheme for neglected dogs of the breed.

The Scheme, which was founded by Mr Bill Pearce some years ago, has as its two-fold aim, the rescuing and placing in suitable homes of unwanted and neglected bobtails. The ages of these dogs range from a few weeks to thirteen years and it is an unfortunate fact that since the inception of the scheme, their numbers have run into several hundreds.

Where a dog is left alone because of illness or death of the owner, the break-up of a marriage, or a new job overseas, he will suffer an initial period of regret for his former owner, but will generally settle easily into a similar home. The dogs which present the greatest problems are the real 'rescue' cases, dogs who have been ill-treated and neglected. These include those who have been abandoned on motorways, dumped on waste ground or tied to trees by owners who go to any lengths to be rid of them. Others are brought to the Rescue Scheme's notice by vets who have healthy bobtails brought to them to be put down. When the vets ask permission to pass the dog over to the Rescue Scheme and thus save its life, the owners generally agree, provided that all responsibility for the dog is taken from them.

The Rescue Scheme may also have to find new homes for dogs that are blind, deaf, crippled, autistic, covered with parasites, emaciated or even positively dangerous. Those that are too ill or too dangerous to go on to new homes are put down, but as far as possible they are rehabilitated. This is not an easy task, and potential owners are interviewed by people who know the breed very well and can match dogs and owners carefully to ensure the transaction has a successful outcome.

The Rescue Scheme does not buy or sell dogs, nor does it advertise them. Dogs are collected by members of the Scheme who give up time to fetch unwanted dogs from all parts of

England, Scotland and Wales. The Committee consists of representatives from each of the registered Breed Clubs so that regional contacts can be made. Once a dog has been delivered to a Rescue Centre, any registration cards or pedigrees which may have come with it are given to the Honorary Secretary and they are not passed on to new owners. There are several reasons for this. Dogs are found new homes under the Rescue Scheme as pets only, not as show dogs or dogs for breeding, because in these last two capacities there is a possible case for exploitation, and the dog has suffered quite enough already. Moreover, it is unfair to the original breeders of these dogs, the majority of whom are caring people who have genuinely tried to place their stock correctly in the first place, to have their names publicized as the ones who have produced a 'rescue' bobtail.

Once the dog has been given a health check and received veterinary treatment if this is necessary, and has been assessed as to character and temperament, he is sent on to a home which has been specially selected for him. In other words, a 'rescue' bobtail is not automatically placed with the next family on the list of people applying for one. With very few exceptions, new owners are not given the address of the previous owner, mainly because the uncaring owner cannot be expected to be of any help in advising the new owners how to cope with the dog. Even caring owners who have had to give up their dog do more harm than good if they visit the dog in its new home. The dog becomes upset and unsettled and all the new owner's hard work may be undone as the result of one visit. The Rescue Scheme tries to keep in touch with new owners, to hear how the dogs are progressing and also to offer advice of any kind if it is needed.

Because the Rescue Scheme does not sell the dogs, they have no direct means of making money, yet funds are always needed for the upkeep of dogs in care awaiting a new home, to cover vets' fees and postage and telephone costs, and to pay petrol expenses for those people who collect and deliver the dogs all over the country. Also needed are people willing to interview prospective new owners, but these must be experienced people who have owned bobtails themselves. It is also possible for an experienced owner to be put in touch, through the Rescue Scheme, with a family who love their bobtail, but who are finding it difficult to look after him because they lack experience in grooming, feeding or training. With some friendly guidance from a knowledgeable person this family can keep and enjoy their dog throughout his lifetime.

If you decide that you would like to be an owner of a rescue bobtail, contact the Hon. Secretary of the Rescue Scheme, Jill Harwood, The Old Farmhouse, High Hameringham, Horncastle, Lincolnshire, telephone: Winceby (06585) 644. You can be sure of advice and support, and you may well feel that, if you are chosen to be the owner of a 'rescue' bobtail, you are indeed privileged to be entrusted with the future welfare and happiness of an animal who has known precious little in his past before the Rescue Scheme stepped in.

Chapter 3

TRAINING YOUR DOG

HOUSE TRAINING

House training is a priority from the moment you introduce the puppy to your home, but it is one which should not present too many problems. Old English Sheepdogs as a breed are generally very quick to understand what is required of them in this respect. Always take your puppy out after every meal and always take him through the same door so that he associates this door with going outside to relieve himself. He should also be taken out frequently during the day between meals. Do this also whenever you see him wandering round and sniffing at the floor or going round and round in circles. Praise him with a pleased sounding voice if he does what you want him to do when you have taken him outside. If you catch him making a mess inside, express your disapproval in a displeased voice and *show* him his mess so that he knows what it is you disapprove of, then take him outside immediately as if to say 'This is where you should have done it.' Severe methods, such as rubbing the dog's nose in it, and smacking rarely seem to have any effect. All that happens is that the dog becomes confused and anxious.

As soon as the puppy wakes in the morning he should be put outside. He should also be taken out last thing at night. There then remains the problem of what to do if he should wake up in the middle of the night and want to go out. One of the best ploys seems to be to place a thick wad of newspaper next to the door he normally uses to reach the garden and he will most likely use this and it can easily be disposed of in the morning. So long as you are prepared to let him out regularly and not leave him shut in for long periods, your puppy should very quickly learn to be clean in the house.

Puppies that are kennelled outside and older dogs that have spent their lives in kennels and are being brought inside to live present a problem in house training. Perseverance is the key word, and the method we have found successful when coping with older rescued dogs that spend a few weeks with us before going on to a new home, is to spread newspapers all over the kitchen floor for the first few nights. The dog generally tends to make a mess (if he is going to make a mess at all) in one particular spot. This place only is covered the following night and he (hopefully) learns to mess on the newspaper. Gradually the papers are moved nearer to the door. Within a week, just one sheet of newspaper is spread beside the door leading to the garden. The last step is to tuck the corner of the sheet under the door and the dog will tend to scratch at this if he wants to relieve himself. This will generally happen at four o'clock in the morning, and you must then get up and let him out. However much you regret the bed you have just left, praise the dog generously, and you will usually find that, once this stage has been reached, house training troubles are over.

Careful planning of meal times, the removal of water bowls by eight in the evening and a walk last thing at night should also help to do away with any night calls.

Training a puppy to use a cat flap in the door is a useful practice while the puppy is small enough to take advantage of it. Of course, the puppy will not realize that he is getting bigger and, one day, may well walk off with the whole kitchen door around his shoulders, so this idea must be used circumspectly. It also requires a certain imperturbability on the part of the puppy's owner who has to be able to carry off the undignified situation of squatting on all fours in front of a closed cat flap talking encouragement to a non-appearing puppy. *You* know he is the other side of the door, but what are the neighbours thinking?

Our puppies are raised indoors in a whelping box on newspaper until they start climbing out at about three weeks old. Then they go into a kennel, the nearest to the house, bedded on soft straw, but a few sheets of newspaper are laid in the puppies' run, and as they are used to making their messes on newspaper in the whelping box, they always go into the run to the newspaper. When the paper is wet and needs changing, I always leave one sheet down, and cover this with clean, dry sheets in order to keep the scent around for that one in the litter who seems to be slower on the uptake than the rest.

Kennelled dogs who mess inside their kennel and refuse to go into the run should be fed inside the kennel, and their food bowl placed next to the area where they soil. The dog will find this unpleasant and may then begin to use the outside run in future.

Training of this kind extends beyond the immediate vicinity of the house, especially for town dwellers. If you have a garden of your own — get the dog to use that before going to the park or recreation ground for a walk where he may otherwise use areas of grass designed for walking, sitting on or where children are meant to be able to play. If you live in a flat, with no access to a garden of your own, kerb training is the only answer — but choose a quiet road, as dogs have been hit by traffic, particularly by buses travelling close to the kerb or pulling up at a bus stop. Even so, it is encumbent on the owner, in the interest of public hygiene, to carry equipment to clear up the mess his dog makes. PRO Dogs sell a complete kit which is both manageable and disposable.

Once trained, Old English Sheepdogs are very reliable; in fact, they become so used to using their own special patch of lawn, ditch or hedgerow that many owners will tell of long days away from home at a show where their dogs refuse all chance of relieving themselves until they return home to their own patch, maybe twenty hours after setting out.

USING A COLLAR AND LEAD

When the dog is about ten weeks old, you can begin teaching him to walk beside you on a lead. Start by putting a collar on your puppy and leaving it on for about a quarter of an hour and then for longer periods. A lightweight nylon collar is better at this stage than a leather one which is inclined to be stiff when new. The dog will be less likely to scratch at a nylon collar, and scratching is to be discouraged as it will impair the quality of his coat.

When he is used to wearing the collar, attach the lead to it and with the dog on your left side, start walking forward, encouraging him to come with you. If he drags behind or runs on ahead, twitch the lead to bring him to you and say 'heel'. Hold him on the lead from the beginning as one does an adult dog, with the loop in your right hand and the lead crossing your body so that your left hand controls the slack about halfway down the left-hand side where your dog is walking. While your puppy is on his lead, talk to him and praise him while he is walking beside you; be patient and refrain from pulling him roughly if at first he refuses to walk quietly beside you. Discourage him from chewing the lead; keep on the move so that the lead is never slack enough for him to take it into his mouth and play with it. While you are in the early stages of teaching your puppy to walk at your left side, always turn to the right yourself when you want to change direction so that you turn away from the puppy. If you turn left while he is at this stage, you may trip over him and frighten or confuse him. Once he really can manage to walk quietly to heel, you can help him to adjust his movements to yours for the left turn.

You may feel that lead training requires a special sort of collar which will give more control over your dog. Dog training classes ask owners to provide a slip collar, or choke chain as it is sometimes called. It works on the principle of tightening as the puppy pulls away from you. Owners of long-haired breeds like the Old English Sheepdog do not normally favour any kind of chain collar because it dirties the white neck hair and is also responsible for rubbing the hair away. If you want a slip collar, it is possible to get a nylon one. An ordinary leather collar with normal fastening may serve your purpose, however, especially if your dog is responsive and learning quickly to do what you want. When choosing a leather collar, buy a rolled collar, not a flat one, as these tend to rub the neck hair rather badly. As your dog grows, you will need a fairly short, stout leather lead; there is no point in having a long one if he is going to walk to heel when led. Long leads are made for low-slung dogs.

You can begin to teach the sit position while lead training is in progress by stopping with a short lead so that the puppy cannot walk on and saying 'sit', while at the same time placing your left hand on his hindquarters and exercising a downward pressure. If your dog is solely a pet, you can continue with this method of teaching him to respond to a hand pressing down on his hindquarters, but if you have a potential show dog in training, remember that in the ring the judge is going to do just this to test his hindquarters, and the last thing he wants the dog to do is to sit down, so your dog will have to learn to respond to the word alone when he sits. A slight upward jerk on the lead and pushing him back against a wall may persuade him to sit, but do so gently and don't frighten him by backing him into a corner.

Once your puppy sits, reward him; a pat and a 'good boy' or a 'good girl' will teach a puppy to respond positively to your command. If he refuses to comply, say the word again accompanying it with a firm push on his quarters. It might help to stand him with his rear end against a wall as, in this way, it is not so easy for him to pop up again once he is sitting.

A reward for a dog is a pleased voice and an approving pat. He does not necessarily have to be fed. If he disobeys, the only 'punishment' he should receive is the withholding of praise. Make a lot of fuss each time he does it right. Your puppy will enjoy pleasing you and will want to experience your approval. Eventually he will sit on the word of command. This is a very important piece of training. There are times when it is imperative for a dog to sit still. Kerb training in town should include the sit. If the dog merely stands and stays, he remains on his feet all the time and might be tempted to make a dash. If he is made to go through the motion of sitting before crossing a road, this effectively slows him up and the physical action of sitting induces a backward movement which may inhibit any tendency to dash forward into trouble.

The stay leads on from the sit lesson, as the puppy can be brought to sit and then to stay in the sitting position. Stand in front of the dog, hold his head or both sides of his collar and say 'stay' firmly. Then leave go and step back a couple of paces. He will want to follow you but you must put him back in the sitting position and give the stay command again and step backwards again, doing this over and over until he realizes what you want him to do. Reward him with fuss and praise every time he responds correctly. Gradually step further and further from the puppy until he will stay while you are at the opposite end of the room or run or wherever you are training him, but do not go out of sight during this early basic training without calling him to you and showing, by encouraging words, that the game is over.

Obviously the next piece of training is to respond to the word 'come', because, once he has stayed, you will then want him to come to you. Call the word in a lively voice, not as flat and final as when you say stay, so that he will realize the command to stay put has been cancelled. Be prepared to work on these three commands for a long time. The bobtail puppy is intelligent, quick on the uptake and anxious to please, but he is also bouncy and full of the joys of life so you will need to be patient and understanding. Be firm, expect obedience, don't give in, but on the other hand don't make the training sessions too long. Reward whenever you can with a great show of affection and approval. Correct by withholding that approval and instead gently and firmly place the dog in the position required accompanied each time by the relevant word of command.

There will be times when you want your dog to lie down and you will have to teach him to do this on the word of command. Get him to sit, and then say 'down' firmly, at the same time lifting his front feet and legs forwards so that he is lying down. Once he is there, keep him there and praise him. This will take some time to accomplish, but he will gradually learn to arrange himself in a lying position without your help when he hears the command.

Remember that 'sit' and 'down' are two separate command words which tell the dog to do two clearly distinguishable actions. So don't confuse your dog or puppy by telling him to 'sit down'. Keep commands to one syllable — sit — stay — down — come — fetch. It is also easier for training purposes if you give your dog a name consisting of one syllable, but this is a counsel of perfection and few owners use success in obedience training as the chief factor when choosing a name for a dog. In fact, one might argue, equally convincingly, that a name of two syllables carries better and further if you call to your dog over a distance. The tone of voice is certainly important, and I have seen dogs trained by tone of voice alone, the handler using the dog's name with various inflections for the commands. In this case, the single syllable name *is* to be preferred.

If you keep a dog in a town, he should always be on a lead when he walks with you on the pavement. Don't be tempted, just because he has learnt to walk to heel, to ask him to do it in town without a lead. There are many distractions in a busy street, or even a quiet one for that matter, ranging from a cat or a bitch in season on the other side of the road to a vehicle which backfires loudly or discharges its exhaust fumes into your dog's face. Don't forget kerb drill either, even if there is no traffic in sight, and then encourage him to walk steadily across the road with you, keeping to heel.

A well-trained dog is just as much of an asset if you and your dog live in the country. There may not be so much traffic, but one car driven too fast along a narrow, twisting country lane is a greater danger than traffic keeping to the speed limit in a town. So your dog should be trained to stay or come to heel the moment you hear a fast approaching car. A dog should always be on a lead if you are taking him through a field or across a common where animals are kept. Unless it is unavoidable, neither you nor your dog, however well-trained, ought to walk through a flock of sheep or a herd of cows in a field, because the very presence of a dog may be disturbing to the animals.

There are some general rules to be followed when training your puppy. First of all, make sure the words you use are distinguishable as command words by saying them clearly and firmly and using each word in isolation. Make things even easier by the use of a different intonation for each command and keep to it. For example, 'sit' should be a short, sharply enunciated syllable, spoken on a level tone. 'Stay' must not sound like another short sharp syllable by saying something which sounds like 'sté'. Deepen your voice and make use of the two syllable sounds of which the spoken word consists. Say 'stay-ee' with a downward inflection on the '-ay' and an upward inflection on the '-ee'. The word 'come' should be spoken in an encouraging, almost excited tone to the young puppy when he is first learning it, and when he comes, fondle him and show pleasure at being reunited with him. However, an excited, inviting tone of voice is not always appropriate. You will have to get him used to a sharper more peremptory tone when you are not merely recalling a puppy from a basic lesson stay but find yourself recalling an over-enthusiastic bobtail who is about to launch himself with powerful exuberance on a non-dog-loving relative.

Owners whose dogs live *en famille* year in year out generally find that their dogs can understand certain frequently repeated phrases or even whole sentences. This is normal, but there is no case for trying to do this with a puppy during basic training. Commands must be short and easily distinguished from each other to avoid confusion and frustration on your part and the puppy's.

While some owners undertake all their dog's training, others prefer to go to specially run dog training classes. Ideally, your puppy should have learnt from you the basics of sit, stay and come before you go, but if you find even these difficult to instil on your own, take him along when he is six or eight months old and see if training classes help you both. However, they won't perform miracles. The trainer will guide you and give you exercises to do in the class, but you will be expected to go home and practise them every day for a week so that you can show some progress at the next class. It is useless expecting the puppy to be obedient only while he is attending the class. It is as bad as going to Weight Watchers but not keeping to your diet in between the meetings. Regular classes are held in most areas, and your local library or local police station should be able to direct you to them. If you are not quite sure about the usefulness of these classes to you, go along one evening and ask to be a spectator. You will generally find the classes divided into three sessions. There will be a beginners' class, an advanced class and possibly a special coaching class for people who are working for Kennel Club Obedience Tests. You may find yourself so interested that you will want to go in for the obedience tests with your dog.

It is essential, if your puppy or young dog is to benefit from these classes, that he should arrive at them in a fit state to make an attempt to do what is asked of him. We know of one very excitable bobtail puppy who was not very fond of car travel at the best of times and who would bark frantically whenever anyone entered the car. The well-meaning owner agreed to call for a friend and her two small dogs on the way to the class which was about twelve miles away. The Old English Sheepdog puppy used to bark non-stop for every one of those twelve miles and arrive utterly exhausted at the class. Consequently, he could do nothing right and the owner had to give up going. However, some members of the breed have done very well in obedience classes and have gone on to take awards in the Kennel Club tests. Many dog shows, including Crufts, now hold advanced obedience classes and draw large entries and even larger audiences.

Before you get as far as aspiring to Crufts, there are Beginners' and Novices' tests to see how good you and your dog are under test conditions.

Beginners' Test
Walk to heel on a lead
Walk to heel off a lead
Sit for one minute with the handler in sight

Down for two minutes with the handler in sight
Recall from sit or down
Retrieve an article provided by the owner

Novices' Test (A)
Walk to heel on a lead
Sit for one minute with the handler in sight
Recall from sit or down while the handler is walking away
Retrieve a dumb-bell
Down for five minutes with the handler in sight
Perform a scent discrimination test

Novices' Test (B)
Walk to heel without a lead
Sit down for two minutes with the handler in sight
Be sent away, down and recall
Retrieve a dumb-bell
Stand for one minute at a distance from the handler
Down for ten minutes with the handler out of sight
Perform a scent discrimination test

Novices' Test (C)
Walk to heel at fast and slow paces interspersed with sit and down
Sit for two minutes with the handler out of sight
Be sent away, down and recall
Retrieve an object
Stay down for ten minutes with the handler out of sight
Perform a scent discrimination test
Show obedience to commands of sit, stand and down at a distance from the handler

Test C is quite a difficult one which involves some of the things dogs have to do for the much more advanced tests. If you don't aspire to extracting this sort of obedience from your bobtail, it is worth watching some of the obedience tests at dog shows in order to see how the handlers use their voices to give the commands to their dogs and to watch how even the most experienced dog enjoys doing something well and being praised for it.

Chapter 4

CARING FOR YOUR DOG

FEEDING

The Dog's Digestive System

If the owner understands something about his dog's digestion, he can better appreciate the sort of diet the animal requires. First of all, the dog's teeth are those of a carnivore. He has four tusk-like teeth, two in the lower jaw and two in the upper, which are shaped to tear flesh from bone. His molars are especially sharp and made for chewing so that he can eat meat in sizeable chunks. Cereal- and grass-eating animals, on the other hand, have flattened molars for grinding and incisors for gathering and they are quite unlike the teeth of a dog. The saliva of a grain- or grass-eating animal contains enzymes which break down starches, but the dog's saliva lacks most of these enzymes. That is one reason why a dog is able to bolt its food in chunks; its saliva does not have to deal with it as part of the digestive process. The dog's oesophagus or gullet can expand to take chunks of meat on its passage to the stomach in a way which would be impossible or extremely painful in man.

The digestive process begins in the dog's stomach which is proportionately larger than man's and capable of greater extension. The dog retains food in his stomach for a long time as much of the process of digestion takes place here. Cereals and fibrous foods are digested in the intestine; men and horses, for instance, can take a fair amount of food in their intestines because of the type of food they eat, but the dog's small intestine holds relatively little food because he is not by nature a vegetarian. In the wild, a dog would gain most of the vegetable matter it required from eating the intestines of animals it killed.

Rennin is present in much larger quantities in the puppy's stomach compared to the adult dog's. Thus it would seem that adult dogs are not able to cope with large quantities of milk in their diet.

Diet

The Old English Sheepdog is a large breed and requires the best feeding from the beginning. This includes pre-natal nourishment which, together with details about weaning and feeding the very young puppy, is dealt with in Chapter Seven, while an outline of how to feed the newly purchased puppy is given in Chapter Two.

By the time the puppy is twelve weeks old, he should be receiving four meals a day. You should gradually increase food quantities over the ensuing weeks, then, when he is eighteen weeks old, reduce his number of meals to three a day, while continuing to increase the amount he is eating. At twenty-four weeks, he will be able to come down to two meals a day. His puppy biscuit can now be left off his menu and be replaced by a larger kind. His meat intake each day at this stage of rapid growth should be about one and a half pounds. A teaspoonful of vegetable oil added to his meals will improve the quality of his coat. If the dog at this age is growing fast, but remains thin, and you are satisfied that he does not have worms, he may need up to half a pound more meat, and boiled rice and egg may be fed as an extra meal.

From six months to about two years the young dog needs to stay on this large amount of food in order to ensure steady, healthy growth. While professional breeders are fully aware of this, some pet owners do not appreciate that the time for maximum feeding is in the first two years of a dog's life, and that the average adult dog in fact requires less meat than the growing dog. Once the dog has reached the age of two, you may want to cut down his meat intake by a quarter to half a pound. An even older dog, over eight or nine years, will not require as much as this and should be given not only less meat, but also less biscuit. However, if a dog of any age is losing weight, and so long as the cause is not worms or a tumour or the onset of some serious disease, he can be given extra food in the form of rice, cereal or biscuits and, of course, your own left-overs.

Feeding routines of the adult dog vary from household to household. Some owners feed their dogs once a day, others divide the dog's daily intake into two sessions. It really does seem to depend on the owner and his ideas about how much his dog can comfortably manage to digest at one meal. Many family dogs are fed twice a day, usually a small meal of cereal or biscuits at breakfast-time when the family eats, and then again later in the day when they are given a meal which contains their main supply of meat.

Having dealt with quantities of food, we must turn to another problem which worries many dog owners, namely, what *type* of food should be given? Obviously, there must be a high meat or meat substitute content in the diet and there is a considerable range available, from varieties of dried foods to tinned and frozen food and raw and cooked butcher's meat.

It is possible to feed your dog on specially prepared dried food whose protein content is equivalent to that of meat. This sort of food is sold under various proprietary names in the form of meal or pellets. The meal is fed moistened with water while pellets are generally fed dry, but drinking water should always be available to dogs on this diet. This food is advertised as complete and containing all a dog requires to keep him healthy, so no other food should be fed with it or at any other time. The pellets bear no resemblance to meat but are usually made from meat, fish, blood and bone meals combined with cooked cereals with the addition of mineral and vitamin supplements and amino acids. Many owners swear by this diet and their dogs look a picture of health, although you may prefer to see your dog eating meat that *looks* like meat, adding nourishing home-grown vegetables and meat scraps from your own table. There are other dried foods on the market including dried meat pieces sold in three different sizes. This is highly concentrated and three-quarters of a pound of it is equal to a pound of fresh meat. You can also buy dried fish pieces. This type of fish and meat comes in bulk, but there are also other preparations of packaged dried meat available; if you use this, remember to follow the directions on the packet. Some stipulate that fresh water must be available alongside the bowl of meal.

There are also many varieties of tinned meats on the market, and it is difficult to assess the varying amounts of cereal and meat in each one. In these days of vegetable dyes and meat substitutes, dark 'meat' and rich brown 'gravy' is not always all that it seems. The most genuine sort of tinned food I know, which advertises its contents on the wrapper, does *not* contain dark brown food. It is expensive and very good. Probably the majority of family dogs are fed on tinned meat and they all thrive. You may have to experiment at first, because some dogs find certain foods too rich, while other brands will suit their digestions perfectly. Never feed tinned meat on its own, always mix in biscuits or left-overs from your own meals, including vegetables such as carrots, beans and cabbage. Some owners complain that the cheaper, sloppy brands pass straight through their dogs, but the addition of a complete biscuit meal mixed well in with the tinned food stops this. Tinned food has the advantage that it keeps well, is convenient and does not require special storage.

If you have plenty of freezer space, you may consider feeding your dog from the packs of frozen food available. Most of them are made from meat, offal and cereal and once they are unfrozen, smell rather strongly, but this is an asset as far as the dog is concerned!

We come finally to the original article, raw meat itself. Red raw meat is the nearest 'natural' food a dog can have, but not all dogs can take meat raw and many owners prefer to cook it. If it is cooked this should be done lightly and slowly; don't boil meat over a raging heat, for it will go tough and be thoroughly unappetizing. Ideally, meat should be served in chunks so that the dog has something to chew. Dog meat derived from butcher's scraps is often minced before it is sold, but ox cheek is usually sold in lumps and some butchers still sell sheep's heads. Offal, such as the paunch or stomach of a bullock, cow or sheep, and various trimmings of a butchered animal not required for human consumption can be given from time to time, but not every day. Liver is best served only once a week and it can be fed raw if it is fresh. Heart and kidney can also be given but these are better cooked. If you serve white meat, that is, chicken or rabbit, make sure that the bones are removed. These bones, if swallowed, will first be splintered by the dog's teeth, and the risk of these splinters piercing the intestine is a very real one.

Your dog will love bones all the same, but only give large marrow bones which will not splinter. Bones are items which some dogs become very possessive about, so if you are feeding more than one dog, give a bone to each. You can ask the butcher to cut a large bone into portions. Whilst your dog is still a puppy you should 'bone-train' him. That is, give him his food bowl, bone or tit-bit and then after a few seconds, take it away, make him wait quietly for a few moments, then give it back. If you do this regularly as part of his training, you will ensure that later in his life he will not snap or snarl if a toddler picks up his favourite toy or bone. After a dog has eaten a large amount of bone, his motions may be hard and white, so be prepared for this and realize that there is no cause for alarm unless you give him so many bones that it happens every day.

Feeding scraps or left-overs has already been mentioned and there is certainly no need to throw all your scraps away, but it is not advisable to feed your dog pieces from the table during a meal because he will come to expect them and will make himself a nuisance at meal-times. The cardinal rule about feeding scraps is that bones should not be included, so do not be tempted to put the remains of a chop or a chicken leg aside for your dog, and of course, scraps are not enough to satisfy the needs of either a puppy or an adult dog. Each dog must have his own specially prepared food, with table scraps as an appetizing bonus. Dogs may also eat fish, white fish being preferable to the yellow smoked or kippered variety. If your dog has had a tummy upset, white meat or white fish is usually recommended by a veterinary surgeon as an alternative to red meat for a day or two.

With their varied diet, some of today's dogs eat food which is a far cry from the natural food consumed by their ancestors, while others follow a regime of feeding where they eat food which is very similar to what they would have if they were to forage for themselves. The herbalists of old were not entirely wrong when they lauded the properties of our native herbs as sources of a natural health-giving diet for ourselves, and our animals too can benefit from natural feeding, remembering that 'natural' to them means the inclusion of meat.

The dog must also have roughage, usually in the form of biscuit, and health-giving vitamins and minerals. A health-food addict will always ensure that his dog is fed good, wholesome wheatmeal or wholemeal biscuits, just as he himself will eat only bread which contains the whole wheat germ. Water is given as a drink once puppyhood is over because, in their natural state, adult dogs have no source of milk and their digestive system is not equipped to cope with it. Vitamins and minerals can be obtained from natural foods such as watercress, parsley and seaweed. Firms which supply vitamins from these and other plant sources tend to concentrate them for convenience in tablet form. If you have a herb garden you can grow your own comfrey which contains more protein than other green vegetables and is almost unique in containing vitamin B12, which is very rarely found in plants. Comfrey also contains other B complex vitamins together with vitamins A and C and traces of the essential minerals, calcium, iron, manganese and phosphorous. Cook comfrey lightly in a little water, having first removed any tough veins from the leaves and mix it, like any other vegetable, with your dog's main meal, adding any liquid there may be over, as this makes a good drink.

An all-purpose health-giving food is honey. As it has already been pre-digested by the action of the bees who produce it, even sick animals can take it. It is a source of energy for a flagging dog

67

or for one whose appetite is not what it should be, and it is always recommended for animals suffering from heart conditions. It is easier to feed the firm rather than the runny variety, and it is best to do it out of doors or on a tiled kitchen floor which can easily be wiped over, for one of the less likable qualities of honey is its stickiness. For this reason it may be unpopular in the case of show dogs because of what it can do to their coat!

For dogs who are off-colour with stomach or intestinal upsets, barley water is recommended. This is not the commercial drinking cordial, which is flavoured with lemon, but is made by boiling one pint of water to which has been added a tablespoonful of pearl barley. Once the liquid has boiled, leave it to simmer for about twenty minutes. Then allow it to cool, strain off the barley and serve it to your dog. Honey can be added if he does not like the new taste.

If you are going to follow a regime of natural rearing, you will be urged to allow your dog to fast for one day out of every seven. The reason for this is that in the wild state a dog would not eat every day. Dogs have to hunt and eat when they can and on days when there is no food around they rest up, drinking but not eating, which gives their digestive system a rest. It does not cease to function, but works merely to eliminate completely all impurities and unwanted residue of food from the body. During fasting, dogs should be encouraged to drink plenty of water to aid this process. If a dog has a minor stomach or intestinal upset, it is advisable to make him fast, and this should be followed by a meatless day, or at least a day of white meat. If his stomach upset continues beyond a day or two, consult your vet.

Natural herbal remedies act more slowly and more gently than chemical ones, and watercress, parsley and sunflower seeds for your dog's coat and yeast and garlic for his general well-being are worth considering. All these things and more can be bought conveniently in powder or table form from many health stores and pet shops which specialize in selling the products of those dog food manufacturers devoted to natural rearing. All the major dog shows have stands where 'natural' foods are sold, and the advertisement columns of the weekly dog papers also contain details about obtaining this sort of food.

GROOMING

The Old English Sheepdog is high on the list of animals which require regular and frequent grooming. Special grooming, required for the show dog, over and above regular grooming, is included in Chapter Eight, but we shall deal here with the basics of grooming which all owners of pets and show animals should know about in order to care properly for the dog's coat.

Grooming has to begin from the moment you own the puppy. If he is about eight weeks old, which is the usual time to purchase a puppy, his coat will be black and white, short and very soft. Generally speaking, the coat of the older puppy and the young dog turns first to a paler grey than the true adult coat, but a visit to any dog show will prove that there are many exceptions to this rule.

The bobtail's coat requires a wooden- or plastic-handled hair brush with well-spaced bristles which can penetrate the adult coat. Alternatively, a brush with a cushion pad like the model made famous by Mason Pearson can be used. A steel comb is also necessary with strong two-inch (five-cm) teeth spaced about one-sixth of an inch (three mm) apart, but make sure the teeth are smooth and round at the points. A shallower comb with teeth half that length is useful for puppies, and such a comb will tend to have its teeth set closer together.

The puppy's coat usually begins to turn colour just above the hocks and on his shoulders, and this is a definite sign that grooming must begin. Before this time, it is advisable to introduce your puppy to the brush and comb with gentle grooming which will not only take out the puppy coat but will accustom him to the feel of grooming and persuade him that it is an enjoyable routine. As your puppy's coat lengthens, comb it regularly in order to prevent the puppy coat from matting, and keep the dead puppy hair moving so that the adult coat can grow through. As the hair grows, it becomes light grey from the source, and ends in brown tips which are the dead puppy hairs. In many puppies these come away with grooming, but in some bloodlines the brown tips persist and need to be removed by finger plucking, just as one would prepare a terrier for a show. A few hairs at a time must be gathered over the left palm and the top inch or two gripped by the left thumb. Then, with the right thumb and forefinger, grip the dead ends and pull down sharply, dropping the brown ends into a waste bin. At no time must any pressure pass down the coat to the body as this will cause discomfort and distress to a young dog and build up resistance to what should be a pleasurable grooming exercise. The use of scissors to do the same job usually results in very obvious straight lines all over the coat; even the use of pinking shears or thinning scissors cannot achieve the same effect of irregular breaks that finger stripping gives. After a thorough brush-out, the dog should, one hopes, have turned from a burnt brown colour to a glorious grey.

Once the puppy coat has gone, there is less use for the comb on the body, especially with the show dog, and more use should be made of the brush. You will notice as the puppy matures that your dog is developing two coats, the soft waterproof undercoat and the harsh, shaggy outside coat. Both are important to the show dog but a dog kept as a pet will be less difficult to groom if the soft undercoat is not allowed to grow too thick. So a good grooming is still part of the pet owner's routine, as combing will take out some of the undercoat and keep it down to manageable proportions.

If you have a strong table, stand your puppy on this for grooming and, particularly if you suffer from back trouble, continue to use the table for the adult dog. Some people prefer to groom the dog on the floor while he lies on his blanket and they themselves sit on a cushion. Large dogs seem to prefer the stability that the floor offers, and it does get round the problem of lifting a hefty, protesting bobtail on to a table. If he appears to like the method of table grooming, there will be no problem as he will get himself on to the table via a bench. Whether you use table or floor, there are parts of his body — the stomach and the insides of the legs in particular — which are much easier to groom if he lies down.

On the floor in front of the fireplace is a good place to groom, because in both summer and winter, whether there is a fire burning or not, a natural draught takes the fine brown dust that comes from the coat up the chimney. Asthma and bronchial sufferers will appreciate what a relief this can be. During the hay-fever season, it is advisable to wear a face-mask when confronted by a long session of grooming on a number of dogs; when it comes to changing the gauze dust-trap it is amazing to discover how much debris one would normally breathe into the lungs without it. Obviously, on warm days, the garden is the best place to groom.

A great deal of bobtail grooming is best done with the animal lying down on his side. The inside and outside of the legs can be done together with the feet and the sides of the body. The chest and stomach can be brushed or combed, and eyes, ears and mouth can also be cared for in this position. If there are mats in the coat, don't tug at them; the dog will not unnaturally object and in any case, you don't want to lose the undercoat in large chunks. Gently tease the mats apart using the index finger and thumb of each hand until you can start brushing or combing again. If the mat is very difficult, hold it with one hand and tease the mat with the end tooth of your largest comb. If it will not separate by this method, you may have to cut it open by scissoring but at no time must you pull away from the body; not only will the dog object, but you will pull out valuable coat. If the mat is really solid, scissoring is the only answer. The way to open up a mat is to use long, narrow-bladed hair-dressing scissors. If the dog is excitable, ask another person to hold him steady and reassure him gently. The lower blade of the scissors must slide under the mat along the dog's body and the cut is made *into* the mat in the general direction of the hairs, at a right angle to the body, never cut across the coat. Always watch out for nipples (even in a male) and of course the penis and scrotal sac. Never pull a mat towards you before scissoring. Nasty cuts can result from such an action. Once a cut is made through the mat, put the scissors aside and start teasing with the fingers again. Although this is a long process, the finished result of a matted dog restored to his former glory is infinitely preferable to shearing the whole coat off, the lazy way out to which so many owners resort.

When brushing or combing the legs while the dog is lying down, pay attention to the hair in the groin; this is a tender area, so be careful not to pull if there are knots, which are often caused by the friction of the dog's legs against his body when moving. Another area which mats easily is behind the top of the fore-legs, and the hair below the hocks can become plastered together with mud if the dog has been for a country walk in wet weather. Parts of the hindquarters can be groomed while the dog is lying down, but the rest of the body has to be finished off when he is standing up. While the dog is standing, make sure that the hindquarter hair is free of matting and that there is no matting of hair along the spine. Check that all the hair on the ears is clear, looking out for small, felted areas which can appear along the lower edges of the ear flaps. Beware of heavy-handedness here. Once mats have been broken up by the fingers, use the finer comb to remove the small 'felts' by combing along the flap and away from the ear. Be very gentle; take the flap in your left hand and guide the comb through slowly, making sure you don't catch the comb's teeth in the ear's skin tissue.

Then, while the dog is standing, give him his final all-over brush. The hair on his front legs should be brushed upwards and the neck and shoulder hair brushed downwards to meet it below the shoulder. Brush the chest hair down also, but brush the hair on the head and face forwards to make the head large and attractively shaggy. Brush the hair on his back down at the sides towards the floor and back along the top towards his rump. Brush the hair on his hind legs upwards and brush the rump hair upwards and outwards to give him a rump-in-the-air, cobby appearance, which is the style of presentation that is favoured by the exhibitor in the show ring.

If the dog is grubby, and particularly if the white hair is dusty or muddy, you will be delighted to find that a good grooming followed by correct brushing will work wonders. Brushing and combing will remove dirt and dust particles and restore the whiteness to the coat. Too much washing tends to soften the coat and washes out the natural oils which give it its characteristic springiness. If the white parts are really dirty, a localized wash may be useful. Grooming chalk and powder, which acts as a dry shampoo, can also be used to give extra whiteness.

There remains the question of how often one should groom the household pet. There are no hard and fast rules, so long as the coat is attended to frequently enough to avoid matting. Some owners prefer to do a little every day. Others prefer a bi-weekly careful grooming, and some save it all up for once a week. This last method may seem tempting, but if time is short and the weekly grooming is left over for several weeks, trouble accumulates. A daily brush and a twice-weekly grooming is probably most satisfactory, but whatever one's routine, there are times when extra grooming is imperative if the house dog is not to bring mud and wet into his owner's home. After a wet, muddy walk, it is a good idea to put each of the dog's feet in turn into a bucket of luke-warm water to remove the mud, and to dry all four legs with a towel before allowing the dog the freedom of the house. A wipe all over with a damp chamois leather is also a useful way of giving a quick clean to muddy coats.

CLEANLINESS AND HYGIENE CHECKS

A large coat of long shaggy hair can hide a multitude of sins. Regular, thorough grooming should eliminate trouble, but where a dog has not been regularly groomed problems do occur, so that beneath the apparently groomed exterior of a pet dog, a whole host of undesirable situations may be hidden. Eyes, ears, mouth, feet, pads, undercoat, genital areas and bottom can be neglected to the point of cruelty. So your dog must be groomed thoroughly, right through to the skin.

Eyes

Examine your dog's eyes daily and be sure that any congealed mucus in the inner corner of the eye is lifted off. This is usually easy because the mucus hardens as it dries. If it is soft, wipe it away with a piece of lint or cotton wool soaked in warm water or tepid tea. General staining can be remedied by the use of 'Diamond-eye' used by white poodle owners and other owners of white headed dogs. Boracic is another old favourite which is safe to use around the eyes. If, when grooming, you notice that your dog's eyes are always wet and running, consult your vet.

Ears

The insides of both ears need regular examination. The skin under the flap should be pink and as clean as anywhere else on the body. Neglected ears tend to be greasy and hold a deposit of dirt on the skin. If you have to wash the skin, do so very carefully, making sure that no liquid or soap gets into the ear itself. A plug of cotton wool, inserted first into one ear and then into the other would save a lot of head shaking. In other words, give your dog's ears as much care as you would to those of your children. Long-haired dogs often grow hair from the interior of the ear cavity, and a division of opinion exists on the subject of whether to pluck hair from the ear canal or not. I can see the force of both arguments. If all the hair is removed, grass seeds, wet and cold air can be let in, and continual pulling at a tender area from a conscientious owner often promotes bacterial and mite infestation.

On the other hand, if too much hair is allowed to grow from this area, a large waxy mat may form which will be painful to remove and may impair hearing. Normally, however, once the top hair has been removed there is an otherwise perfectly clear ear canal, so I therefore advocate a 'middle-of-the-road' approach, which leaves the longer guard hairs to protect the ear opening, and removes the smaller, wax-covered hairs by careful plucking with artery forceps, these being smoother edged than household tweezers. Deep plucking should only be done by a veterinary surgeon and then usually under anaesthetic so that the dog does not shake his head.

Mouth

One of the most discoloured areas of a bobtail's coat is around the mouth. The hair often mats because food remains in it, so this part of the face needs to be watched and washed regularly, and combed with a wide-toothed comb after meals.

Teeth

If your dog's teeth are badly coated with tartar you will need professional help from your vet, but it is possible to keep the teeth clean with a damp rag dipped in salt. Some owners use toothpaste designed for smokers and Zepto sticks to scale off tartar, but a canine brand of toothpaste is available.

Feet

Hair will grow between the dog's pads, and if this is not scissored away back to skin level, it can form a mat containing grit and soil which will cause the dog to suffer from sore feet. In snowy weather, the dog's feet and the hair around them will collect large balls of snow which will solidify into ice. Even when returning to a house or a warmed kennel, these ice balls take some time to melt and in the meantime can cause discomfort. You can speed up the melting by placing each paw in turn in a bowl of tepid water and rubbing the feet dry with a towel. A dog's pads must be watched for cracking and drying. This can be a source of considerable discomfort to the dog and the pads will require washing in warm water and lubricating with vaseline or lanoline. Watch the dog's nails, particularly if you keep him in the country or in a kennel where the run is on grass. The nails of a town dog or a dog with a concreted kennel run tend to get worn down and rarely become over-long in consequence, but the country dog's nails have a chance to grow and will probably require cutting from time to time. Long nails can cause pad spreading which is a deformity in a bobtail. It is possible to cut the dog's nails yourself with nail clippers made for the purpose. Never use ordinary scissors as they tend to split the nail and often will not cut through them anyway. Be sure to cut only the dead nail, which is a pale greyish-yellow colour, leaving the part where the pink quick can be seen. It is harder to see the quick on dew claws and any black nails, so exercise a great deal of caution as the quick, if cut, bleeds profusely. If in any doubt about nail cutting, it is far safer to seek professional advice from a veterinary surgeon or a breeder.

Hindquarters

Your dog's hindquarters need to be looked after carefully. With plenty of physical exercise and a regular, balanced diet, he should not have too many intestinal upsets, but as with all long coated animals, any difficulty in the evacuation of faeces will usually result in soiled hair around the hind parts. This is not only objectionable to the family with whom he lives but decidedly unhygienic, for the improperly evacuated faeces adheres to the dog's hair as he sits on it and becomes firmly caked so that any further evacuation of waste products is virtually impossible or at least painful and difficult. Sometimes it is possible to comb him clean and a puff of talcum powder dries out the hair, but in bad cases the coat must be scissored away around the anus and the dog must be washed. It is an unpleasant task but one which must be faced. Rubber gloves and plenty of fresh air help. The Old English Sheepdog is naturally clean in his habits and hates to be dirty, so never scold him; if you are sympathetic and gentle and get him clean and comfortable as soon as possible, he will certainly be very grateful.

HOUSING

Indoor Housing

Housing a dog indoors is a comparatively simple matter because the basic requirements of warmth and shelter are already there. The main problems to be resolved concern the extent of the house the dog is going to share with the family, the type of bed he is going to have and where he will stay when he comes in from a walk with exceptionally wet and dirty feet. Being such a large dog, the Old English Sheepdog is going to take up a fair amount of room both waking and sleeping. The normal, commercially produced dog bed is not nearly large enough for an adult dog. He may be able to curl up on it, but he will not be able to stretch out as he should do. Provided that it is not placed in a draught, a perfectly adequate bed can be made from blankets or rugs placed on a folded sleeping bag or old eiderdown. Bedding should be of the washable sort and it is helpful to have two lots, so that while one set is being washed and dried, the second can be used. If you cut up an old blanket and quilted sleeping bag or eiderdown, you should get two sets of bedding unless the dog is abnormally large. From the point of view of washing the bed, a terylene filled quilt is easy to put in a washing machine or spin drier. You would probably have more trouble with feather fillings.

Hopefully, you will encounter no more than mud and a certain amount of grease from the dog's coat which has to be washed out of the bedding. However, it is very easy, particularly in the summer, for your dog to pick up dog fleas. They live in the dog's coat until it is time for them to breed when they go into the dog's bedding to lay their eggs. Once the eggs have hatched, the fleas are ready to return to the dog's coat. So if your dog has fleas, treat his bedding as well, disinfecting it with flea powder and in severe cases, washing it in a disinfectant liquid like Emsil, designed to combat parasites, which can be obtained at pet stores.

Try to place the dog's bed somewhere that he can feel is his own special territory. As dogs like lying with their backs against a wall a corner position is good, but if no corner can be spared try at least to place his bed against one wall. As already noted, many dogs appear to like lying under tables, and as long as the family are not going to sit round a table regularly and kick the dog with their feet, under a table against a wall is often an ideal spot to locate the dog's bed. Remember that because of his heavy coat he will not thank you if you put his bed beside the Aga. In fact, he will probably refuse to use it if you do, choosing instead to lie in the coolest spot to sleep, on tiles or flagstones, for example.

The house dog's feeding arrangements are usually best contained in the kitchen or utility room. Although the Old English Sheepdog is not a messy feeder, water can be spilt, pieces of food dropped and biscuit crumbs scattered. A heavy water bowl helps avoid most spills, but a sheepdog can upset even that if he accidentally puts his foot on the side of the bowl. How much of your home is your dog going to share with you? Even if you are prepared to share the whole house, there will be times when your dog is too dirty to go into some rooms until he has been wiped down and dried off. So you will have to devise ways of confining him, and obviously it is very unsociable to shut doors in your dog's face. A gate across the bottom of the stairs will keep the dogs out of the bedrooms, and a 'toddler gate' would probably work just as well if there are children in the house, so long as it is strong enough to withstand the onslaughts of a determined bobtail who wants to spend a siesta on your continental quilt.

There are also times when you may want to confine the dogs to the kitchen, without shutting them off altogether from people in the living-room, and you might hang a wrought iron gate, made to your specifications, across the kitchen doorway for this purpose. The kitchen door can be left open and the iron half-gate closed, and the dogs can gather round and look into the living room.

If your dog is sharing your living quarters to a major extent, you will have to exercise strict rules of hygiene. (Certain unpleasant conditions like ringworm and a type of mange can be transmitted to adults and children.) If your dog's coat should become badly infested with fleas, you will have to disinfect the carpets and furniture. Details about de-infestation of premises can be found in Chapter Five under the section on parasites. You will also find PRO Dogs literature on the subject very helpful. However, if you take reasonable precautions over cleanliness, the Old English Sheepdog will prove a wonderful house dog who lives very well alongside a family under the same roof, and if you have no more than two or three dogs it seems a shame to kennel them because you will be missing marvellous companionship.

Most breeders have their kennel dogs and their house dogs, usually in order of seniority, with older dogs moving into the warmth as they grow old and require more of their creature comforts. Some, like ourselves, have the dogs around us all day. The majority are kennelled at night while the older ones sleep indoors, each in his own favourite spot. Temperament is an important consideration if you adopt this method; a family bond develops between the dogs and sometimes there is a definite 'pecking order', but the owner must always retain the position of pack leader in order to keep the peace.

Outdoor Housing

A great deal of thought has to go into the design of outdoor kennels. A single kennel is necessary for a bitch with puppies or for segregating a bitch in season, but otherwise, double kennels are more companionable. Basic requirements are good ventilation, warmth, absence from draughts and weatherproofing. There must also be enough room for the dogs to move around when they are inside. The kennels should be erected on a well-drained site so that the runs have a chance to dry out quickly after heavy rain, and with hot weather in mind, you need to place them where there will be some shade for the dogs in summer.

Most kennels are built of wood with a raised wooden floor

which can easily be scrubbed clean. One end of the kennel can be converted into sleeping quarters by building a raised platform about six inches above the floor. If the whole kennel can be lined with something like hardboard it makes a warmer, cosier home for the dogs and prevents them from chewing the framework. The well thought out placing of doors and windows also adds to the comfort of the outdoor home. Don't have a door in one wall opposite a window in the facing wall as this is a potential source of draughts. Keep the door and the window down one end of the kennel so that the far end is a little darker, and place the bed platform here.

The window should be large enough to provide both light and air and ideally it should always remain partially open unless the rain is blowing directly in. If the window is placed fairly low, about two feet from the floor, the dog will be able to see out and won't spend his time jumping up or standing on his hind legs to look out, which is not good for his joints. Keep the dog away from the actual heavy gauge glass by having wire fencing across the window on the inside. There are various ways of arranging window openings. Some kennel owners prefer windows which open outwards and upwards. These have the advantage of keeping the rain out most effectively. Other owners make use of sliding windows. Either way seems more desirable than wooden shutters because, once the door is closed and the shutters fastened, the dogs are in the dark and shut away from all that is going on around them.

Many kennel doors are made as half doors so that the bottom half can be fastened to keep the dogs in, while the upper portion remains open to admit light and air. While this is in some ways a good idea, it means that your dogs are probably going to spend a lot of time on their hind legs looking out if they think what is going on outside is more interesting than in their own quarters.

Inside the kennel, you are going to need somewhere to put feeding or grooming utensils, so shelving, convenient for you but out of reach of the dogs, is going to be very useful. Never store cleaning agents, the dog's medicines or gardening aids such as weedkillers or slug bait, on the kennel shelving, even though it might be a handy place, as bobtails can jump very high and, if bored, might find one of your containers a nice toy.

In the summer months, the dogs will have little need for bedding and will find their raised platforms are all they need for a night's rest. In the winter, wood shavings or wheat straw, which is generally cleaner than other types of straw which tend to hold parasites, is suitable as a bedding material. During very cold winters an infra red heater will take the chill off and of course infra red lamps are necessary in the whelping kennel with newly born puppies, so you should arrange for an electricity supply to be laid on to the kennels, with the switches placed high up on the walls so that the dogs cannot switch them on or off by jumping up at them. The wiring, of course, should be run at a height where it cannot be chewed.

If whelping is going to take place in a kennel, further provision will have to be made for bedding, so that the litter cannot fall off the bedding platform. I prefer to whelp my bitches indoors, in the ordinary square whelping box with farrowing rails all round (details of which are given in Chapter Seven). Not only is it easier to control the temperature indoors, but the bitch also has a chance to get away from her kennel mates, for at a time of stress like this she may regard them as rivals and a danger to her puppies. We also put a camp bed alongside the whelping box and sleep in shifts for the first week beside the bitch and her pups — which would be a difficult exercise in a small kennel! But if your kennels are substantial buildings, where you can maintain tranquillity around the bitch and a steady, warm temperature, and if they are vermin-proof (especially from rats) and above all draught-proof and dry, you are set for a trouble-free whelping out of the house.

Environmental Health Officers who, in most districts, have the job of issuing Breeders' Licences under the Dog Breeding Act seem to prefer a completely separate whelping kennel with facilities for a higher level of hygiene than one would accept in an ordinary kennel. It is very important that you notify the local Planning Officer of any buildings you may intend to erect if your kennel plans show foundations or brick walls. Wooden kennels of a small construction usually termed 'free standing' are classified as temporary buildings and do not need planning permission or have to meet building regulations, but once you start to erect covered runs, you are approaching the borderline, so have a word with your local Town Hall, to avoid any problems later on.

The kennel run should form an integral part of the entire kennel space, so that the dogs can move freely from inside to outside when their door is left open. If the dog is never allowed into the house, or outside the kennelling area for exercise, the run ought to be made as large as possible, larger than the length or width of the kennel. If it can incorporate features such as trees, so much the better as it all adds interest to the dog's environment. Bearing in mind the strength of the Old English Sheepdog, these runs require stout chain link fencing held by strong posts set well into the ground. The dogs are going to launch themselves against the fencing countless times every day of the year, and vertical posts supporting fencing six feet (1.80 m) high are not enough; horizontal posts must also be incorporated to withstand the onslaught.

The gate into the run needs to be designed with care. This requires two strong posts to support it, and the gate itself must be built to withstand the weight of more than one dog. It must also have a fastening the dogs cannot learn to open.

If you are about to establish kennels, a word with an established breeder of any large breed in your area will prove very beneficial, as apart from all the useful hints and tips he may be prepared to pass on to you about the construction of his kennels, and faults he may find with his own arrangements in practice, he will also know what the local Environmental Health Officers require, and will be able to guide you about estimated costs. Make sure that you arrange such a meeting by appointment, as there is nothing worse for a breeder than trying to feed a crowd of hungry dogs while he attempts to answer questions at the same time. Of the typical hints that come to mind, one is the construction of support posts on the side away from the dogs. This means that they cannot chew the wood (and this applies especially to young dogs), and is helpful when the yearly creosoting comes round as you don't have to lock the dogs away for a whole day while the application dries, but only for the short time it takes to do the actual creosoting. Moreover, it will, of course, strengthen the wire if the posts take up the strain of the dogs' weight on the fence, rather than the metal staples if the posts were on the other side. If your bank balance will stretch to angle-iron supports, sink these and the bottom few inches of wire into a raised trench of concrete which can be made by shuttering the sides with odd lengths of floor boards. An added advantage is that this four-inch (10-cm) step holds in your kennel run surface whatever it is you use — shingle, earth, pulverized fuel ash, turves or paving — and prevents the most fox-like of bobtails from digging out.

I am not an advocate of concrete for the actual run area as not only does it get very hot in summer if there is no roof cover, but a strong mixture will sometimes precipitate the powdered cement and this can crack the pads and create sore feet. It is better to use paving slabs all around the edges of the run (the part the dog uses most) and from the gate to the kennels and wherever wear will occur. Second-hand slabs, either broken or whole, can be picked up quite cheaply from the Local Authority Highways Department, and these old pavement slabs prove, on inspection, to contain chips of stone formed under pressure into a cement mixture which does not harm the pads. Of course, careful choice from a good range of craftsman-built kennels with a well-designed run and coloured ornamental paving slabs can turn a utility area into a very attractive garden feature, if you can afford it.

Bed your slabs on to sand, and brush sand into the joints and this will enhance drainage. A narrow strip of concrete can be mixed and laid immediately in front of the kennels. While the concrete is still wet, lay an old piece of plastic guttering into it and use it to form a gully which should fall away over the kennel frontage to an area which the dogs will not frequent; dig a soakaway here, that is, a deep pit filled with old rubble, half bricks and large stones from the garden. You can always stand a garden butt (make sure it has a lid) over the top and collect the rain water from the kennel and run roof at the same time, but if it is standing over a soakaway and should overflow there is no harm done. This pit will take away all the kennel hosings if the channel has a fall of about one inch (1.5 cm) every six feet (1.80 m), and your guttering on the kennels and run (if needed) should have the same sort of fall. It will also prevent the run area from getting unnecessarily wet after its regular cleaning session.

Before you lay your run, consider the supply of services to the kennel. Will you need electricity or water? Are you likely to have an office or a caravan nearby? Most local ironmongers can supply polythene water piping and British Standard Institute electric cable that can be sunk into the ground at least eighteen inches (45 cm) down. If you think that piped water and electricity are unnecessary expenses, you may be inclined to change your mind when you find yourself trying to carry two buckets of water as well as a torch on a dark night from the house to the kennels. Moreover, hoses trailing up the garden can be a nuisance; dogs chew them; you trip over them, they are unsightly, and infra red lamps won't work on batteries.

If your kennels are in a built-up area, you will have to consider your neighbours when deciding upon the siting of the kennels. Trees and shrubs help to deaden the noise of barking — and have the added advantage of providing shade for the dogs in summer and affording some protection from wind and rain. Always consider the effects of wind and driving rain on your dogs' comfort. A verandah or a simple extension of the roof of the kennel may suffice, but if a dog is going to be left in the run for long periods, the run itself could be halved by the addition of another gate and some more fencing, and this smaller area adjacent to the kennel could be covered over. Corrugated sheets of perspex which let the light in may be used, and are ideal for small areas, say six feet (1.80 m) square. A larger area would not only work out very expensive, but has the added disadvantage that on a hot day, when there is no breeze, the heat in the run can prove quite exhausting to the dog.

If you construct covered areas to your runs, or if you leave the kennel door open when the dog is in the run, don't expect your bobtail to take himself inside during a downpour. My experience is that they will lie out in rain, wind and snow and go into the kennel when we are sunning ourselves in the garden.

Another factor worth bearing in mind is that dogs can jump over very high fences. Chain link mesh gives them a very good purchase when clambering over a six-foot (1.80 m) fence, so do not leave a gap between the top of the fence and the roof. A dog could get over in order to get at a bitch in season, or you may find you own a Houdini like our old lady who, even at the age of nine, climbs out of every restraint we put on her. When a stud dog is kept with bitches, it is well to place his kennel some way off from theirs, so that he is not driven frantic and tempted to climb out each time a bitch comes into season; also arrange that he exercises in the opposite direction from the bitches' kennels, taking his walks to leeward, rather than windward.

CARE OF THE AGEING DOG

The expected life span of the Old English Sheepdog is around twelve years, although some live for a shorter time and a few go over the twelve-year mark. As with humans there will be some deterioration in health and some slowing down as old age approaches. Some bobtails become progressively, and eventually totally, blind. A dog who has a happy, stable home life adapts to his fading vision; he finds his way around the house and garden with no difficulty and can be taken for walks on a lead.

Blindness and general slowing-down would present real problems in a working dog. Working sheepdogs of any type do not take kindly to retirement, and many are so obviously upset at finding themselves no longer able to drive cattle and sheep that the owner has to put them down to relieve their distress. On the other hand, there is no need to have the elderly family pet put down so long as he is not in obvious pain, can move freely and enjoy his food and human company. If he is blind, help him to find his way around the house. If he appears to be disobedient, suspect deafness rather than a change of character. Regular half-yearly health checks with the vet are in order, but you are the best judge of his general state of well-being and can notice any deterioration in health or change in behaviour. As you groom your older dog, you can look out for the condition of his eyes, ears, feet and backside. Never clip off the coat of an elderly dog. They need the warmth a good thick jacket of fur can offer. Kidney problems are very common in old age and one could consider a dog coat if the natural one is sparse. Regular grooming gently undertaken keeps his coat in good order and also allows you to check for unexplained lumps (which the vet should examine), bad teeth and sore gums. Keeping an eye on your dog when he relieves himself is a check on the normal, regular working of kidneys and bowels.

The older dog may put on weight and will not need so much food. Cut back on the amount of carbohydrates and give leaner meat with not too much fat. Generally, keep up the protein and provide more water. Probably two small meals a day are better than one large one. Sympathy and understanding eases his old age. If he is sleeping, don't disturb him unduly and don't let children pull him about and expect him to play as much as a young dog would. Cut back gradually on exercise and make his walks shorter. The older dog also needs — theoretically at least — more warmth and should be kept out of draughts. Of course, the dog may decide otherwise; an elderly dog may have a penchant for frosty moonlight nights and may escape from the house, if he can, to sleep outside on a piece of concrete, but this is far from advisable, as dogs of advanced years are prone to rheumatism and arthritis.

As soon as it is obvious that the old dog is in pain, or that movement is too much for him, the kindest thing to do is to have him painlessly put down by your vet. One of the last things you can do for him is to take him there yourself and hold him while it is being done. It is a heart-breaking experience but your dog will surely appreciate your presence at the end when he is very ill or very old, and it is also easier for your vet to have someone to hold the dog while he does what is necessary.

A marvellous antidote for losing a dog is to buy a new puppy. No dog can replace the old one because every dog is different, but the puppy will take up so much of your time and attention that there will be no time to spend mourning your old dog, even though you can never forget him.

Chapter 5

HEALTH AND FIRST AID

CONTAGIOUS DISEASES

There are four contagious diseases which are common among dogs, and an animal suffering from one of these generally becomes very ill and usually dies. If he does recover, his general health and stamina will probably have been undermined for the rest of his life. Fortunately there is a very simple precaution the dog owner can take by having his animal vaccinated to provide immunity from all four diseases. Two doses are usually given as injections, the first when the puppy is approximately twelve weeks old, provided that he is healthy, and the second is administered two weeks later. Inoculating the puppy any earlier than around twelve weeks old is often a waste of time and money. The puppy will have taken a natural immunity against distemper from its mother's milk, and these antibodies react against the vaccine. Some breeders use a measles vaccine from around three weeks old and this gives the puppy an immunity for up to five months. But what is not often appreciated is that if the mother herself was given a measles vaccine when a puppy, the antibodies are passed on to her puppies and the measles vaccine they receive will be ineffective. If the breeder insists on having the puppy vaccinated before you take him at eight weeks old, a second full dose of vaccine must be given without fail at twelve weeks of age.

Most of the vaccines are marketed under trade names. Which kind your dog receives will depend on the type your vet is currently using. The laboratories issue vaccination or inoculation certificates which are filled out for you by your vet after the second dose of vaccine has been administered, giving the owner's name and address, the dog's age, breed and sex, together with details of the vaccine used. These vaccines generally give life-long protection against two of the contagious diseases, namely distemper and hepatitis, although some dogs may lose their immunity to distemper during the first two years following the administration of the vaccine. For continuous immunization against the other two, leptospira canicola and icterohaemorrhagiae, booster injections must be given annually or every eighteen months. There are spaces on the form for your vet to fill in the date when the booster doses are due and for him to give details of the dosage given each time the dog returns for further immunization. These forms are generally issued as booklets with hard covers or plastic jackets so that they last the dog's lifetime.

Signs and Symptoms of Canine Distemper and Hard Pad

Distemper produces a diphasic temperature; the dog's eyes and nose discharge mucus and he coughs and appears to find breathing difficult. The disease is also accompanied by gastro-enteritis. The dog's nervous system is affected and he may suffer from fits and convulsions. In especially virulent forms of the disease, the skin will erupt, hair will fall out and pads will become hard and sore. Once your dog has contracted the disease, it is difficult to inject anti-serum effectively and death usually results. Earlier this century a very high percentage of puppies of all breeds died of distemper, but with the increased use of preventative inoculation, the disease is now virtually unknown in puppies.

If you are buying a puppy to replace a dog that died from distemper, and you are proposing to bring the newcomer into the same house or kennels, you must quarantine your home for at least two months to all dogs and burn all the previous dog's possessions, bedding and brushes. If the puppy is booked to come to you by a certain date within this two month period, ask the breeder to kennel him until the quarantine has ended. If the breeder cannot do this for you, arrange for a friend to take the puppy until you can have him.

Canine or Viral Hepatatis *(also known as Rubarth's Disease)*

This is a disease which attacks the liver. The symptoms are gastro-enteritis and excessive thirst. Fever generally follows and jaundice sets in. Unfortunately, long before the disease is obvious, the condition is too far advanced for the dog's life to be saved. As the disease is highly contagious, it can spread through a kennel and carry off complete litters of puppies.

Leptospira Canicola

This is a disease affecting both kidneys and liver and, except in mild cases, the dog rarely recovers if the disease is too far advanced before it is detected. The symptoms are ulcerated gums and mouth with brown staining on the teeth. There is also brown slime on the gums. Treatment must commence early in the course of the disease to be successful, but despite treatment, permanent kidney damage is likely.

Leptospira Icterohaemorrhagiae

This is extremely infectious and the commonest cause is the urine of rats. The symptoms are listlessness and loss of appetite, great thirst and vomiting. The dog's motions tend to be a pale clay-like colour. Jaundice follows, eyes, gums and skin turn yellow, and the dog usually dies. If dogs receive regular annual boosters, it is extremely unlikely that they will contract either of the leptospiral diseases.

Canine Parvovirus

A recent infectious disease beleived to have arrived in the UK from the USA. Related to the virus which causes feline enteritis and is most serious in young puppies, often resulting in whole litters dying between four and eight weeks of age. The symptoms are diarrhoea, vomiting and often bleeding. The condition can cause both enteritis and myocarditis. There is a new vaccine available which is specifically for the disease, but many vets are using feline enteritis vaccine to give some protection.

HEREDITARY DEFECTS

In many breeds, and the Old English Sheepdog is no exception, the demands of fashion have led to various inherited weaknesses of both physique and temperament. The Old English Sheepdog, being a large animal, suffers from various types of hip abnormality common to large breeds and classified under the general name of hip dysplasia. The Old English Sheepdog also suffers as a breed from two types of eye condition, entropion or in-growing eyelids, and progressive retinal atrophy (PRA) which eventually results in blindness. It is most likely that your dog will never suffer from any of these conditions, but they are described together here because they are three defects to which the breed is prone through heredity.

Hip Dysplasia

This is a general term which actually means a badly formed hip joint but encompasses various abnormal conditions of the ball and socket joint formed by the acetubulum and the head of the femur. The main feature is a varying degree of looseness at the joint (laxity) which can lead to the head of the femur not seating at all in the socket (sublaxation). This results in differing degrees of shallow acetabulum and flattenings of the femoral head, which inevitably lead to osteo arthritis. Joint laxity is genetically controlled, but a number of environmental considerations vary the severity of hip dysplasia.

Since hip dysplasia can be present as an abnormality at any

time in the first two years of your dog's life, it is wise to watch your puppy for any sign of reluctance to rise from a sitting position. Look also for other signs, such as a dog resting his weight on one back leg only, or generally appearing weak in the hindquarters.

The surest way to diagnose hip dysplasia is by X-ray, the very worst cases being detected from two weeks old, although a routine X-ray to check on the condition would not normally be taken until the puppy is over twelve months old, because by this time the bones have set or ossified, the adult hard bone taking the place of the softer puppy frame.

In 1965, the British Veterinary Association and the Kennel Club jointly launched a scheme to try to control the spread of this condition. A panel of experts scrutinize X-ray plates that have been submitted to them by conscientious owners, through their vets, and if perfect hip formation is found, a clearance certificate is issued to the owners. A report is sent to the relevant vet, whatever the result.

Unfortunately comparatively few dogs have gained such a certificate, and when one considers that the panel studies six areas of the right hip and seventeen graded conditions of these areas, marking their interpretations to three degrees on each of these specified conditions, and then do the same for the left hip, it can be seen that standards are high. The scrutineers also take into account the quality of the plate itself and the position of the hips on the radiograph. Then they make one of three decisions:

i.   The findings fall within the agreed limits of normality and a certificate should be issued.

ii. The findings do not fall within the agreed limits of normality and a certificate should not be issued.

iii. The findings do not fall within the agreed limits of normality and the certificate should be withheld, but a 'Breeder's Letter' may be sent.

A Breeder's Letter states that the dog showed borderline changes which placed it outside the range of normality; then follows a short piece of guidance on the choice of dogs to use to eradicate the defect from future generations.

The Old English Sheepdog Club has started its own hip-grading scheme. Using two veterinary surgeons, working on a principle similar to the Kennel Club scheme, they assess the X-ray plates of members' dogs and assign the following grades:

1. The very best for breeding dogs without hip dysplasia. Recommended for submission to the KC/BVA Scheme.
2. The dog has a practical working joint which should last its lifetime.
3. An adequate joint giving a little trouble towards the end of the dog's life span. Recommended to be used with a mate awarded Grade 1 rating, when bred with for other points.
4. The dog is of no real interest in a breeding programme.

It is a great pity that only a few breeders use these schemes to screen their breeding stock. It is true that many have their dogs X-rayed and seek their own vet's opinion, but the majority of people breeding puppies do nothing to eradicate the condition. The greatest problem is trying to convince owners that hip dysplacia has no clinical symptoms. It is only after the X-ray plate has been seen that the condition is discovered in many dogs which show no apparent signs of suffering from it; movement may be perfect, which can be explained by the fact that the faulty joint has stabilized and the bone growth is completed and during this time, the dog has managed to compensate for its dysplasia. Plates have been seen where only the pelvic muscles have held together the wayward bone structure.

Recent figures clearly show how the incidence of hip dysplasia was reduced when selective breeding took place. With both parents within 'normal' limits, 64 per cent of progeny could be certified as normal. Where only one parent was within normal limits, 54 per cent of progeny could be certified, and with neither parent normal, 37 per cent of progeny could be certified. Two normal parents can produce offspring with severe hip dysplasia because it is a disease with a polygenic mode of inheritance, that is, several genes are involved in the transmission. The main point, however, is that with normal parents, on average over a number of litters, fewer dysplastic puppies will be born. Proof can be further provided, by bringing normal grandparents into the pedigree, that hip dysplasia is hereditary and not solely due to environmental factors. Dr F. Nicholas has tabulated his findings over an admitted small number of dogs and found that with three grandparents and two parents 'within normal limits', 100 per cent progeny are normal; with two grandparents and two parents within normal limits, 71 per cent of progeny are normal; with one grandparent and two parents within normal limits, 68 per cent of progeny are normal.

Genetics apart, both nutrition and exercise have been shown to affect the frequency and degree of hip dysplasia. The desire of some breeders to promote rapid growth with resultant overweight is not conducive to sound hip formation. Similarly, over-exercise in a young puppy and standing up at windows tends to add stress to the joints.

The owner of a dog who discovers that it has hip dysplasia should let the breeder know, offering proof in the form of X-ray plates or a vet's report. In acute cases, where the dog is in pain, the only humane thing to do is to have him painlessly put down. However, there are cases where the family pet with a slight malformation is able to lead a happy, carefree life.

Progressive Retinal Atrophy *(PRA or Night Blindness)*

This can usually be diagnosed by a very careful inspection of the eye by a veterinary surgeon using an ophthalmoscope. An owner may recognize early signs by detecting an increase in pupil size and a tendency on the dog's part to stumble against objects when in an unfamiliar environment. This condition is more serious for the working sheepdog, as it signals the end of his useful life; working dogs do not take kindly to a life of leisure and pine so much to be back at work that they sometimes have to be put down.

For the family dog or the retired show dog, the condition is one which can be lived with by most. As the onset of the disease is gradual, the dog adapts to this condition of failing or restricted vision and by the time he is really blind he is able to find his way around the home without having to rely on his sight. He can even go for walks over familiar territory without much trouble, although he should always be on a lead in traffic or among a lot of people. This defect on its own is certainly not a cause for putting an otherwise healthy dog down as long as he is obviously not distressed by his condition.

This appears to be something to which members of the breed are especially susceptible where line breeding is used. It is a more difficult condition to eradicate than hip dysplasia in that it usually becomes apparent only in older dogs, by which time it is too late to lay an embargo on breeding. As with hip dysplasia, the Kennel Club has a scheme whereby dogs examined and passed as clear are given a temporary certificate. Once the dog reaches an age laid down for the breed by the scheme it is checked again and a permanent certificate issued. Full details of this and other schemes run by the Kennel Club's Abnormalities Sub-committee, with a list of dogs passed as clear, can be obtained from Clarges Street.

Entropion

This is a congenital defect in which the eyelids turn inwards. Either the upper or the lower lid may be affected, or even both together. This condition causes the eyelashes to brush against the cornea, causing intense irritation which produces keratitis or inflammation of the cornea, accompanied usually by conjunctivitis. An operation can cure this, but any responsible breeder would not breed from affected stock or bloodlines known to carry the condition.

GENERAL HEALTH PROBLEMS

Abscess

This indicates a collection of pus and where an abscess can be seen beneath the skin, it is generally the result of some wound which has become infected; it may even be caused by the dog scratching a spot or sore place with a dirty claw. Keep the place clean and bathe it frequently with warm water. You can add Epsom salts in the proportion of one teaspoonful to one pint of water. This should bring the abscess to a head by about the end of three days. Once it bursts, continue bathing to remove all pus. If the abscess does not heal, or if many abscesses erupt over the skin, specialist help should be sought at once. When dealing with an abscess or any kind of skin wound in a bobtail, it greatly helps cleansing if the long hair around it is clipped away.

Anal Irritation

The major cause is due to the blockage of the anal glands, which are sited at each side of the rectum. The dog experiences pain or irritation and may delay evacuation or rub his anal area along the ground. Each of the two glands opens just inside the anus slightly below and to one side, and the liquid that is exuded not only helps the passing of motions but also acts as a scent to other dogs. Some dogs regularly suffer from impacted anal glands and it is possible to empty the glands yourself, although most pet owners leave it to the capable hands of the vet. If you do it yourself, be warned that the secretion, which is usually clear, will, in a case of blocked anal glands, be a thick, evil-smelling pus. You will need a large piece of cotton wool and having placed it over the anus, squeeze with finger and thumb at the 'twenty to four' position. If the dog reacts violently — or if you do — take him to your vet for treatment.

Other causes of anal irritation are inflammation of the prostate gland in dogs, abscesses, diarrhoea and inflammation of the rectal wall. If your dog or puppy continually rubs his backside on the ground, nibbles himself or seems unwilling to pass urine or faeces, consult your vet.

Bad Breath

Bad teeth will cause bad breath, as will tartar on the teeth or a gum disease like pyorrhoea, or ulcerated gums. Certain diseases of the heart and stomach also give rise to bad breath, and even inactive anal glands can cause breath odour. If the breath smells of acetone, it is an indication that there may be a disturbance of glucose control of the body. Cases of bad breath should be reported to a vet, who will diagnose the cause.

Constipation

One cause of constipation in the Old English Sheepdog can be a blocked anal opening if the dog's coat is neglected in this area. Faecal material sticks to the hair, the dog sits down and gradually the whole area is blocked. The dog finds evacuation of stools increasingly difficult and painful, delays evacuation as long as possible and, as a result, becomes constipated. Dosing with milk of magnesia, together with exercise and grooming, should sort the problem out. A balanced diet, water and exercise should prevent constipation but if the condition occurs and persists, veterinary advice should be sought because it may indicate an obstruction caused by a foreign body or a tumor.

Cough

There are many causes of coughs. A loud, dry, hard cough usually indicates laryngitis; excessive barking can cause this sort of cough. Inflammation of the pharynx is indicated by a short, dry cough. Wheezy coughs accompanied by laboured breathing are often a sign of emphysema (wind) or hay-fever. Some deep coughs indicate a heart condition. A recurrent cough should be referred to a vet so that he can diagnose and prescribe antibiotics, antihistamines or whatever is appropriate.

Diarrhoea

If there is no accompanying rise in body temperature, this usually indicates a digestive upset. Many owners starve the dog of solid food for twenty-four hours and then return to feeding white meat (i.e. rabbit or chicken) for a day or two instead of red meat. A kaolin mixture will prove a useful remedy, but if the diarrhoea persists beyond forty-eight hours, a vet should be consulted, as a digestive upset, corrected by fasting and a change of diet, should respond more quickly than this. Puppies often suffer as a result of worms, or a change in environment, water or diet, or some stress factor. Withhold milk for a day, but always offer boiled water that has been allowed to cool, as dehydration is possible in a bad case.

Diseases of the Ear

INFLAMMATION OF THE EXTERNAL EAR
The Old English Sheepdog has more hair in the external ear canal than breeds with pricked ear flaps and an accumulation of wax and hair can cause inflammation. The ears should be inspected frequently, and great care should be taken with regular grooming. During grooming, excess hair can often be pulled out gently without hurting the dog; if it *does* hurt, he soon lets you know. If hair has been allowed to grow and form into a hard ball with wax, we have found that the best way to remove this hardened wax is by slowly pulling and rotating. In bad cases, one can remove a complete wax impression of the outer ear canal plus all the excess hair in one simple operation. Long-nosed artery forceps and Q-tips will help in clearing up any loose hardened lumps. The ear canal itself, after the removal of this debris, usually appears quite clean and free of any infection. If the dog's ear is really painful, he may need expert treatment under a light anaesthetic. In a well-groomed dog, the situation will never get this far.

Other causes of inflammation are grass seeds in the ear or infestation by ear mites. It can also be brought on by draughts, especially if the dog is allowed to hang his head out of a car window as he is travelling along. Never attempt to put anything in the ear to alleviate the condition, but seek veterinary advice at once.

INFLAMMATION OF THE MIDDLE EAR
This may follow inflammation of the external ear if the infection reaches the ear drum. In other cases, the infection may spread from the throat. Once the infection has spread this far, the dog's balance is usually affected and he tends to walk in circles. This is of course a case for veterinary treatment.

CANKER
This ear disease is accompanied by a discharge. It is a chronic disease of the external ear, involving the auditory canal. It is possible to obtain canker powders and lotions from pet shops, or you can go to your veterinary surgeon. Many breeders swear by a canker powder called Thornit, available only from Miss Bett at Thornham, Hunstanton, Norfolk PE36 6NB. It is basically a herbal remedy and for certain conditions it can be heartily recommended.

Cataract

Cataracts are common among ageing dogs. A gradual whitening of the lens occurs until the eye looks opaque. Surgery is possible in some cases. Where this is not possible, the dog gradually becomes blind, but, as long as he is not a working dog, he adapts to his condition and becomes adept at finding his way around his own home territory.

Fly Strike

For the majority of owners this is a remote problem, but very sad cases of neglected Old English Sheepdogs have been recorded where the ungroomed dog has maggots breeding in festering sores. Flies are first attracted to sores and matted rear ends, they lay eggs there and the maggots hatch out in due course.

PARASITES (EXTERNAL)

Fleas

Although the dog flea lives on the dog's body, it lays its eggs away from the animal, so if your dog has a severe infestation of fleas, you must use flea powder not only on the dog's coat, but on his bedding and in those parts of the house frequented by the dog. If the dog is kennelled, the premises must be impregnated by flea powder or scrubbed out with a disinfectant which has anti-parasitic properties. In the home, fleas tend to lay their eggs in floor cracks, under skirting boards or along the edges of carpets and rugs. Dust flea powder on any chairs the dog uses and spray edges of carpets, skirting boards and chair and table legs. In bad cases, repeat this spraying every ten days for about a month, or, if you are constantly troubled by fleas, you can call in the help of the Local Authority.

Fleas on the dog tend to migrate towards the head, neck and ears, so these parts need careful dusting. Avoid shaking powder into the eyes and ears. The base of the spine, where the tail would join the body if a bobtail had a tail, is also a favourite place for fleas to gather. Some dogs are more sensitive than others to fleas in their coats. It is quite ruinous if a dog scratches his coat, for he will tear out the soft undercoat and decimate the hair of the top coat. Scratching can also lead to sore areas on the skin and if the dog's claws are dirty as he scratches eczema may break out.

Lice

Unlike fleas, lice spend their whole life cycle on the dog. Lice eggs among the dog's hair look rather like scurf. Most eggs tend to lie on the hair around the neck or in the hair under the ear flaps. Adult lice can be destroyed by insecticidal powder. When eggs are detected they are best destroyed by cutting off the hair on which they are laid. Then this hair must be burnt. If your dog is infected by lice, use an insecticidal powder daily for four weeks as the life cycle of the louse lasts from a fortnight to four weeks.

Ticks

These are usually picked up from grass. They are blood-suckers which bury their heads into the dog's skin. You can recognize the tick by the sac-like body which remains above the skin and which becomes black when it is swollen with blood. It should be pulled from the skin, very carefully so as to bring the head away with it. Surgical spirit or paraffin will cause the tick to unburrow and you can remove it easily. A head left beneath the skin could cause an abscess to form.

Harvest Mites

These are also picked up from grass, and country dogs are more likely to suffer from them after a walk through the fields. They are minute red insects which remain on the ears, between the toes and on the undersides of the body. Their presence can often be detected because the dog nibbles and bites himself. Insect powder will kill them.

As a means of ridding your dog of these external parasites, a bath in a brand of flea and lice wash may be necessary, and your vet will be able to supply you with an appropriate one. Alugan is the best and is what most vets will give you.

PARASITES (INTERNAL)

Round Worms

Most puppies are born with round worms, even though the bitch is free of them, because dormant eggs remain in the older dog's

101

muscles until she becomes pregnant, after which they activate and enter the bodies of the unborn pups. The larvae migrate to the intestines and some are adult by the time the new-born puppy is a week old. Give puppies a worming dose when they are three weeks old with a repeat dose every fourteen days. As it is possible for the larvae of round worms to live in the human body, cleanliness should be observed when there are children in the family. PRO Dogs Literature is very useful here, and hopefully your breeder will have supplied one of their worming certificates when you took the puppy. Round worms are recognizable as being round, white and anything in length from half an inch to three inches. Pups may vomit them up, but they are more often passed in the puppies' motions. Most adult dogs appear not to have round worms, but some owners like to worm their dogs regularly once a year on the principle that prevention is better than cure.

Tapeworms

A tapeworm has a head equipped with hooks and suckers with which it attaches itself to the wall of the dog's intestines. Behind the head grow yards of segmented body and it is the passing of these segments, pearly white or pinky-red in colour, in the faeces which alerts owners to their dog's condition. For total elimination, the head must come away with the body and tapeworm tablets can be obtained which effectively do this.

As the immediate host of the most common of the many tapeworms which dogs carry is the dog flea, it is obvious that the elimination of the internal parasite must be accompanied by the extermination of the external one, although it does not necessarily follow that a dog who has fleas also has a tapeworm.

Tapeworms and round worms take goodness from the dog's digested food so it is obvious that a badly infested dog will tend to be a skinny, unhealthy animal because much of the nourishment provided by his food is taken by the parasite to which he is playing involuntary host.

There are various proprietary brands of tapeworm tablets on

the market. Some are too weak to be effective if taken in the dosage prescribed, others on the other hand have a very harsh effect. It is generally more satisfactory to consult your vet and ask him to prescribe a dose.

SKIN TROUBLES

Eczema

There are two types of eczema, both non-contagious. Dry eczema gives rise to scaly or scurfy inflamed patches on the skin. Wet eczema, as its name implies, shows a wet, raw skin which bleeds when the dog scratches himself. It may be caused by diet deficiency or by an allergy, or it may indicate some kind of digestive disturbance. Eczema can also be caused through excessive scratching with dirty claws. In almost all cases of eczema, not only must the skin complaint be dealt with but also the primary condition which is causing it. Hair should be clipped away from the affected area and the patches swabbed with cotton wool soaked in warm water, which should be burnt afterwards. A little coal tar soap can be used when swabbing away any pus or crusty areas. Then apply a cream specially prepared for the purpose. There are brands on the market, or you may obtain ointment from your veterinary surgeon. If the eczema is around the eyes do not use soap, use an eye lotion prepared for veterinary use or cold weak tea and warm water.

Ringworm

This is a fungus disease, and kennelled dogs are probably more at risk from it than house dogs, but if your kennels are kept hygienically, you should avoid the problem. Unlike eczema, ringworm is highly contagious, and it is infectious to humans. Unfortunately, it is not easy to detect on the dog, and the first sign that dogs are infected is that a human member of the family is seen to be suffering from ringworm. When ringworm does manifest itself on a dog, it usually appears as bald patches on parts of the dog's body; sometimes too there are scaly areas of skin, not necessarily in ring formation.

Mange

Sarcoptic or common mange, contagious to dogs and humans, can be treated and eradicated, but follicular or demodectic mange, not contagious to humans but contagious to other dogs, is more of a problem. If your dog scratches and hair begins to fall out, you may suspect mange, particularly if the affected areas are covered with small spots. The dog will usually aggravate his condition by nibbling at himself, which causes scabby areas on his skin. You should eliminate the trouble obtaining powder and ointment from your vet, but it is often necessary for humans who are in contact with the dog to have their own clothing dusted with powder too.

TUMOURS

As in humans, tumours may be malignant or benign and only specialized inspection can distinguish the two, so any unaccountable lump you can feel should be reported to your vet. Dogs are more subject to tumours than most animals.

Interdigital Cysts

As their name implies, these appear between the toes and are inflamed swellings mainly affecting the forefeet. They usually burst and heal. These cysts should be treated, as soon as they become evident, with hot fomentations. Place the foot in warm, salted water and soak it for ten to fifteen minutes. Press the cyst gently from time to time to encourage it to burst. Dry the foot after soaking but do not bandage it. It will do the dog no harm if he licks it, as he probably will. If these cysts are infected, you will need help in the form of antibiotics from your vet. The Old

English Sheepdog with his hairy feet is a candidate for these cysts so look after his feet, keeping the hair between the toes cut and clean.

Warts

These are small solid tumours and are very common all over the body. Cutaneous warts tend to occur in older dogs, growing singly or in groups. Some owners recommend castor oil externally applied; others have their own rather idiosyncratic ways of eliminating them, bordering on 'magic', as is the way with the disposal of human warts.

On the more scientific side, it is possible to vaccinate, using a serum prepared from bovine wart tissue. A surgical operation is also possible, but after some time the wart generally reappears, accompanied by others. It is thought that some warts are congenital, certainly some are infectious. In puppies, a spate of warts can appear around the face and mouth and then disappear as quickly as they have come.

MALIGNANT TUMOURS

These are cancerous and spread to surrounding tissues and other parts of the body. They may occur anywhere. A general symptom is weight loss and the dog becomes very thin; other symptoms often occur, depending on where the tumour is located and the particular organ or organs it is affecting. For instance, jaundice may be a sign that there is a malignant tumour affecting the liver. Drugs and deep ray therapy may act beneficially, but one can no more rely upon a cure in dogs than one can in humans. It is kindest to the afflicted dog to have him painlessly put down.

VOMITING

Sickness in a dog may be merely a sign that he has eaten something which has disagreed with him. Once he has rid himself of the disagreeable substance he will be as right as rain again, although his owner may decide to put him on a light diet for twenty-four hours. If vomiting is persistent, this means that something other than a mild tummy upset is the matter. If it is accompanied by other symptoms, the problem is easy to diagnose but if you are at all in doubt, consult expert advice at once because it may be a warning system that all is not well.

FIRST AID AND ACCIDENTS

When a dog is ill or injured your best friend is your vet but there are times when it is necessary to do something in the way of first aid to the dog yourself.

Traffic Accidents

As with road accidents to humans, one's first reaction is to run out to the rescue, but watch out for traffic or you will be another road accident victim yourself.

A dog who has had a road accident will almost certainly be in shock and will probably be in pain. Even the best tempered bobtail may be excused biting and snapping at his rescuers in such a situation, so a useful precaution before attempting to move the dog is to tie his mouth with a belt, tie or headscarf.

The Old English Sheepdog is a large dog to lift at the best of times and if he is injured, awkward lifting can obviously aggravate the injury. One of the recommended ways to move an injured dog is to slide a large towel, rug or coat gently beneath him and lift him on this.

He is a sturdy dog and can take a number of hard knocks with nothing worse than a few bruises. After any road accident, however unharmed your dog may appear to be, it is as well to have him checked by your vet. He can assess the amount of shock the dog may be suffering and knows how to look for any internal injuries.

Shock

Shock lowers the blood pressure and there are other malfunctions of the body which may arise from your dog being in a state of shock following an injury. Other causes of shock are: poisoning, extensive burns, surgery, exhaustion, starvation, chronic diarrhoea and weakness caused by distemper. Serious shock can cause death, and in all conditions of shock veterinary help must be sought. While waiting for the vet to arrive, keep the dog warm with a blanket.

Concussion

A blow generally causes concussion of the brain but it may cause concussion of the ear and subsequent deafness. Concussion causes shock and partial unconsciousness. The pulse is feeble and the breathing shallow and there may be involuntary passing of urine. Eye pupils are usually dilated and show a poor response to light and there may be bleeding from the ears or into the eyes. The dog must be kept warm and veterinary help obtained immediately.

Bleeding

MINOR INJURIES

Place a sterile gauze pad over the wound and apply light pressure for a few minutes until bleeding stops. Once the bleeding has stopped, the pad will probably be sticking to the wound. Don't pull this away or the bleeding may begin again. Place a second piece of gauze or lint over the wound and, if necessary, keep it in place with a bandage.

Some minor injuries occur in places where it is virtually impossible to staunch the bleeding except by the application of a caustic stick, which is the job of someone more qualified than the average dog owner. If a dog is scratched on the nose by a cat, for example, the bleeding may be kept going because the dog is constantly licking the area. It may be the tiniest puncture but it can bleed for twenty-four hours or more if steps are not taken to stop it.

TOURNIQUETS

A tourniquet is an extremely dangerous device and should be used with the greatest care and only in extreme conditions. It may have to be used when pressure with a finger or pad is not enough to stop copious bleeding. If a tourniquet seems to be the only way to stop a dog from bleeding to death, it must be loosened briefly (the time depends on the amount of bleeding), at regular intervals of not more than ten minutes. Get the dog to a vet as soon as possible so that the tourniquet can be removed.

Making a Tourniquet

When this is used to stop arterial bleeding, the tourniquet should be tied, never *on* the wound but above it, that is between the wound and the heart. If you know that it is a big vein that is bleeding, the tourniquet should be placed with the wound between it and the heart. However, excessive bleeding is usually arterial, so if in doubt, treat it in the first place as if you know it is an artery. Use a large handkerchief, a cloth belt or tie but *never* wire, rope or rubber cord, and tie it tightly in place. Alternatively, a tourniquet may be made by tying less tightly and slipping a stick or pencil beneath the knot and twisting it to tighten the tourniquet.

Poisoning

In all types of poisoning, it is necessary to determine the type of poison which has been taken in order that the most effective antidote can be prescribed. Poisoning can cause shock, so until expert attention arrives, the dog must be kept warm. The usual quick cure is to make the dog vomit and a tablespoon of dry mustard in half a cup of water, a cup of warm soapy water (not detergent), or a large crystal of washing soda are all effective methods to induce vomiting.

Acid Poisons
The antidote for most acid poisons is a tablespoonful of bicarbonate of soda to a cup of water. If the need for an antidote is desperate and there is no bicarbonate of soda available, crushed egg shells or even plaster from the wall have been known to be effective.

Alkali Poisons
Three to four tablespoonfuls of vinegar or lemon juice help allay alkaline poisoning.

Rat Poison
Warfarin is a common rat poison and is often mixed with rolled barley, but as the Old English Sheepdog is not by nature a rat-catcher, he is less likely to eat a warfarin poisoned rat than, say, a breed like a terrier. As warfarin causes internal haemorrhage, the symptoms do not generally show in time to save the dog's life. If you do suspect that your dog has swallowed warfarin-poisoned bait, induce vomiting immediately. Vitamin K is a known remedy and will be administered by the vet, and blood transfusions will have to be given if the bleeding has been extensive.

Arsenic
The signs of this type of poisoning are watery or bloody diarrhoea, salivation and staggering, ending in convulsions and vomiting. If a substantial quantity is swallowed there is no time for the signs to show up and death is almost instantaneous. One to two ounces of milk of magnesia with crushed charcoal (about a teaspoonful) is effective in milder cases of arsenic poisoning, followed by half a cup of strong tea.

AGRICULTURAL INSECTICIDES
These may be inhaled or swallowed, but this sort of poisoning is most often brought about by absorption through the skin and feet pads, and veterinary treatment is necessary.

SLUG PELLETS
Many packets of slug pellets carry warnings that they are harmful to animals and children. Even the best-fed dog may eat from a bag of pellets if they are left within his reach in the garden shed, or scattered around young plants. If slug pellets do not cause death, they have been known to bring on a state of coma lasting up to twenty-four hours. If your garden is slug-infested, try a liquid slug killer like Sluggit which is watered on to and around plants. It is highly effective and yet is invisible to the dog. As long as you don't leave a watering can full of the solution near a thirsty dog, your animal is safe.

BULBS
Many bulbs are poisonous to dogs: hyacinth, daffodil and narcissus bulbs can all kill a dog who eats them. Adult dogs generally leave these sorts of things alone, but a puppy may chew up bulbs which are lying around waiting to be planted, or which may have been placed in a dark cupboard for winter flowering.

SNAKE BITES
The only poisonous snake in Great Britain is the adder or viper. Dogs are often bitten when they stumble on an adder sunning itself on a quiet cliff top or area of moorland. The bite is not usually fatal if treatment is quick following a correct diagnosis. The dog will become very excited at first and the bitten limb will swell considerably; he will show you where the bite is by licking at the wound. Get the dog to a vet immediately so that he can give an injection of anti-serum. If you are miles from nowhere and on foot, the old fashioned method of making a criss-cross cut on the 'heart side' of the bite and binding around the limb above the wound and the swelling and then sucking out the

venom and spitting it away is the best treatment. The venom is quite harmless in the mouth provided you have no cuts or sores. You will be unlikely to have any potassium permanganate crystals on you, so use cold water pads, if you can get to any water. Keep the dog warm and use a coat to carry him back to the car, then get him straight to the vet.

Burns and Scalds

The dog who is often in the kitchen stands more chance of suffering from burns and scalds than does the kennel dog. These external burns will mainly be caused by hot fat or hot water. Another source of domestic burn comes from spitting coals or logs.

Superficial or first degree burns which affect only the outer skin layer can be treated by bathing the skin in a strong solution of tepid or cold tea, or any burn preparation suitable for human use. Fortunately for the Old English Sheepdog, his thick coat is very protective, and in this respect he is less likely to suffer from minor burns than some other breeds.

A second degree burn presents a more serious problem, for in this case, the outer layers of the skin are burnt and blisters form. Strong cold tea externally applied is a soothing remedy and hair will have to be clipped away so that it does not become flattened into the scab. Second degree burns can be serious or even fatal if they cover over half the dog's body.

Third degree burns, where blood plasma is lost, require immediate veterinary treatment. The dog suffers from shock as the blood pressure decreases, and this shock must be treated quickly if the dog is to recover. If third degree burns cover more than 20 per cent of the dog's body recovery is doubtful. Moreover, hair will not grow where skin has been badly burned, and this factor, coupled with the pain the dog endures, makes it kinder in certain cases to have the dog put down.

Choking

This is generally caused by swallowing a large object which becomes lodged in the oesophagus, or may be occasioned by a bone or some object which is stuck in the back of the throat. If the object has not actually been swallowed, and is still in the throat, a finger or a blunt-ended object which will not snap or break if the dog bites on to it, may be able to dislodge the obstruction, but be sure not to push it further down if using this method. Serious cases should be taken at once to a vet.

Bandaging

This is one of the hardest things to do oneself. Dogs tend to tear and bite at bandages as soon as they are put on, so their owners tend to bandage too firmly and too tightly, which can damage circulation. Bandaging is therefore best left to the professional expertise of your vet, but it is advisable to have some sort of bandaging at home for emergencies. At least three widths of bandage ought to be available with various widths of adhesive tape to keep the bandaging together. Safety pins are not safe with dogs because they work at them until they come undone, but elasticated metal grips can be very useful.

Liquid Adhesive

This should only be used by a veterinary surgeon when being applied to the wound itself, but it can be used by the dog owner to keep a dressing on a wound. Clip the hair around the wound, cover the wound with a gauze pad and glue the edges of the pad to the skin surrounding the wound with liquid adhesive.

The Ruff Guard

This is an adaptation of the Elizabethan ruff, as its name implies, and can be made from a circle of stiff card, corrugated cardboard or an old lightweight plastic bucket with a collar attached. Cut a neck hole a little smaller than the size of the dog's head, making the ruff eight to ten inches deep from neck to outer edge. Make a cut in the card from the neck hole to the other edge to allow the collar to be slipped on to the dog. The ruff can be closed in a variety of ways. The two edges of the card can be overlapped and stapled together or stitched or a strip of card can be stapled over the cut to hold it together. If thin, stiff plastic is used, eyelet holes can be made on either side of the cut and the sides be drawn together with tape or a shoe lace.

This sort of collar limits the dog's head action and prevents him from reaching his injury and biting at the bandage or the stitches after surgery. He will also be prevented from scratching his ears and face while wearing the ruff.

Protective Coats

If the wound is on the body, a cylinder of lightweight linoleum may be used as a restrictive coat to prevent scratching with the hind legs. The use of such a coat on a bobtail may depend as much on the weather as the wound, because it could be excessively hot. The tailor-made coats available for bobtails and obtained at major dog shows have a use here, which they were not originally meant for.

Administering Artificial Respiration

Respiration rate varies according to the size of the dog; the larger the dog, the lower the respiration rate, that is, breaths per minute. The Old English Sheepdog is therefore a relatively slow breather. Sometimes an owner has to offer first aid in the form of artificial respiration, particularly in the first moments of the life of a new-born puppy, which has been whelped with fluid blocking its nasal passages. The puppy should be held head down in the palm of the hand and thrown forward (while you keep a firm grip on the puppy and make sure the neck is not whipped over the end of the fingers), so that the fluid is expelled. Although the nasal passages are thus cleared, breathing may not start up naturally, and artificial respiration

113

must be given. This can be done by using the mouth-to-mouth resuscitation method, which is safer than using the hands to press the lungs into action because external pressure on the ribs of a newly-whelped puppy can cause severe damage. However, never suck in air during the mouth-to-mouth method as this could cause a collapse of the puppy's lungs — just blow gently into the pup's mouth.

Restoring Respiration in Older Dogs

With older dogs, rhythmic pressure against the chest is successful in restoring respiration in cases of near death from drowning or from shock. One has to guess at the rate of normal respiration under normal conditions, then increase the rate up to one half as much again.

Laboured and Uneven Breathing After a Road Accident

If your dog has been struck by a car, his diaphragm may be punctured and a vet should be called in at once. Another cause of lung collapse or difficulty in breathing may be the inhalation of chemicals such as domestic cleaning sprays or insecticides, and veterinary treatment is necessary.

The Dog's Body Temperature

A dog's body temperature is a useful indication of his state of health and well-being. A rise or fall from the norm can indicate that there is cause for alarm and, conversely, if the dog's temperature is found to be normal, fears for his health are generally allayed. The body temperature should always be taken at the rectum, using a rectal thermometer, smearing the end first with vaseline to make insertion easier. The average body temperature of the bobtail is 101.5°F (38.61°C). Puppies may have a slightly higher body temperature, up to 101.8°F (38.77°C). A slight fever is indicated by a temperature of 102°F (38.88°C). A seriously high temperature is one which is 105°F

(40.55°C). Anything registering over 106°F (41.1°C) indicates collapse and probable death if the body temperature cannot be quickly brought down. During the last few days of pregnancy, even for the last week, the bitch's temperature may drop to about 99°F (37.5°C) and around twenty-four hours (or sooner) before whelping it can go down to 97°F (36°C).

Dogs do not sweat through the skin as humans do, but only from the pads of the feet. Excess heat is got rid of by panting, a sight we all know is the long pink tongue dripping saliva. Dogs shut up in cars on sunny days cannot lose heat quickly enough and the dog could easily die from hyperthermia. The 1976 heatwave saw many dogs, even at dog shows, staggering in the heat. This is one of the symptoms of heat stroke. The dog collapses and can go into convulsions. You must get the dog into the shade and get cold water on to the head, neck and body. Some kennel owners seeing this happening to a dog kept under plastic-sheeted runs turn the hose on to the sick dog, to get the dog's temperature down quickly.

PROBLEMS RELATED TO THE DOG'S BEHAVIOUR OR APPEARANCE

Depraved Appetite

It is to be expected that a puppy, like a small child, will take a lot of unappetizing and non-digestible things into his mouth. In most cases the puppy will tear and chew at things without swallowing too much. If you suspect that your puppy has swallowed anything large or sharp or otherwise indigestible to the serious detriment of his general health, recourse to knucklebones and rawhide chews may help, but as the condition may be symptomatic of a dietary deficiency, or some other condition requiring treatment, consult your vet. Coprophagy or stool eating may rise from vitamin deficiency or severe debility after illness. A course of vitamins under veterinary supervision may be the answer. If your dog persists, the obvious remedy is to keep the kennel run or garden clear and provide hard biscuits and chews to replace the more unsavory diet.

Some country dogs horrify their owners by eating horse droppings and cow manure. Although this is a repellent practice by human standards, it generally does the dog no harm and is a way of obtaining readily digested grass and cereal. One of the most unpleasant aspects, especially with cow dung, is the smell which is retained on the mouth hairs for a long time afterwards. Washing is necessary if he is to coexist with humans. Manure and dung attract flies and larvae and altogether is a habit which dog owners ought to discourage.

Dew claws

The dew claws are found on the inside of each foot and are best removed within a few days of birth. They are generally attended to when the puppy is docked. The Breed Standard makes no mention of dew claws, but situated as they are, they are in constant danger of being ripped away from the foot if they are allowed to remain. It is much easier to groom your dog's legs if they have been removed, because you can give a clean sweep of the brush or comb without fear of catching the claw. If a dog catches and rips a dew claw which has been left, it will usually bleed profusely, but a pad and bandage will soon stop it.

Docking

If the tail is incorrectly docked, the stump will look ugly as the dog matures, giving him a lengthy looking back; moreover the stump can become sore from constant rubbing. The Breed Standard is explicit about docking, which must take place very early in the puppy's life before the removal of the tail can cause a great deal of pain. That it does cause some pain is certain because the puppy cries, and Old English Sheepdog owners have come under fire for allowing the practice to continue, while in the horse world, the distinctive docked tail of the cob

116

has virtually disappeared. The breed would obviously lose one of its outstanding characteristics if docking were discontinued, and the traditional sheepdog which this breed has perpetuated for over a century with very little deviation from the original docked rear-quarters would be a thing of the past, which would be regrettable. With conservation a by-word and zoos and special farms rearing endangered species, the sheepdog owner might well argue that the tail docking required of the Old English Sheepdog was a form of conservation anyway, and certainly the ancient nickname of bobtail would have lost its meaning.

CASTRATING AND SPAYING

For the owner of the pet dog particularly this is a subject which has to be thought about. If the dog is not going to be used for breeding and the owner is constantly embarrassed by having to apologize to owners of local bitches for his dog's unwanted overtures, he may well decide to have recourse to castration or a vasectomy for his animal. Similarly if the owner of a pet bitch who is not going to be used for breeding does not want the risks attendant of each six monthly heat, he should have her spayed. Dogs and bitches suffering from hereditary defects might also be rendered infertile in order to avoid any accidental matings.

Castration and Vasectomy

Castration is the term used for the surgical removal of the testicles and is obviously a much simpler operation to perform on a puppy than on a grown dog. Vasectomy involves the cutting and tying of the small tubes that carry sperm. This last method has several advantages over castration: The dog does not put on weight; his temperament does not change; the dog still has his sexual drive, though sterile; the operation itself is simple; because vasectomy is an easier course to take than castration for the older dog, breeders can send an older dog with known heredity faults to a new home, safe in the knowledge that he cannot breed.

Spaying

The uterus and the ovaries of the bitch are removed by a surgical operation. Opinions are divided about the best time to spay a female. It is considered by some that the older the bitch, the more difficult the operation, so they advocate spaying early, at around five months old, before the bitch ever comes on heat. But it might be felt that subjecting a young bitch so early in life to a surgical operation is putting an unnecessary burden on her. Unless a bitch is really old, in which case any operation is a risk, spaying can usually be carried out long after maturity has been reached (i.e. usually after the first heat period).

OBESITY

Both castrated and spayed animals tend to put on weight if they are over-fed, so their diet must be restricted. Owners of such dogs and bitches need to watch more carefully and feed more sparingly to avoid an overweight animal.

EATING GRASS

Dogs frequently eat grass, choosing usually the broad bladed, coarse type which they will eat in large quantities. People generally say that grass-eating is a sign that the dog is unwell, but this is not always the case. The grass may be providing the roughage in order to expel a tapeworm; in fact any sort of irritation of the alimentary tract may cause a dog to eat grass, but as patently healthy dogs also eat it, ill health is not the simple answer.

Chapter 6

THE FAMILY DOG

DOGS AS MEMBERS OF THE FAMILY

Dogs and children generally get on together very well, but if you are planning to buy an Old English Sheepdog, and a new baby is also expected in the family, it is advisable to buy a puppy or adult dog from a breeding kennel or Rescue Scheme only *after* the arrival of the baby and once its routines have been established. If the dog arrives first, he is generally made the centre of attention and does not take kindly to being ousted by a newcomer. There is no breed of dog that can really be trusted if that situation develops, whereas if he comes into the family and finds the baby already there, he accepts the situation as normal. Well-established family dogs on the other hand, take human additions in their stride, becoming very attached to them and ready to defend them if necessary.

An Old English Sheepdog is such an engaging animal that once you have one in the family, you may think about getting a companion for him. Although, obviously, two dogs cost more to keep, there are advantages in having more than one. The Old English Sheepdog is not a breed given to whining or barking when alone, but two dogs are company for each other if the family is out during the day. In many households, once the children are at school, both husband and wife go out to work, and it is much more satisfactory to leave two dogs at home than one on his own.

Large breeds like the Old English Sheepdog require a

considerable amount of exercise to keep themselves fit and healthy and can cheerfully carry on walking for miles after their owner is ready to go home and put his feet up. Two dogs usually get more exercise than one because they play together and chase one another once they are let off the lead. If you are using a public park to exercise your dogs, read the bye-laws before you let your animals run marathons around the grounds; it may be illegal to let them off the lead. There are fewer problems about exercising dogs in the country, so long as they don't disturb livestock or trample over growing crops. While dogs enjoy playing chasing games with each other, they also appreciate a proper walk and this is a very good chance in these days of car travel for the owner to get his exercise too.

Two dogs are company for each other if you have to leave them in boarding kennels when the family is on holiday. They are probably glad to be together in a strange environment. The expense is not exactly doubled, for if your dogs share a kennel, you will normally be given a slight reduction over the cost of two separate kennel places. For the owner who lives alone, the great advantage of having more than one dog is that the relationship between owner and dog tends to be less intense and is a more relaxed one. One dog living with one owner tends to become spoilt and is expected to react more like another human than is good for it.

For some families, keeping two Old English Sheepdogs would be just too expensive, although they might agree in principle with the idea of having two dogs. In that case, they might like to know how well the breed mixes with a member of another breed, because for many families, a second dog, like a second car, has to be a smaller one.

The agreeable nature of the Old English Sheepdog extends to all other dogs. They may be a little stand-offish and uncertain for two or three days — they are even with puppies of their own breed — but very soon the newcomer is accepted and can usually be found completely relaxed and curled up with his large shaggy companion, the best of friends. We have had complete success with introducing Lhasa Apsos and Maltese to sheepdogs. A bundle of grey and white fur on the floor indicates a sheepdog with a Lhasa Apso or Maltese curled up against it, although the small one is usually indistinguishable. Dog books written about Apsos and Maltese praise them as dogs that are excellent for flat dwellers as they require so little exercise. Ours obviously think that they are Old English Sheepdogs because they tramp for miles with their large companions and enjoy fast games of tag in a two-acre field.

We know of many combinations of terrier-type and spaniel-type dogs and poodles living with Old English Sheepdogs. The only breed I have come across so far which is not too happy with the bobtail is the Basset Hound. The larger dog is perhaps too boisterous, and its tendency to play low-jump over the Basset's back is definitely not appreciated. The long, low-slung back of the Basset Hound is very vulnerable to injury and, understandably, they do not like heavy dogs skimming over them. However, there may be readers of this book who have found that the combination of Old English Sheepdog and Basset has worked very well.

If you already have a staid, elderly small dog it would hardly be fair to the incumbent to introduce an Old English Sheepdog puppy. His enormous size and unbounded energy would almost certainly be too much for it.

If you want to keep an Old English Sheepdog along with a cat, the problems are probably no greater and no less than with any other breed; if anything they would probably be less, because the breed is not notably a chasing or hunting type. Some dogs leave cats alone, but the well-established rule, 'if the cat moves, chase it', more generally applies. In obtaining a successful dog-cat co-existence, the onus always seems to be on the cat. If a cat can keep its cool, and sit it out or arch its back and spit, the dog generally gives in. The most diminutive kitten can guard a doorway in the best Horatian tradition against the largest, shaggiest sheepdog so long as it sits tight and hisses. So, if you have problems, talk to the cat, not the dog.

THE DOG AND EXPENSE

Veterinary fees will be high if your dog is unfortunate enough to be ill, which is why it is worth paying for vaccination at the outset and keeping up the booster doses, but good feeding and grooming and adequate exercise coupled with comfortable and hygienic housing should keep your dog in good health. A major expense will, of course, be food. The dog has to be well fed and be given an adequate amount of food, so pet owners would do well to learn a lesson from breeders and kennel owners; they buy their food in bulk and so can the ordinary pet owner. It is worth exploring all the possibilities in your area, interviewing butchers, pet shops, animal food suppliers and even slaughter-houses, but you have to be strong-minded to enter even the most humanely run abbatoir if your arrival happens to coincide with a consignment of live stock.

The cheapest sources of food are slaughterhouses and the next cheapest are butcher's shops where they are willing to sell dog scraps and offal from animals they slaughter themselves. This probably applies to country butchers rather than those in cities and towns. If your local butcher can count on your buying a large amount of dog meat in bulk regularly, he may be persuaded to take a few pence off the price he is asking of the casual customer.

Local slaughterhouses often supply lights and tripe at a minimal charge for a huge bagful, but you will find that preparing it is a messy business. The lights, which are the lungs of the animal, have to be separated from the trachea and surrounding fat, and washing tripe (which is the cow's compound stomach) entails the smelly job of separating grass and mess from the parts you are going to feed your dog. Tripe is also smelly if you intend to cook it, although if you use a pressure cooker it cuts down on 'smell time' in the kitchen. If you can put up with the mess and the smell, you may be tempted to feed your adult dog exclusively on this because it is so cheap, but veterinarians have expressed doubts about the food value of a diet based solely on lights or tripe. Butcher's scraps are better, being more nutritious.

If you are unable to buy in bulk from your butcher, look around and see if you can buy kennel packs of tinned or dried meat from a pet shop or a supplier of animal foodstuffs. Some firms which used to specialize in bulk supplies of horse and farm animal foods now also sell packs of tinned meat and dog biscuits. Buying a box of, say, twenty-four large tins of meat is cheaper than buying the tins separately from the shelves of the supermarket. If you prefer commercially produced frozen dog food, it is also possible to buy that in large packs. Biscuits and meal are cheaper bought by the quarter- or half-hundredweight sack, or its metric equivalent of twelve or twenty-five kilos and most pet shops can supply you with as much of this as you want.

Bulk buying means that you need a car to transport the food and if you live in the country a considerable journey may be involved, so the cost of petrol has to be set against the money you will save on the food thus bought. It may be possible to join up with a neighbour who also has large dogs and thus share the time and expense of car journeys.

If you go in for bulk buying, you obviously need to have adequate storage facilities. A deep freeze is necessary for storing meat, and if you have a chest freezer and can spare one compartment for the dog, you will find that several boxes or packs of meat can be stored together. Biscuits and dog meal ought to be taken out of their paper sacks and cardboard boxes and stored in plastic dustbins to discourage mice. Dried meat and other sorts of dried dog food should also go into a special bin.

Before cooking frozen meat, I prefer to thaw it out slowly, just as I would meat for human consumption. The small blocks of pre-cooked frozen meat such as Woffle, need at least eight hours to thaw out right through to the middle, and tripe in block form takes even longer, so pre-planning of mealtimes is essential, but make sure that all meat which is defrosting is out of the dog's reach.

WHEN THE FAMILY GOES ON HOLIDAY

Holidays for most families these days involve car travel. Many new puppies suffer from car sickness and although they usually grow out of it, they may take up to a year to adjust to travelling in it. Journeys with a car-sick dog are made easier if there are rubber gloves for the owner (by definition, the one who has to clear up the mess!) and plenty of paper tissues and old newspapers to cover the back seat and the floor. A plastic bottle of disinfectant and a fresh air spray are also useful additions. Some puppies travel better on the floor of the car (see p. 42), but some obviously do not like the feeling of confinement which that brings with it. You may feel that the dog needs more air and certainly an open window may help, but don't let him ride along with his head out of the window because dust can get into his eyes and both eyes and ears can suffer from the draught he is in. Ideally, long before you go on holiday, you should have made every effort to get your dog used to car travel by taking him first on short journeys and then making them progressively longer as he gets more used to the sensation of car travel. Regular stops on these journeys to enable him to get out and walk around a little also helps the puppy to avoid being sick in the car.

Whether the dog is prone to car sickness or not, a window should always be left open when you leave your dog in the car, especially in hot weather. A dog in a car where all the windows are shut can suffer agonies in sunny weather and may even die of dehydration. It is possible to buy window guards which allow air in and keep dogs in as well; they also help to keep car thieves out, but once your dog has grown to his full size, he will deter anyone from breaking in by his bulk alone. You can help your dog by choosing a shady place in the car park if there is one, but remember that the sun moves and at the end of a long meal in a restaurant, the car that was in the shade may be in the full sun, so open both the windows to get a through draught. In really hot weather, leave a bowl of water on the floor of the car.

An Old English Sheepdog takes up a lot of room in a car and his size will drastically cut down the cubic capacity normally given over to luggage if you have an estate car. Owners of large dogs who also have a family generally have to invest in a roof rack or trailer.

Owning a dog can cause problems when the family wants to go on holiday. While a cat will often be better left at home with a pussy flap for entry and exit and a kind neighbour to feed it, a dog requires more care, for he cannot be left to his own devices in the way a cat can. Quite apart from the cruelty of leaving a dog on his own while you go on holiday, an owner can be prosecuted under the Abandonment of Animals Act of 1960 if he goes away without making arrangements for somebody to look after his dog in an adequate manner. So a dog must either accompany his owners or be placed in the care of a friend or in boarding kennels.

If you can take your dog on holiday, do so. As an important member of the family he shouldn't really be left out, and his enjoyment of the holiday will add to yours. If it is going to be a hotel holiday make sure beforehand that the hotel you have chosen will take dogs; never leave this to chance, but ask about dogs when making your bookings. It is no good turning up at a hotel which does not allow animals and hope to force their hand. If you are allowed to enter the hotel you will certainly be made to leave your dog in the car and should he object to this or take it upon himself to bark at visitors to the parking lot, you may be asked to leave; certainly you will never be able to relax for worrying about whether your dog is making a nuisance of himself. Although about five million homes in this country are said to contain dogs, there is a fair proportion of the population which does not like them and they have a right to expect that a hotel which says 'no dogs' is going to honour its commitment. Many hotels which do allow dogs let the owner take them to the bedroom to sleep but do not, quite understandably, allow them in the dining-room. Booksellers and newsagents shops are well-stocked with books giving details of holiday accommodation throughout the British Isles and Regional Tourist offices can provide further information. Many of these books provide lists of campsites, farmhouses and self-catering holiday sites and include information about their acceptance of dogs.

Where dogs are allowed on to campsites, the general rule is that they should be kept on a lead at all times and that they should never be exercised on ground adjacent to where campers are living. In case of an accident, a small shovel or trowel is a vital piece of equipment. A dog owner who apologizes and is ready to clear up his dog's mess is much appreciated by his fellow campers. The ideal campsite is one where you can place your tent or caravan close to an exit leading to woods or an unfrequented lane where the dog can be taken for early morning and late evening exercise; there are a few places like these and they are very popular with dog owners.

An Old English Sheepdog's lead is generally a short, stout one, quite adequate for use when walking the dog, but nowhere near long enough to attach to a stake or peg in the ground. If the dog is to sit outside with you and you are to conform to the rules, he will need a length of chain (rope can be chewed through) attached to a well driven in metal tent peg or the car bumper. Alternatively, you can buy huge corkscrew-like pegs with a handle on top for attaching a long lead. These are sold in most pet shops and at dog shows. The chain should be long enough to allow him to lie down in the shade and also to reach his water bowl. On the other hand, don't be tempted to make his chain too long. If something causes your dog to dart forward he may foul a guy rope and pull your tent or someone else's about his ears. If he has too much rope, he may wrap it round your table or camping gaz stove. Campers ought always to have a fire extinguisher among their equipment, but prevention is better than cure.

The most convenient foods for holiday time are the tinned variety. Some pet owners like to boast that their dog never eats tinned food, but if you are in the habit of taking your dog on holiday with you, it is not a bad idea to accustom him to tinned as well as fresh food so that he won't refuse it on holiday when you probably have nothing else to give him.

Many dogs sleep in their owner's car quite comfortably. Even if you have two dogs there is plenty of room for them to stretch out in an estate car with the back seat folded down. Some dogs sleep in part of the family's tent or in the awning of a caravan. If they are well tethered and can be relied on to keep quiet, they can even sleep outside the tent if the weather is fine, but they are still going to have to contend with dew, however warm the day has been. In wet weather groundsheets become very cold and damp and the dog ought to be off the sheet on some kind of matting or sleeping bag to avoid rheumatism.

If you are having a seaside holiday, you may be disappointed to find that your dog is not an enthusiastic swimmer. Some members of the breed like the sea, but the Old English Sheepdog is not generally noted for its love of sea water. While other breeds like the labrador will cheerfully play and swim in the water with the family, the bobtail will usually prefer to stay on the beach guarding your clothes, which is not a bad thing as salt water plays havoc with the undercoat. Sand doesn't help either, and our family caravan is filled with sand from the dogs' coats after a week on the beach.

If you are taking your dog away with you using public transport, different conditions apply according to the type of transport used.

Rail Travel

If you travel by rail you will have to buy a ticket for your dog and the price is the same as a child's fare. You will be allowed to take the dog into your compartment so long as he is not a nuisance to other passengers. As the Old English Sheepdog is so large, he is more likely to be tolerated in a crowded carriage if he is well behaved and knows how to sit still. Rail travel may be unavoidable, but it is not the most convenient way of transporting a large dog like the bobtail, particularly if the train is crowded; both owner and dog are likely to be on edge if he seems to be taking up too much space or if he gets restless on a long journey, added to which, it is the sort of breed which attacts well-meaning but unwanted attention from other passengers so that the dog is constantly being disturbed and excited. If you can avoid rail travel with a bobtail, do so.

Dogs are not allowed in the dining car, so you must arrange for a member of the family to stay behind with him or decide to picnic in the compartment. If you are using a sleeper, the dog cannot accompany you to a sleeping compartment and will have to spend the night in the guard's van.

If you are using the London Underground, you will be confronted by a notice to the effect that all dogs must be carried! It is in the dog's interest of course that he should not have to negotiate stepping on and off a moving staircase and most stations have a central stone staircase which meets the case.

Sea Travel

If you are travelling to islands within the United Kingdom, you can take your dog on board and keep him with you on deck, but he will probably be excluded from cabins and dining areas. As with rail travel, he will have to be paid for at the child's rate. The different ferry services and shipping companies have their own regulations concerning dogs who travel on board, so when booking your passage make inquiries about your dog.

Air Travel

Most major airlines operating within the United Kingdom will accept a dog who is accompanying a fare paying passenger. The dog must travel in the cargo hold and be paid for as excess baggage. He must travel in an adequate container which you may buy, make or hire from the airline (for specifications about dog crates, see Chapter Nine). The cargo hold is pressurized, so your dog will suffer no ill effects. Some companies do ask for a certificate signed by your vet, declaring that the animal is in a fit and healthy state to travel.

It may not always be possible for your dog to accompany you on holiday. This obviously applies to families who are going abroad. You can take a dog out of the United Kingdom and into

1. 'Winter Time' by George Morland circa 1800. Many nineteenth-century sheepdogs are depicted with the long rough coat which was to develop into the profuse, shaggy covering associated with the Old English Sheepdog of today. *Reproduced by courtesy of Sotheby, Parke Bernet & Co*

2. Ch. Aberfells Georgey Porgey at Richmond Championship Show 1979. Seen with his owners Sheelagh and Jeff Curd, having gained his 35th CC and setting a new breed record

3. Ch. Pendlefold Prince Hal, born 1967, owned and bred by Brenda Riddiough.

4. Ch. Oakhill Peter Pan, born 1966, owned by Mr and Mrs Ashcroft, bred by Mrs Hargreaves.

5. Lead training a young dog

6. Barnolby Artistic of Amblegait taking first prize in the Junior Bitch Class at Crufts, 1978. Note the use of the nylon show lead

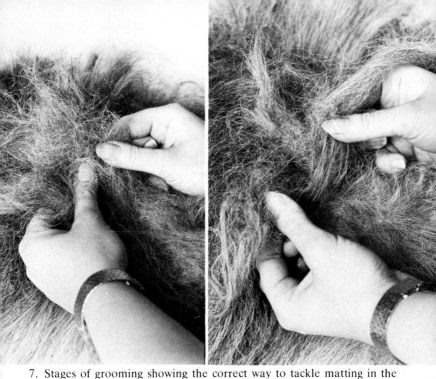

7. Stages of grooming showing the correct way to tackle matting in the coat. Gently tease the mats apart using the index finger and thumb of each hand until you can start brushing and combing again

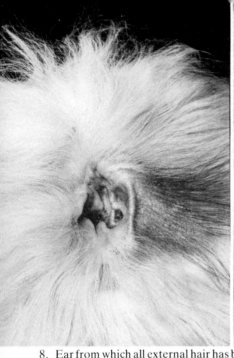

8. Ear from which all external hair has been clipped to allow air to circulate
9. Good, dark brown eye showing an excellent ring of pigmentation
10/11. Good, tight scissor-bite showing clean white teeth with no tartar

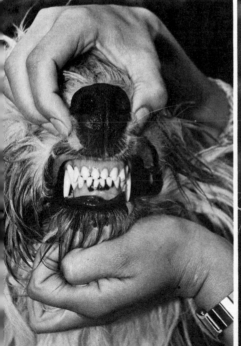
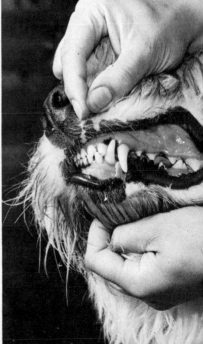

12. Pads. *Right*: clean and clipped; *left*: hairy and matted
13. Good rear end showing low-set hocks and parallel position of back legs
14. Body coat clipped away to reveal poor rear end and cow hocks

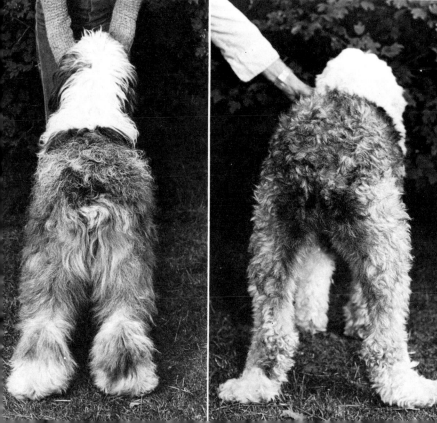

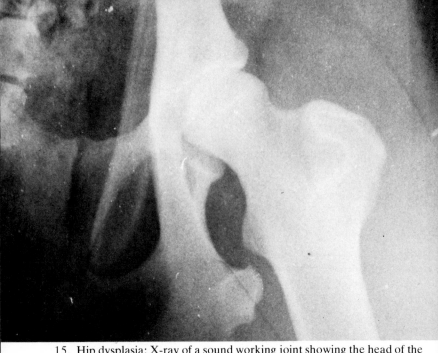

15. Hip dysplasia: X-ray of a sound working joint showing the head of the femur sitting snugly in the socket

16. Hip dysplasia: X-ray of a poorly formed joint, showing a shallow socket and slight flattening on the head of the femur

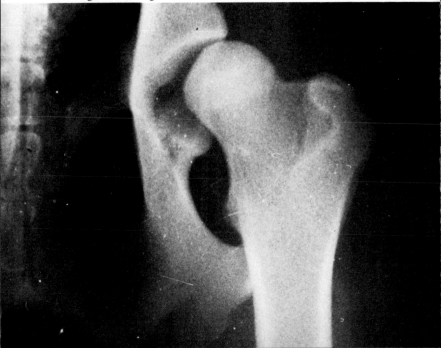

17. Puppies at nine months and at three weeks old relaxing in the shade on a hot summer's day

18. An early introduction of children and puppies teaches gentleness

19. Typical arrangement of out-door kennels

20. Ch. Keyingham Double Daisy being prepared for a show in the benching area

21. A regional Breed Club Show where young dogs are able to compete in a Minor Puppy Class

22. Bitch Class at a Championship Show

23. Mrs Zoë Wyatt, secretary of the South-Western Old English Sheepdog Club, with her spinning wheel and Sam. *Bristol Associated Press*

24. King Hotspur of Amblegait at work with Eric Morecambe making a TV programme. *BBC copyright photograph*

most other countries quite easily, but on returning to Britain the dog will face a compulsory six months in quarantine kennels on account of our anti-rabies laws. Few dogs enjoy parting from their owners, but most are far happier in boarding kennels than many owners realize, or perhaps care to admit. If you are kennelling two dogs together, their happiness is further assured.

The only way to feel satisfied about boarding your dog for the first time is to visit the kennels and see them for yourself before the holiday begins. Good boarding kennels welcome inspection by prospective clients and usually suggest a sightseeing tour if such a request is not made by the dog owner. Many of them are proud, and rightly so, of their excellent facilities. Before committing your dog to the care of the kennel, ask about inoculation regulations. Most kennels require that your dog should have been vaccinated against the common transmissable diseases (see pp. 88-91) and will need your assurance, in the case of an adult dog, that the booster doses have been kept up. You should have the card to show them. If you are boarding your dogs during the winter months, ask about winter quarter arrangements. If the weather is very cold, even bobtails appreciate some heat, especially dogs who have been used to living in centrally heated houses. Most boarding kennels now have heated winter accommodation for this very reason.

Look at the individual kennels themselves to assure yourself that there is a raised plain wooden platform bed because this eliminates the fear of draughts. If you do not kennel your own dogs at home, the kennel quarters will look pretty bleak to you, but the dog's own bedding in the form of a piece of quilting or a rug can go on to the platform. If the kennels has straw down, ask for it to be removed as it may harbour parasites. A plain, wooden bed with the dog's own rug is far to be preferred. Leave him an old slipper or something he is used to having at home.

The interior of the kennel should be dry and waterproof with a reasonable run so that the dog can get exercise even when he is confined to his kennel, and also so that he can move away from the immediate vicinity of his sleeping quarters if he cannot wait to relieve himself until his official exercise time. Ask about the amount of exercise he is going to receive each day and where it will take place. He should be taken out every day several times to a safe place to run and exercise.

If you are concerned about food and diet, ask what food is used. The Old English Sheepdog is normally an adaptable feeder and enjoys his food so much that he will generally take what is offered him. Because dog food is such an expensive item, you will be asked to pay more for boarding an Old English Sheepdog than a small breed. In other words, fees are graded according to the size of the dog. Ask about boarding fees so that you know just how much you will owe at the end of a holiday. Boarding a pair of Old English Sheepdogs can add considerably to the holiday budget.

If the dog needs to have any medication while he is in kennels, discuss this with the proprietor, who will carry out your instructions. If you have a bitch who will come into season while she is in kennels the proprietors must be informed so that she can be placed with other bitches in season well away from dogs.

You may want to visit more than one kennels before you are satisfied that you have found the one that suits your dog. While one does not want to be over-sentimental about one's animals, it is no use spoiling a holiday by worrying about a dog's happiness and comfort. What one owner may find acceptable in a boarding kennel, another may not. I personally dislike the type of kennel where all the dogs are housed in one large hangar-like building with a narrow walkway running down the centre from which pens for the animals lead off on either side. When all the dogs bark in this roofed space, the result is bedlam. Their access to the outdoor run is through a trap door behind their beds. The dogs are let out each morning to relieve themselves, and in some instances, in order to save time, they are allowed only five minutes before they are sent back so that the dog in the next pen can come out. This does not always give a dog time to relieve himself and he has to perform in his indoor kennel. It is to be hoped that all owners find somewhere they are happy to leave their dogs while they are away.

When you leave your dog at the kennels you will be asked to fill in a form giving his name, age, sex and details of inoculation. If you have a holiday address or telephone number that is also recorded together with the name of your vet. Having supplied this information you will then be asked to sign an agreement that you leave your dog in the kennel's care and that you empower the kennel to see to any emergency treatment your dog may require. Some kennels, for a fee, will groom and wash your dog for you while you are away.

YOUR DOG AND THE LAW

The Dog Licence

The owner of a dog over six months old must obtain a licence from a post office which has to be renewed each year. This licence at the moment costs 37½p, being the equivalent of the old 7s 6d dog licence. It is probably the only thing which has not seen a price increase since pre-decimal days.

Exceptions for which no licence is needed are:

Guide dogs for the blind.

Two farm dogs on a farm who are bona fide working dogs.

Farms of over 400 acres may keep more unlicensed dogs depending upon the size of the farm and the number of sheep or cattle kept. Extra licences are obtained by application to a magistrates' court.

Hounds under twelve months old which have not been used with a pack, provided that all the other hounds in the pack have been licensed.

Dogs Attacking Livestock

The back of the dog licence carries these words: 'Do not let your dog worry sheep, cattle or poultry. If you do, it may cause a great deal of harm for which you may be held responsible.

Keep your dog under control whenever there are sheep or cattle near and do not let it stray at any time on to fields or pastures where such animals are grazing, or poultry are kept.'

The owner of a dog which attacks livestock, and this includes horses, pigs and goats as well as the animals mentioned on the dog licence, can be made to pay damages for what his dog has done, unless it can be shown that the incident happened when the livestock in question strayed on to the dog owner's property. If a farmer sees no other reasonable way of stopping a dog from attacking his livestock, he is within his rights to shoot the dog. Stray dogs who have been known to worry sheep or other livestock and whose owners cannot be traced may be shot by the owner of the livestock if they remain in the area unclaimed. Anyone who kills or injures a dog, whether it is because of sheep worrying or any other cause which may be accidental, must report the incident to the police within forty-eight hours.

Dogs Causing Injury or Damage

All dog owners have a legal duty to take reasonable care that their dogs do not cause injury or damage. If they fail in this respect, they may be liable for prosecution.

Dogs owned by a person under the age of sixteen are considered the legal responsibility of the head of the household.

An owner is responsible for his dog if he escapes, even though he may have escaped through no fault of the owner.

If an owner can be proved to have been negligent, he is held responsible for any damage his dog may do. Wording on the back of the dog licence relating to this reads: 'Many accidents are caused by dogs roaming uncontrolled on the road. If your dog causes an accident which kills or injures someone you may be blamed for not looking after your dog. No matter how well your dog is trained keep it on a lead in traffic'.

Collars

All dogs in public places are required by law to wear a collar which must contain details of the owner's address. A telephone number is a useful addition but the dog's name is not required and it is advisable not to include it. Most pet stores can provide various types of address medals or containers which can be attached to the collar. Remembering that your puppy is going to grow into a large dog, pick a large size medal for him to wear so that it can easily be found among his long hair.

Insurance

It is possible to insure against possible costly bills for damage caused by your dog. Most insurance companies can arrange this type of insurance if you ask for it. A personal liability policy will indemnify the dog owner against compensation he may have to pay if his animal causes death or injury to a person or damage to property. Members of several of the Old English Sheepdog Clubs have the opportunity to insure their dogs, however many, and themselves against third party claim for the sum of one pound. This gives cover of £100,000. Full details of the scheme can be had from Graham Handley, Commercial Union House, 39 Pilgrim St, Newcastle-upon-Tyne. Tel. 0632 20755. There are other schemes which cover dogs for veterinary fees and a dog's life may be insured. A life insurance policy can also be made to cover theft of the dog and this is worth looking into if you own a valuable dog which is a show dog, or a valuable stud dog or bitch from which you breed.

Quarantine

All dogs entering the United Kingdom are required by law to spend six months in approved quarantine kennels in order to make sure that they are clear of the rabies virus. The cost of landing, transporting and keeping a dog in quarantine kennels must be borne by the owner. If you take your dog out of the country, these rules apply when you bring him back into the country. You can take your dog to Ireland, the Isle of Man and the Channel Islands, as they are subject to the same strict rules as other parts of Britain.

Quarantine kennels have regular visiting hours, but it may be more unsettling for the dog to see you and then lose you again after each visit than to be left alone for the whole quarantine period. Quarantine kennels will send written reports to owners and send news of any problems concerning the dog.

Rabies

The dog licence carries a warning to owners about rabies. 'Any case of rabies must, by law, be reported to the police at once. Symptoms: An infected dog may try to hide, froth at the mouth and tear up cloth, mats, wood etc. It may trot for long distances, snapping at other animals, persons or objects in its path. Precautions: A dog which has a wild and neglected appearance or which behaves unnaturally should be avoided. Rabid dogs will not usually attack persons who leave them alone.'

Rabies is a virus disease which can attack not only dogs but all mammals including man. While it is commonest in dogs, cats, foxes and squirrels also catch it easily. The infection is usually spread by the bite of an animal because the virus is located in the saliva. The virus affects the brain and death is almost certain. The first sign of rabies in dogs is a change in temperament; quiet dogs become aggressive and normally aggressive dogs become unnaturally quiet. The second stage comes when the dog runs wildly about attacking anything or anybody which comes in its way. The final stage is paralysis when the dog loses control of its lower jaw and limbs. It finally collapses and dies. Rabies in dogs usually takes a week to run its course, but a dog with rabies is not generally allowed to live that long. As the dog licence reminds owners, rabies is a disease which must be reported to the police.

A dog suspected of having rabies must be quarantined until its condition has been diagnosed. Dogs who have been exposed to the disease should be quarantined for six months and the period will be extended if these dogs are known to have been bitten by a rabid animal. The United Kingdom is free of rabies, as are Australia and New Zealand. The quarantine rules may seem harsh but they have kept these countries free of the dreaded disease, and when one thinks that the horrible fate of a rabid animal could be shared by a member of the family, the rules make sense. People who consider it clever to smuggle the family pet to the continent and back on a private yacht are behaving in a highly selfish and irresponsible manner. However, the Old English Sheepdog is not a dog to be smuggled through the customs under somebody's fur coat!

Moving House

There are disconcerting stories of dogs who will not settle in a new house with their owners and who run back, often many miles across country, to their old home. Fortunately, the majority of dogs prefer to stay with their family wherever they happen to be. All the same, moving house for dogs as well as humans can be something of an unwelcome upheaval. At that time dogs always sense that there is something unusual afoot and there are one or two things you can do to make the transition from one home to another go as smoothly as possible with the minimum of upset. The great thing is to try to maintain the dog's normal routine of walks and feeding-time if you can, and keep his bed in the same place right up to the time of moving.

On the actual day of moving in, try to spare one member of the family to take the dog for a walk in order to give someone else the chance to get his bed fitted up in the place where it is going to be, so that he has something familiar to return to when he enters his new home.

If you are moving away from your former locality, don't forget to find out where is the nearest vet. If neighbours can't help you, look in the yellow pages of the local telephone directory or ask at the library or the police station. You will also have to remember to change the address on your dog's collar.

If moving house also involves moving kennels, the task

assumes even greater responsibilities towards the dogs. Our last move involved six adult dogs and two litters of two and four weeks old. They were transported in various cars and lorries, and the first week was devoted to getting the dogs safely settled in. Old chicken houses and spare bedrooms were all utilized to house dogs and pups while permanent quarters were being prepared. Not until all the animals were properly housed did we start on our own house. In a case like this a team of helpers is essential as you do not wish to protract this unsettling time for the dogs.

Chapter 7

BREEDING

Some owners tend to think that it is only the professional breeder who needs to concern himself about studying the form of the stud dog and brood bitch and the intricacies of genetics. This is certainly not the case. All Old English Sheepdog owners who take up breeding have a responsibility towards maintaining the standards of the breed. Successful breeding is a highly skilled job and it takes at least three, often more, generations of known stock to be able to predict at all accurately what the result of any particular mating will be. Thus it seems very unfair to the breed and to those breeders who have put such a lot of hard work into the task to undo so much by careless and haphazard breeding.

For one thing, if you own a bitch from whom you want to breed, or have a potential stud dog, he or she must be clear of hereditary conditions such as hip dysplasia and entropion (see pp. (91, 95), which in the case of the former, means having the animal X-rayed to obtain a certificate of clearance. By the same token, if the dog or bitch comes from poor stock, or is badly mis-marked, you should abandon the idea of breeding because some at least of the litter will retain the defects of the parents, and when these puppies mature, some of them may be used for breeding and so the faults are further fixed and perpetuated.

If you own a well-bred bitch, seek the advice of a professional breeder over the choice of the stud dog. The best person is usually the breeder you bought your bitch from in the first place. What one is aiming to do is to select a pair of dogs who will produce a litter which will inherit all the good, desirable characteristics of the breed and as few as possible of the poorer traits. In choosing the stud dog, you will need to study the fore-bears of both animals in order to succeed in retaining desirable characteristics and breed out faults. An experienced breeder who knows the dogs in your bitch's pedigree can give you just the advice you need. If you are hoping to become a professional breeder yourself, you must get to know the breed by attending dog shows, following up good animals and studying their offspring over a period of time.

The systems most used by breeders fall into three categories.

In-breeding involves the mating of very closely related stock such as mother to son, father to daughter, or brother to sister. This method 'fixes' characteristics quickly, both good and bad, so a thorough knowledge of the dogs making up the pedigree is needed together with a severe determination to cull any poor stock which results.

Line-breeding is similar to in-breeding, only the net is spread wider to include other relatives, in an attempt to fix back on to a particularly outstanding ancestor, usually a grandparent, who could be used in the breeding programme whilst he is still young enough.

Out-breeding or *out-crossing* sometimes becomes necessary when the other two methods fail to bring about the looked-for results. This is the mating of two unrelated animals and with this method any desirable qualities are apparent and usually dominant in this first cross, so breeders operating this system find a particular unrelated dog or a young bitch who has the characteristics or qualities they are looking for and use the mating to fix the trait in their own bloodlines. Afterwards, they return to in-breeding and line-breeding with the resulting progeny. The novice breeder using this method must bear in mind that he has two unrelated sets of genes to juggle with and, once again, must be prepared to discard resultant bad stock from his breeding programme.

Whichever system one adopts, the ultimate success will stem from the original breeding stock and the question most commonly asked is whether to start off with a dog and a bitch from related bloodlines. My advice is to purchase a bitch initially from your chosen kennel, ideally from stock you have seen and admired at a show, possessing all the characteristics of the breed known as 'type' and conforming as closely as possible to the Breed Standard, with the possible exception of 'cobbiness'. If she is slightly long in the back, this should not bar her from your considerations as, in fact, some breeders prefer this in a potential brood bitch. Perhaps the most important item that often gets overlooked is temperament. Any nervousness, bad temper or aggression could be inherited, and superficial show points should never override the correct bobtail temperament. Too many dogs today are being bred with unreliable characters, so extend your inquiries to include the progeny of your chosen animal. By handling the dogs and questioning the owners, you will be able to make your decision.

THE STUD DOG

The choice of a male dog by a novice hoping to launch him on his stud career requires some careful forethought. A quality bitch has the choice of every proved stud dog in the country that fits her pedigree and the only way to ensure a supply of quality bitches for your particular dog is to put him in the show ring for all to see. Coupled with a successful show career, of course, must come the all-important clearance from hereditary defects, so when your dog is thirteen months old you will have to arrange with your vet to have him X-rayed in order to ensure that he is clear of hip dysplasia. Remember to keep one X-ray plate for yourself which you can show to interested bitch owners.

Stud dog owners must maintain their dog in top condition in order to keep his virility at peak level. Good grooming will obviously be regular throughout a dog's show career but this should be maintained after the dog has retired from the ring to stud. It is a marvellous sight to see a veteran who has added something to the breed parading in a condition that threatens his juniors and progeny. The stud dog's condition is also maintained by correct feeding. A high protein diet is called for with the addition of vitamins E and B. Some dogs are easily put off their food by the mere whiff of a bitch in season, so forethought must be given to the siting of the kennel and exercise area. Frustration caused by smelling bitches he cannot get to can lead to severe weight loss and consequent loss of condition and virility. At the other extreme, an over-fed, over-weight dog can also cease to be fertile, so a balanced diet with vitamin supplements and a contented existence are essential to a successful stud dog.

Among the biggest mistakes, stemming from the erroneous idea that a stud will quieten down a boisterous dog, is to use him when he is too young and to make use of his services too often. A dog with potential for breeding should have his first proving stud at ten months with a carefully chosen bitch, suitably related or carefully out-crossed, who has had at least one previous litter and who is placid and able to help the young dog. The dog should then be rested until after his X-rays have been taken at thirteen months. Stud work is mostly seasonal and a successful run at shows will result in the dog being in great demand. When beginning to use a young dog, close the interval between studs very gradually, ideally seeing every litter he sires, until by the age of two to three years old, a dog can be used twice a week in a seasonal burst without any drop in fertility. Much credit goes to exhibitors who manage to show a dog with successful consistency and maintain a regular flow of quality litters. A careful use of a good stud dog can result in his services being used throughout his lifetime. Some owners can boast of dogs siring litters at thirteen years of age with no sign of loss of quantity or quality.

A certain amount of the Casanova syndrome is obviously a desirable characteristic in a stud dog and this keenness must not be blunted if the dog shows an interest in his mother or bitches that he is not intended to mate. Continual correction may over-impress him and result in his being afraid to perform at a planned mating. The dog needs to be both keen and well-trained so that he can be persuaded by his owner to cut out lengthy playing sessions with a bitch which can result in exhaustion for both animals without a mating taking place.

The owner of a stud dog will find that he is involved in a considerable amount of paper work for he must obtain mating forms from the Kennel Club and he must always have copies of the dog's pedigree to hand to the owners of the bitches who visit his dog. He must also be prepared to explain the intricacies of the Kennel Club Registration Scheme to pet owners who are rarely conversant with it. He must also expect the inconvenience of having his own personal and social life upset. Bitches that are ready can obviously only be mated at a specific time and they show no consideration for your theatre dates or dinner parties.

THE BITCH IN SEASON

The bobtail bitch is rarely ready for her first mating before her third season, the usual time being when she is about two years old and mature enough in body and mind. A bitch normally comes into season for the first time when she is about ten months old and then at fairly regular intervals of approximately six months, although every bitch is an individual in this respect and you can never forecast accurately because even the weather, especially a cold spell, can upset the menstrual clock.

The season or 'heat' lasts for about twenty-one days and is marked at the beginning with a clear mucus-like discharge from the vagina which can be seen on careful examination. The bobtail is a very clean, fastidious animal and owners are more likely to notice the licking operations before they spot the discharge. This stage lasts for a few days, and if a mating is planned the stud dog owner should be informed at once. After about seven days, the vagina has swollen to quite a size but is still firm to the touch. By now the discharge is bloodstained and can be quite copious. If the bitch is a household pet, she should be confined to areas that can be mopped easily, or she can wear a pair of old briefs or special sanitary briefs made for dogs around the house, which will prevent stains on the carpet. The absence of a tail makes it a lot easier to keep the briefs in place, but in case of difficulty you can always clip or peg them to the coat. Whatever you do, try not to laugh at her as I'm sure she feels as silly as she looks. From eight days onwards the discharge eases up and the vulva starts to soften and turns pinkish in colour. When the vulva is at its softest and the discharge has turned from blood-red to a straw-yellow the time is right to take her to the stud dog. Even so, one cannot make this a hard and fast rule. Some bitches are ready earlier and others are not ready until the nineteenth or twentieth day, although they are perhaps exceptions. Discharges can stay blood-red right through the heat period and hardly any noticeable swelling of the vulva can be detected. The only sure way in this case is to take the bitch to the dog and let him decide.

The dog will be attracted by the scent given off by the bitch. Of course it goes without saying that the unwanted attentions of other dogs will be received, and for the three weeks of her season, strict surveillance must be maintained. A determined dog will get over or under any barricade, so close confinement for the period must be observed. Exercise can be taken away from the house by putting the bitch in the car and driving to a suitable exercise area. Always use a strong collar and lead during exercise; often the urge to be mated is as strong in the bitch as in the dog and a keen bitch may well run off in search of a mate if not securely tethered. This could still happen after a successful, planned mating, so continue your regime of surveillance for at least a week after mating has taken place.

THE CHOICE OF A MATE

When looking for a stud dog, be guided by what the stud dog owner has to say about your bitch, and if he recommends a different choice of dog, accept his advice. The top winning Champion in his kennel may not necessarily produce the best puppies from your particular bitch. Don't take it badly if a young dog is offered, provided he is proven at stud (which means that a litter, sired by him, has been born). In fact, apart from the financial difference, a litter brother to a winning dog or a near relation of the dog often does produce better stock. Whichever dog you use at stud, you must obtain a copy of his pedigree complete with his registration details and blue certification of mating form completed by the stud owner. This form doubles as the litter registration document and must be carefully kept for the next nine weeks until the litter is born.

One often sees in an advertisement for stud the expression 'approved bitches only'. This is stipulated as a precaution in case your bitch, on inspection by the stud owner, reveals a glaringly serious fault which could well be inherited. He can then turn your bitch down on two counts. Firstly, he has the future of the breed at heart and does not want to propagate faulty stock, and secondly, he will not want to risk his dog's good name on the puppies' pedigrees as past experience has shown that people invariably blame the dog for the poor quality in their puppies. So before embarking on a mating adventure that possibly has been conducted over the telephone or at long range, ask your vet to check your bitch over, not only from the anatomical point of view, but with the Breed Standard in mind. Most vets are only too pleased to offer their opinion on your bitch's overall suitability for mating. Another person to ask, and one who should be well equipped to deal with your inquiry, is the breeder from whom you bought your bitch in the first place if he or she is a professional. By exercising these precautions you are saving both yourself and the stud dog owner possible embarrassment when you meet.

THE MATING

Before mating can take place successfully, the eggs must have descended ready for fertilization. If the mating is timed correctly, you should get a good sized litter. Some bitches will stand for a longer period than others, so timing is critical. A forced mating on the early side may mean that only a few eggs are ready to be fertilized, whereas a later mating can catch a good number of eggs. Timing is more especially difficult for bitches who have to travel a long distance to the stud dog, so mating arrangements may involve the stud dog owner kennelling the bitch, or the bitch and her owner staying in the area in a hotel. Some owners ask for two matings in order to make sure that a sufficient number of eggs are fertilized and there could be two days between the unions. Opinion is divided as to the benefits of this procedure. If the first mating is successful in producing a good 'tie', there is little point in a further mating, but if there is no tie (and I would add that many a large litter has been born without) a further mating can be tried about twenty-four to forty-eight hours afterwards, but no later.

The bitch that is ready for mating will flirt when confronted with a dog or even another bitch, spinning round and springing up and throwing her rear end towards the dog; when she is standing she will roach her back and muscular tremors can be seen quivering along her back and sides. When her rear end is sniffed, the vulva will swing round in search of the dog's attentions. If the bitch is doing this with other dogs and bitches in her own kennel, the time is pretty sure to be right for the planned mating to go ahead.

When the bitch arrives at the stud dog's kennels, give her time to rest and relax after the journey and let her relieve herself in a place indicated by the dog's owner. A widely recommended time for mating is early in the morning as both animals are fresh and rested, but obviously this depends on the bitch's condition and readiness.

The dog and bitch should be introduced to each other on leads. If the bitch is not quite ready, she may snap at the dog; a hair slide keeping back the dog's fall will give him a chance to see better and to cope with any eventuality. If the bitch persists in snapping at the dog, the dog owner may well muzzle her or use an old pair of tights or a tape to secure her jaws. Continued aggression from the bitch usually indicates that she is not ready for mating or that she is past the day, so she should not be forced into mating.

An outbuilding or an empty garage is often used for the actual mating, as not only are you in private there, away from all distractions, but also the dogs are contained in case you need to release them for a short period of courtship. Letting the dogs romp through the meadows may appear very romantic but often play overrules the reason for the visit and a flighty bitch may well tire out a seasoned stud.

As soon as the foreplay is over, the bitch will stand four square and the dog will mount her. It is advisable for the bitch's owner to assist here. For one thing, the bitch—particularly a maiden bitch — needs someone she knows to be with her and to reassure her. It is also a good thing to have the owner present so that the mating can be witnessed and confirmed. Once the dog has mounted, the bitch should be firmly held round the collar by the owner who should talk to her reassuringly if she seems alarmed. The bitch may stand steadily for the dog, but be prepared to hold her up if she is one of those bitches who seem to want to do the whole thing while sitting down. The stud dog owner will usually put a knee under the stomach of the bitch, not only to stop her squatting but also to raise her, if she is on the small side, to help the dog. If the dog is having to stretch, a rolled up hearth rug for him to stand on is of great assistance.

After several thrusts, the penis is held by the bitch, due to constrictor muscles locking down behind the posterior gland, and this causes the two dogs to be tied. The dog is unable to withdraw until the bitch releases him, usually after about fifteen to twenty minutes, but be prepared for a longer period. It is tiring for the dog to remain in the mounted position and he will bring one foreleg and one back leg over the bitch's back and they will remain standing back to back until the bitch releases him. If the dog does not turn himself, his owner should assist him gently into the desired position. Both animals must be watched during this time because they may get tired and want to sit down, resulting in serious injury to both.

As soon as the dog is released, the bitch can be carried away and rested in the car. Do not give her a chance to rid herself of the semen inside her. Some stud owners lift the rear legs of the bitch to help the flow towards the womb. In all matings let the stud dog owner control the proceedings as he alone knows his dog and any idiosyncracies must be tolerated.

STUD FEES AND BREEDING TERMS

Whilst the bitch is resting, take the opportunity to settle the paper work. The stud fee is payable at the time of service. An experienced stud owner will probably already have sent a copy of the stud conditions. If the bitch should 'miss' and no puppies result from the meeting, most breeders give a free service the next time the bitch comes into season, if the dog is not booked at the time, but there is no legal obligation for the owner of the stud dog to agree to this. Stud fees today are high, and rightly so, reflecting the cost of campaigning a winning dog and his general upkeep. So you are paying for the services of an excellent dog expensively reared, the result of specialized breeding from whom you expect to get a litter of very good puppies which you will probably sell on the strength of the dog's good name and reputation.

I would strongly advise paying the stud fee outright and avoiding entering into a contract whereby the stud owner has a pick from the litter. Invariably, the one you want to keep is the one puppy he will choose and often arrangements are misunderstood or ignored by both parties. If you do decide to undertake such an agreement, make sure that all the details are entered on to a special Kennel Club form and registered at Clarges Street. A small fee ensures a legally binding contract and one that both parties will have to abide by.

As soon as the financial details have been settled, the bitch can be taken straight home to a meal. I prefer to give only a small drink as it is wise not to let the bitch urinate for a few hours. Remember that the bitch could still mate with another dog for up to a week and that if this happened complications both physical and administrative could occur. If two dogs of the same breed serve a bitch during one heat both dogs must appear on the registration document as it will be practically impossible to tell who sired what. If another breed or a mongrel should get to your bitch it may still be difficult to tell which are the pure-bred pups.

PREGNANCY

The time between mating and the birth of the pups is on average sixty-two days. Bigger litters tend to arrive early, but puppies born a week premature seldom survive. Some bitches go over their time; a wait of several days may indicate fertilization at a second mating. A careful watch on the bitch's habits and regular use of a thermometer will give valuable indications.

It is very difficult to diagnose pregnancy in a working breed such as the Old English Sheepdog. The bobtail carries her pups high up in the rib cage and although the embryos can be felt as they pass through the pelvic girdle at around the twenty-fifth to twenty-eighth day it is not recommended that novice breeders should prod around, as damage can so easily be caused to a developing foetus. Neither is X-ray diagnosis to be recommended, since only in the last weeks of pregnancy can anything be seen and by then outward signs are much more obvious. The teats will have enlarged, the puppies by now can be felt, and as the bitch lies on her side movement can often be seen. A general filling out is noticed from the fourth week onwards, and the appetite starts to become voracious. The earliest sign of a successful mating is provided by the vulva. Normally it returns to its usual size and colour following a season, but after a successful mating it will appear slightly puffy and darker in colour. Another indication is the bitch's behaviour, as she may become quieter and start to pick at her food. This then quickly gives way to an increased appetite.

You may be disappointed if, after a display of the typical signs and symptoms of pregnancy, no puppies appear. Many bobtails, perhaps because of their temperaments, go broody, and this is known to breeders as phantom or false pregnancy. The bitch will make a 'nest', pick up her favourite toy and mother it, even producing milk for it. This is a sad sight, but it is best to leave the bitch alone to get on with it, and after a week or two she will return to normal. If this broodiness is coupled with a difficulty to get her into whelp proper, you might consider the possibilities of her becoming a foster mother. Your local vet or canine society often know of harassed owners who may have orphaned puppies of any breed who would welcome your bitch's attentions.

Feeding the Pregnant Bitch

From the day of mating until weaning, the bitch has to supply all the requirements needed by up to twelve puppies. Bobtails are known to produce large litters and an average of six to eight puppies should be anticipated. Many factors can influence this number, but no expense should be spared to give the bitch the very best of food and additives. The developing puppies take all their nourishment through the placenta from the mother's blood, so vitamins and body- and bone-builders should be given in quantities according to the manufacturer's instructions, as soon as possible. Do not overfeed your bitch; in fact, quantities should not be increased until the fifth week of pregnancy. So for the first four weeks, good-quality meat, complete cereals, eggs, cod-liver oil and calcium such as Stress should be given in their normal quantities. The bitch will want more at five weeks, and I find that splitting the meals into two per day helps her because pressure from a full stomach after a heavy meal can be uncomfortable as the whelps develop. Milk in the form of Litterlac is a good addition to the diet from now onwards.

Never let the bitch become fat or lazy. Muscles should be kept in a hard condition as she will need them for the actual whelping; an over-weight bitch will experience difficulty in expelling puppies. Exercise stimulates the bowels and the bitch needs to rid herself of the waste products of the developing puppies as well as her own, so regular, gentle walks — preferably away from her kennel mates who may rough-and-tumble her — are advised.

A worming dose at around three weeks repeated ten days later ensures that you are feeding the bitch, not the roundworms. If you need to visit your vet to buy your tablets, stock up, for as the litter will need dosing about three weeks after birth and thereafter at regular intervals, quite a few tablets will be needed.

WHELPING

As the day approaches, consideration must be given as to where the bitch is to have her pups. An area out of the way of everyday hustle and bustle is essential. Under the kitchen table might be cosy, but is hardly practical for the next eight weeks.

The Whelping Box

Professional breeders usually have a whelping kennel fitted out with all the luxuries of canine midwifery, but basically all that is needed by the bitch and her puppies is heat and security. A spare bedroom will be warmer than the garage or shed as cold draughts can be a killer of young puppies. A good investment is an infra-red lamp. The dull-emitter type is ideal; never use the bright light type because when the pups' eyes open the light intensity is too great. This can be hung over a whelping box which should be made ready for the bitch to use at around the seventh week of pregnancy. You should use good-quality wood which will take plenty of scrubbing, and buy enough to make a box at least four feet square. This may seem large, but remember that the bitch is going to lie down and nurse puppies for several weeks in this box, although the pups will probably clamber out from four weeks old. Breeders swear by the use of 'farrowing rails' which can be added around three sides; new broom handles serve the purpose and prevent puppies from being crushed against the sides. The front should be made as an entrance with the facility of adding boards to increase the height as the puppies start to crawl around. The sides should be at least a foot (30 cm) high in order to stop draughts and contain the infra-red heat, and flat, clean sheets of newspaper laid down quite thick will make an absorbent and warm bed. A heavy duty enclosed thermometer tacked into one corner is useful to regulate the heat which will need to be up as high as 80°F (27°C) in the box. Never have the lamp placed so low as to burn the bitch's head when she stands up.

Preparations for Whelping

Once the box is in place and the bitch enticed to use it to sleep in, some thought should be given to preparing your utensils for the whelping: scissors that are sharp can be sterilized, not the rusty pair from the grooming bag, a clinical rectal thermometer, cotton wool, vaseline, old, rough, but scrupulously clean towels, a bottle of Dettol, stainless steel dish, strong cotton or thread and a cardboard box and hot water bottles, complete with old towels to cover them. An alarm clock in the whelping area is useful plus a camp bed if you intend to keep an all-night vigil. A notebook and pen are essential for recording times and provide a valuable guide to your vet in times of trouble. Get your neighbours to collect their old newspapers as a large litter will keep the dustbins full for many a week. (Soggy newspapers make terrible bonfires and upset neighbours.) Many breeders use the new whelping blankets that allow wet to pass through and reflect the body heat back to the puppies. For efficient use one must buy two as one blanket is always needing a wash, and for the infrequent litter the expense may not be justified. The final job before whelping is to remove the coat around the nipples and any long hair that the puppies might hang themselves in. A show coat that is to be retained should be tied up in crackers, which can be undone at regular intervals and brushed out.

Labour

Bobtails are usually easy whelpers, and the correct build-up to the day will ensure a trouble-free time. Notify your vet that labour is imminent, although hopefully you will not need his services. The first signs are usually the bitch digging a hole in the prize flower bed or scratching up the carpet, so take her to the whelping box and let her carry out this natural function on the newspapers. Once she settles down, take her temperature by smearing the bulb in some vaseline and gently inserting the thermometer with a rotating action into her rectum. At all times hold the thermometer and the bitch steady for about thirty seconds and note the reading. A dog's normal temperature is 101.5°F (38.6°C) and if whelping is imminent a fall to as much as 97°F (36.5°C) can be expected. This restlessness can be evident for as long as two days, but as soon as straining is first noticed a note should be made of the time. Contractions in a maiden bitch can go on for up to four hours whilst the cervix of the womb dilates, but if they continue any longer, your vet should be telephoned.

Most bitches like to relieve themselves prior to whelping, and you should accompany her to the garden, taking a torch and a towel with you at night; we have had a puppy born in the snow whilst the bitch was straining to pass a motion. Left alone in the garden, your bitch may well decide to have her pups in the most inconvenient place (to you), so have a lead handy in case you need to drag her back into the warmth of her whelping box.

Some bitches always choose the middle of the night to whelp, in which case you should take it in turns with somebody to sit up through the night. Never leave the bitch to get on with it especially in the case of a maiden bitch who is usually completely perplexed at the sight of her first whelp. A feeling of confidence is soon transmitted to the bitch, and the moment you notice the swelling of the vagina and a lubricating discharge, start to reassure her. If *you* feel panicky, make yourself a cup of coffee and occupy yourself while waiting for the first arrival by filling the hot water bottle, wrapping it in a towel and placing it in the cardboard box next to the whelping box. This is the box which will receive the pups as they are born until the whole litter has arrived when they all go back to their mother. Sterilize the scissors and cut a dozen lengths of cotton for tying the cords of the puppies and place them in a mild Dettol solution in the stainless steel dish.

At all times be observant, watch for straining. The bitch will be panting by now. This is natural and is in no way a reflection on the heat of the room. Keep the temperature up between 75° and 85°F (23.8° and 29.5°C) in the box.

The puppies are born each in its own bag or sack, followed by its own afterbirth. Sometimes the bag bursts as the puppy is expelled, but sometimes puppies are still inside the bag after birth. Normally the bitch sees to this and bites the bag open, thus releasing the puppy. If she fails to do this, you must do it for her, tearing it open gently but firmly with your fingers because it is essential that the puppy takes its first breath of air and cries as soon as possible. The bitch herself severs the umbilical cord and devours bag, afterbirth and membranes. If she fails to bite the cord, you will have to take the scissors to the puppy and cut through the cord at least two inches from the body; always cut through the white part of the cord, *never* the red parts near to the puppy. If the bitch takes no interest in her first puppy, break the bag, wipe the fluid away from the puppy's head with the rough towel, cut the chord and leave the afterbirth on the paper. Take the put in the towel and dry it vigorously between both hands. If it fails to squeak or cry out, mucus may be blocking the nasal passages. You can clear these quickly by holding the whelp in both hands with the head resting on the tips of the fingers and dropping the hands from head height to the knees. The whelp's neck suhould be very firmly to avoid it being whipped during the operation. This procedure usually clears the fluid and the whelp, once crying, should be offered to the mother's face for her attention. Normally, the bitch will clean the puppy herself licking it all over. It will look as if she is doing this very roughly, but a vigorous cleaning on her part helps both the circulation and the breathing.

If the bitch severs the cord herself, it is recommended to tie the ends of the cord with a length of the sterilized cord or thread in a reef knot, cutting away the excess thread. If you have cut or broken the cord yourself, it still needs to be tied in the same way. Do not over-handle the whelps, and as soon as they are breathing without bubbles appearing at the nostrils, let nature take its course. The pup will instinctively make for the 'milk bar', although its progress is usually hampered by the bitch's continuous vigorous licking which, besides aiding circulation, also stimulates the puppy to pass its motions and to urinate.

Once the first puppy is obviously contented and suckling, make a note of the time, the pup's markings (for later identification) and its sex. Note also whether the afterbirth was expelled, because at the end of the whelping you must be able to account for as many afterbirths as there are puppies in order to be sure that none have been left inside the bitch. The next pup may follow on quickly after the first, so watch out for the next lot of contractions. If all seems to be going well, offer the bitch some warm Litterlac. I have always found that my bitches appreciate a few mouthfuls, if only to remove the taste of the proceedings. As soon as the contractions become strong, and it is obvious that another puppy is on the way, remove the first puppy to the warmth of the cardboard box. In her restlessness, the bitch could tread on and damage it, so repeat this transfer to the cardboard box for each member of the litter.

Normally whelps are delivered every half hour, but every bitch reacts differently. Some bitches produce their pups with no difficulty every fifteen minutes. These are the easy whelpers. Others may go an hour or more between births, ending up completely exhausted. If the placentas are retained by the bitch delay is often occasioned because they obstruct the descending puppy. Rests are taken by the bitch and it is only when she strains and strains without obvious result that you need to worry.

Some puppies are born feet first; these are known as breech births but have never caused us any problems. A large-headed dog whelp may need a helping hand, and a well-scrubbed finger exploring the passage can usually locate and put right the problem. If you need to assist the bitch, pull very gently on the puppy's leg and pull with the contraction. The main thing to remember is that the puppy may have come away from the placenta and is consequently relying on its oxygen supply from normal breathing and not from the bitch's blood supply, so it needs to be removed without delay.

Abnormal Whelpings

Professional help must be secured for all but the simplest of problems. A telephone call to the vet and your provision of all the necessary facts and symptoms may save not only a puppy but the dam as well. Listening to the advice of knowledgeable friends can never replace the good working relationship of breeder and vet.

The main problem concerning the bitch relates to uterine inertia. This is when the contractions become too feeble to expel the puppy or are absent altogether. It is caused either by sheer exhaustion or a lack of hormones. The vet will have to decide whether he is going to administer drugs or whether a caeserian section will be needed to free the remaining puppies. Puppies can cause problems by reason of their size, or by choosing to enter the world in a wrong position. The pelvis is the main barrier to a puppy, with the brim defying the strongest pushes from the bitch. Once a puppy has entered the pelvis, some correction can be made on a poor position by the vet, who can manipulate the offending head or leg into a better one.

Never be put off by the colour and condition of some pups at birth. The black and green slimy discharge is quite normal and can be wiped away. If a puppy is finally delivered after a hard period of labour it may be necessary to get the lungs going by artificial means. Gently press the ribs in a regular rhythm of a one second squeeze, one second rest. Artificial respiration is dealt with on pp. 113-14. A drop of brandy on a pup's tongue often starts him breathing normally. Some breeders pop a puppy under the hot tap and then rub vigorously against the grain of the coat with a hot towel. Never give up on a puppy, they are quite hardy little things and I have revived many a forlorn case.

AFTER WHELPING

Once a bitch has delivered her litter she will appear quite calm and serene. She takes on an air that is difficult to describe, but an owner who really knows his or her bitch can tell that she is pleased with herself and that all is well. Hopefully the vet has not had to call, but it is wise to telephone during surgery hours and get him to pay a visit to administer an injection that will clear out any remaining afterbirth retained by the bitch. He will check over the litter making sure that there are no cleft palates or malformed puppies that might be better culled.

When whelping is over, let the bitch out to relieve herself and I recommend that you accompany her to see that all is well. By now she will have acquired all her maternal instincts and will want to rush back to her box without delay. Keep all other pets, especially cats, away from the room and children are not really welcome either until the puppies are a few weeks old and can stand the inevitable picking up which goes on once your back is turned.

Weigh the pups as soon as possible after all the chores are completed and keep a record of each individual puppy. Plotting a graph of weight against time can often point out a problem long before a casual observer would notice it. The regular handling which weighing entails will also benefit the puppy in later life.

The bitch will discharge for a couple of weeks after whelping. This is quite normal even if the discharge appears heavy. Keep a regular check on her temperature during this time and report any rise from the normal at once to your vet, who will give an antibiotic injection.

It is advisable to wash the rear end of the bitch immediately she has finished whelping. Stand the rear legs in a bowl of warm, mild Dettol and be prepared to repeat this exercise fairly frequently during the first two weeks, as the bitch's motions will be loose and very dark in colour. The nipples should be wiped with a clean cloth soaked in diluted Dettol, and the feet should also be wiped every time she comes in from exercise before she touches her puppies. Never soak the bitch as she will become sore but keep her clean and dry and maintain her grooming periods as the amount of calcium, vitamins and other goodies you are putting into her tend to make her nails grow more quickly and her undercoat thicken.

A camp bed remains in the whelping room for the first week with the two of us taking turns throughout the nights to doze beside the family because pups are likely to be laid on, stepped on, caught in the bitch's coat or smothered in the whelping blanket. In fact, it is a good idea to use *only* newspaper in the whelping box at all times. A few hours of disturbed sleep is a sacrifice worth making for the welfare of the litter, and soon pinpoints any problems.

When the vet came to look at your bitch immediately after whelping you should have booked a date for four days later to have the puppies docked and their dew claws removed. If they are heavy-boned, large puppies, three days is often better. A weaker, smaller puppy can be left a day or two later. Some vets are reluctant to remove tails, so it is not always politic to stipulate how you wish the operation to be carried out, but the vet must realize that the whole tail has to be removed. There are many methods, but possibly the best is where the skin is pulled back towards the body, the clippers make a cut and then are held in the closed position for a minute or so, followed by a quick check on the wound and a single stitch put in to stop any gaping that can follow the mother's inevitable licking. An antiseptic cream placed around the wound combats infection. The method of rubber banding to remove the tails extends the discomfort over a five- to seven-day period, whereas cutting is swift and usually heals in two or three days. Whichever method is used, check on the puppies' rear ends regularly, right through until they go to new homes.

FEEDING

Now is the time to step up the bitch's milk supply and calcium intake. Any deficiency will produce a condition known as eclampsia or milk fever for which the vet has to inject the necessary doses intravenously until the bitch recovers. Symptoms of this condition manifest themselves when the bitch appears to be off balance and staggers around.

A high-protein diet which aids milk production is essential. Raw meat should be offered even if you normally feed substitutes. The diet indicated for her in-whelp period should be fed three times a day and plenty of clean drinking water should be provided with the addition of a sulphur block in the bowl. Some bitches prefer their meals to be sloppy during the early post-natal period, so a rich gravy can be poured over the food. In fact it is a good idea to pander to her whims and fancies in order that she should eat well. The heavy demands of a large litter can quickly bring down a nursing bitch if you stint on her food over the next eight weeks.

REARING PUPPIES BY HAND

Hopefully you will never need to make use of the advice in this section, but sometimes a bitch will reject a puppy for reasons known only to herself, or worse still, puppies may be orphaned at birth. A foster mother of any breed would be ideal but one is seldom available when wanted, and so you have to resort to a man-made bitch's milk substitute. I have used Whelpi, Litterlac and Lactol successfully on different occasions and the convenience of these easy mix preparations is especially appreciated at the 2 a.m and 4 a.m feeding times. A rota system with a friend or relative is essential, for no sooner have you fed the last pup than it is time to begin preparing for the next feed.

The same room temperature of 75° to 80°F (27°C) must be maintained around the pups, and if stone or rubber water bottles are used in the box, make sure they are well-covered because puppies are adept at scrabbling away a small towel. The temperature of the milk in the dropper (we use an ordinary eye dropper) should be at the bitch's body temperature of 101°F (38°C). All utensils such as droppers used in hand-rearing should be sterilized before use. Never over feed; it is easy to see and feel the stomach filling up. Take it slowly and place each puppy in another box as you complete the feeding. Wind the puppy and finally take a piece of cotton wool, dip it in some warm water and stroke from the puppy's stomach to between the back legs. This will simulate the bitch's licking, and a bubbly brown dropping and a little urine will be left on the cotton wool. Check that no puppy is constipated or suffers from diarrhoea. Noisy puppies are usually either hungry or in pain. Four drops of canine milk substitute fed slowly every two hours is usually sufficient. It is absolutely essential to follow the mixing instructions exactly and never add a little extra powder as it can do more harm than good; too much food is as bad as too little.

PUPPY REARING AND WEANING

While the vast majority of litters are reared successfully, tragedies can occur. A pitiful wailing may signify a 'fading puppy'. Much research is going on into why whole litters can die off gradually after three days from birth. Although timely veterinary attention sometimes saves one or two puppies, the loss is generally heavy and frequently includes the whole litter. At ten to fourteen days the puppies' eyes start to open and any stickiness may be bathed with mild Optrex. Eye colour is impossible to determine until about five to six weeks and even then only the wall eyes are apparent. Shades of brown continue to deepen up to eight weeks.

At three weeks of age all the puppies and the bitch should be wormed and the dosing repeated at fortnightly intervals. At this time also the milk teeth are beginning to come through, and, being weary of sharp teeth and sharp claws, the bitch may well start to leave the puppies for longer and longer periods. For the mother's sake, keep the puppies' nails blunt; the white tip that needs to be removed is very obvious. At this time check the bitch's underside for any scratches or bites which might need attention.

At three weeks old, the puppies can be given their first proper feed. They will have to be taught individually how to lap, so prepare some canine milk to the consistency advised on the packet and offer a tablespoon per puppy on a shallow saucer. They take to it readily; in the case of any slow learners, put a drip on to their lips and as they lick it off, lower the chin into the milk.

The bitch always appreciates our intervention around this time, as the booster meal we give the puppies first takes the ferocity out of their suckling.

During this third and fourth week the milk feeds can be thickened up by the addition of a baby weaning food such as Farex. Often chemists sell off slightly out-of-date boxes quite cheaply, which is worth bearing in mind, as a healthy litter soon polishes off a box and any economy is appreciated.

At four weeks introduce finely minced beef to the diet. Some breeders scrape the beef, but if you find this an arduous task, try some of the specially marketed puppy foods. A large bowl is not a good idea as one puppy tends to dominate and one gets pushed out altogether. Try two to a bowl and eventually you will hit on matched pairs.

Sometimes the bitch regurgitates her own food, and the puppies tuck in. This is an entirely natural reaction and you must decide for yourself whether you are going to tolerate it.

By now the pups are everywhere and may benefit from some fresh air and exercise in the sun, if possible. Water should be available at all times but beware of the bowl becoming a plaything. Electric leads will also be chewed if you leave them lying around.

At six weeks our bitches go through the night with the pups but rarely feed them during the day. At breakfast time they have Litterlac plus Farex; at lunchtime, minced meat with a fine puppy meal which has already been soaked in hot gravy for about ten minutes, added to it to take the chill off, plus Stress powder and vitamin supplements; at tea-time, milk and eggs beaten together; at mid-evening, the meat meal is repeated, with the omission of the Stress and vitamins, and at supper-time the bitch is put in with them for the night.

Some bitches refuse to leave their pups, so facilities should be made where she can either jump a low fence or climb on to a sleeping board well above them if she needs to get away from their demands. She may well start to dry up although the opposite is often true and milk oozes out, and the vet has to give milk suppression tablets long after the pups have left.

We prefer to wean early and place the pups in new homes at around eight weeks. Although this can be costly, and a large litter, well fed and cared for, needs a considerable amount of financial backing, the puppy will settle easily if a diet sheet listing exactly your methods of feeding is given with the pedigree and documents.

Vaccinations to help the puppy combat the four major canine diseases are best given to a healthy puppy at ten or twelve weeks of age (see p. 88). The mother's milk would have given the puppy immunity until that time. Some breeders use a measles vaccine at an earlier age, and vaccines are being brought on to the market that vary the time given and the number of injections needed. Take your vet's advice, especially where pups have been hand-reared and so lack protection through not having any of their mother's milk.

Chapter 8

SHOWING

Dog shows have become increasingly popular with owners over the last fifty years or so. Indeed, dog shows have become a way of life with many bobtail owners, and many family pets have made it all the way to championship status. There is no pastime, sport or hobby which acts as a better 'leveller' of man than dog showing, and every weekend at shows up and down the country one can see people from all walks of life rubbing shoulders in the ring.

Before you can show your dog at a recognized Kennel Club show, he must be registered at the Kennel Club, or at least the registration applied for (in practice it can take a long time to get your document processed and returned to you), and the dog must be over six months old.

REGISTRATION

Registration systems have changed frequently over the past few years at the Kennel Club, and with the onset of computerization one can only state what the procedure is at the time of writing.

When you buy your puppy at eight weeks, the chances are that you will get your pedigree form but no registration document because of the time lag caused by the early days of the new system. When this document does arrive the named owners will probably be the breeders, so you will need to transfer the ownership. A small white form will probably

161

already have been supplied and duly signed by the breeders. Send these two documents with the £4.60 fee back to the Kennel Club to complete the transfer. If you are taking the dog abroad and intend to show or breed there, you will need an Export Pedigree. This is an impressive looking document certifying your dog's three-generation pedigree and listing the fourteen dogs and their registration numbers plus other related information with the Kennel Club's official seal in red. It will enable other affiliated Kennel Clubs around the world to accept your dog's registration into their system.

Your dog's official name will probably bear the breeder's prefix and is the equivalent of a human surname. These names are maintained by the Kennel Club and paid for by the breeder for his sole use. You may not change the registered name of a dog, but you may add your own affix to it if you decide to apply for your own Kennel name at a later date.

If your puppy has not been individually registered, you should receive from the breeder a partly filled in form from the litter registration pack which should have been applied for shortly after the birth of the pups. The breeder would have obtained a blue form from the Kennel Club (Form 1) and at the time of mating, the owner of the stud dog would have signed and completed the male dog's details and confirmed that the mating took place. Once the puppies are born, the breeder fills in the bitch's details and the number in the litter of dogs and bitches and sends this with the appropriate fees (£4.60 per puppy if he registers them all) to the Kennel Club.

If your puppy has not been registered individually you must choose a name; this is not an easy job, as all the names on the pedigree may have prefixes and affixes you cannot use, but generally you can get an idea of the sort of names breeders tend to choose. You will find a choice of names is required and if none of them is available after submission the Kennel Club staff will fill one in for you.

With your paperwork now in order, what do you do next? I would suggest you find out where your local all-breed canine society meets. The address of the secretary can be obtained from the Kennel Club. A note dropped into your envelope containing your registration and transfer documents or application form marked clearly to the shows department may get a helpful reply. If not, your vet, police station or town hall may help, or you could ask at a local kennels, which is always a source of canine knowledge.

We say all-breed society because most of these clubs have a meeting once a week where members can train their dogs (and the committee members train you) in ringcraft and obedience. Most clubs split the two facets of competition, so that 'beauty' and 'obedience' have their own followers. We would not recommend an aspiring beauty champion to attend obedience classes (unless you wish your dog to sit quietly outside the shops). And conversely, those intelligent working types who have aims of retrieving dumb-bells and sitting still for seven minutes need not bother themselves with the whims and fancies of the showring.

The practical aspects of handling a dog can be learnt from any seasoned instructor, whatever breed he owns and shows, so don't be dismayed if you find you are the only bobtail owner in the class. They will be able to pass on many tips about the rights and wrongs of showing procedure and how to show off your dog to the judge in the ring. Once you have learnt the basics, it is a good idea to join your regional bobtail club. The meetings will probably be monthly, although some clubs meet less frequently, and you will meet other bobtail owners and pick up tips directly relevant to the breed and gain advice on how to get the best out of your dog. There will be other novices and people with plenty of experience who will be only too pleased to advise the newcomer. If the general advice is to try your luck, or if you feel you want to show your dog, whatever you have been advised, then the next step is to order either *Our Dogs* or *Dog World* from your local newsagent. The forthcoming dogshows are advertised towards the back pages. You may be puzzled by all the different types of show you see advertised. All levels of show in this country are licensed by the Kennel Club and come under their rules and regulations, with the exception of the exemption show. Although still needing a licence from the Kennel Club, it is exempt from the usual rules and regulations and cross-breeds and mongrels can compete in the novelty classes which follow the four pedigree classes. These shows are ideal for putting your newly learned skills into practice and at the same time your entry fee is usually going to a good cause as they are mainly run for charities. You may have tried your hand at the monthly match organized by your local all-breed society. Here an aspiring all-breed judge either judges the dogs or the handling of the dog by you, in a knockout system, one dog against another, several rounds producing a Best in Match and often a Best Puppy in Match. Sometimes the club has a Christmas party where all monthly winners meet in a grand final for Dog of the Year. These two types of show are ideal for schooling young dogs and for the novice, although competition is still very fierce and huge entries are attracted at exemption shows, particularly on a sunny Sunday afternoon, so take along a picnic tea.

Your all-breed society may well organize a Sanction Show or you may see one advertised at a town nearby. This type of show schedules only up to twenty-five classes and the top winning dogs are barred once they pass beyond Post-Graduate level (see definitions on pp. 166-8); you will have to join to exhibit, if you are not already a member.

Membership is also required for the Limited Show. This is never a problem as you pay with your entry fee. This type of show is often run by the Breed Clubs early in the year in order to draw in the membership. A very good classification is scheduled with minor puppy classes and well divided classes for the two sexes. Champions are barred, as are dogs who have an award which counts towards the title of Champion.

Open Shows are held almost every weekend somewhere in the country, and if you are prepared to travel a little distance, you may find a breed specialist judge and possibly four classes for Puppy, Novice, Post-Graduate and Open Old English Sheepdog. If no breed classes are scheduled then you can enter into the variety classes where an 'all-rounder' judge will officiate. You do not have to be a member to exhibit, but you may find the entry fees are lower if you are.

The top level of show is the Championship Show. It is only at these shows that you can start your dog's career as a champion. Challenge Certificates are on offer; one for best dog and one for the best bitch, and your dog will need to win three, one each from three different judges, to qualify as a Champion. Only thirty-four sets of certificates are on offer in a show year, which means that competition is fierce, especially as the open class will contain existing Champions, so your aspiring Champion will have to be placed in front of these in order to gain that prized certificate.

Of course, you need not aim so high at first, indeed you have to learn to walk before you run, so why not try to gain your Junior Warrant? Assuming your dog is between the ages of six and eighteen months and shows promise, you have one year in which to amass twenty-five points. They can be gained by achieving First Prize in a breed class at an Open Show — one point — and First Prize in a Championship Show breed class — three points. Exhibitors who eventually gain their dog's Junior Warrant have probably travelled hundreds of miles, as in practice dogs stand most chance of winning puppy classes when they are between ten and eleven months, junior classes when sixteen to seventeen months old and, as a minor puppy, about eight months old, although these minor puppy classes are less frequently scheduled and of course your dog's age has to fit in nicely as to when the shows are on, the majority being in the summer months of May to September. When the dog or bitch has acquired the full twenty-five points, the owner must inform the Kennel Club, furnishing evidence of show dates and classes, and the Kennel Club having certified the claim, will award the dog or bitch its Junior Warrant.

So with your appetite for showing now whetted and your plans for the dog's future crystallizing in your mind, you need to get hold of a schedule for the show you have seen advertised. Sometimes they are available at the club nights, if not, telephone the show secretary and give your name and address and breed and take note of the closing date for entries. Sometimes the show committee require as long as six weeks in order to compile the catalogue and do the necessary paperwork, so beware, for you could easily have your entry returned if the postmark is a few days later than the advertised date. The form enclosed in the schedule is fairly straightforward and most of the details required can be copied from your dog's registration card; the only decision you have to make is what classes to enter, and you must sign to say that you will abide by the rules and that your dog is not suffering from a contagious disease (and has not been in touch with a dog who is). Naturally your dog is not vicious or, if a bitch, will not be in season on the show day.

The different kinds of class are shown in the following list. (The word 'dog' is used to include both sexes.)

Minor Puppy For dogs of six and not exceeding nine calendar months of age on the first day of the show.

Puppy For dogs of six and not exceeding twelve calendar months of age on the first day of the show.

Junior For dogs of six and not exceeding eighteen calendar months of age on the first day of the show.

Special Yearling For dogs of six and not exceeding two years of age on the first day of the show.

Maiden For dogs which have not won a Challenge Certificate or a First Prize at an Open or Championship Show (Puppy, Special Puppy, Minor Puppy and Special Minor Puppy Classes excepted).

Novice For dogs which have not won a Challenge Certificate or three or more First Prizes at Open and Championship Shows (Puppy, Special Puppy, Minor Puppy and Special Minor Puppy excepted).

Tyro For dogs which have not won a Challenge Certificate or five or more First Prizes at Open and Championship Shows (Puppy, Special Puppy, Minor Puppy and Special Minor Puppy excepted).

Debutante For dogs which have not won a Challenge Certificate or a First Prize at a Championship Show (Puppy, Special Puppy, Minor Puppy and Special Minor Puppy excepted).

Undergraduate   For dogs which have not won a Challenge Certificate or three or more First Prizes at Championship Shows (Puppy, Special Puppy, Minor Puppy and Special Minor Puppy excepted).

Graduate   For dogs which have not won a Challenge Certificate or four or more First Prizes at Championship Shows in Graduate, Post-Graduate, Minor Limit, Mid-Limit, Limit and Open Classes whether restricted or not.

Post-Graduate   For dogs which have not won a Challenge Certificate or five or more First Prizes at Championship Shows in Post-Graduate, Minor Limit, Mid-Limit, Limit and Open Classes whether restricted or not.

Minor Limit   For dogs which have not won two Challenge Certificates or three or more First Prizes in all at Championship Shows in Minor Limit, Mid-Limit, Limit and Open Classes, confined to the breed, whether restricted or not, at shows where Challenge Certificates were offered for the breed.

Mid-Limit   For dogs which have not won three Challenge Certificates or Five or more First Prizes in all at Championship Shows in Mid-Limit, Limit, and Open Classes, confined to the breed, whether restricted or not, at shows where Challenge Certificates were offered for the breed.

Limit   For dogs which have not won three Challenge Certificates or seven or more First Prizes in all at Championship Shows in Limit and Open Classes confined to the breed, whether restricted or not, at shows where Challenge Certificates were offered for the breed.

Open   For all dogs of the breeds or varieties for which the class is provided and eligible for entry at the show.

Special Beginners   For dogs shown by an exhibitor whose dogs have never won a Challenge Certificate in the breed. Note — It is the exhibitor who has to qualify, not the dog.

Veteran   For dogs over five (N.B. Often stated as seven years, according to the particular show committee) years of age on the first day of the show unless otherwise stated in the classification.

Special Breeders   For dogs and bitches bred by exhibitor.

167

Brace   For two exhibits (either sex or mixed) of one breed or variety belonging to the same exhibitor, each exhibit having been entered in some class other than Brace or Team.

Team   For three or more exhibits (either sex or mixed), of one breed or variety belonging to the same exhibitor, each exhibit having been entered in some class other than Brace or Team.

One should read through the rules and regulations covering the show and the other information that is laid out explicitly in the schedule, so that all you have to do is write out the cheque or postal order made payable to the society and post the form and money, 'First Class' well before the closing date.

Now that you have a target date to aim for in order to finalize your handling expertise, buy any extra grooming aids or equipment and find out at ringcraft training if anybody else is going to the show, so that not only will you have moral support but somebody to share the petrol expenses (and jubilation or even disappointment) with. We have not said 'start your grooming preparation or feeding for the show'. Your puppy, if bought from a reputable kennels would have been started on the road to the top long ago with the feeding, care and selection of the parents, the mating, feeding, whelping of the mother and the nurturing of the puppy from its first day. You would of course have maintained that regime, and grooming will be a natural addition to the puppy's routine. The puppy should be on the slim side, firm but not fat, and worm-free; the coat may be just starting to change, with the grey plainly visible at the roots; hopefully the adult teeth are sitting upright in the gums (some pups are slower with dentition than others), but you still have another four weeks or so before the big day.

For a show dog most breeders would recommend a thorough, weekly grooming session. They tie this in with a show and so plan accordingly, the routine varying according to your own personal situation and common sense. For example if the weather forecast says rain all week, leave the bath your dog will need until the night before the show; otherwise, sunshine permitting, bath thirty-six hours before, so a Saturday morning in the show ring means a bath on Thursday evening and chalk on his white at the showground early Saturday morning. The operative word is early: you will be expected in the ring for the first class at an Open Show at 10 a.m.

All the heavy brushing is done at home. Mats are broken up if they exist by careful teasing as explained earlier in Chapter Four, and the light bristle brush takes out the loose coat. Naturally you are helping your puppy coat along by regular brushing and even combing on the very dark coats. Most judges are not severe when judging puppy class coats, preference being given to the construction and other points. You naturally know your puppy's good points and will be trying to bring them out by careful grooming and presentation. The judge is usually a bobtail owner of some experience; he will appreciate your exaggerations but will also find your dog's failings. All judges have their own individual idiosyncracies. Some judges dislike the dogs being 'strung-up' — heads held high on tight leads — others dislike slicked-down necks, preferring to feel for the length of the neck below the mass of neck coat. Some like the rear ends natural, once again feeling for the length of back, and others like a slightly trimmed area around the stump, fanning out, giving a chamfered appearance to the rump coat. The judge's fancy varies as much as the dictates of show ring fashion and only by many years of experience will you get to know the majority, and new ones are coming along all the time, so the best advice is to prepare your dog to the best of your ability; stand him up in the ring and say by your hard work and endeavour 'here he is, I just hope you like him!' Some days you may win, some days you'll lose, but eventually you will create a style that is your own, influenced no doubt by other views and opinions. But basically, any judge worth his salt judges the dog and not the cosmetics, and gets the presentation in perspective.

The body coat seems to give most people most problems. It is preferable to leave the head and front to last, starting grooming at the shoulder points and working along one side to the rear. Begin with a flick through with the bristle brush, parting the coat and checking for any mats that need teasing apart with the fingers — this can be the shortest or longest of jobs, depending on the age of your dog and therefore the length of coat, or the condition he has been kept in over the past weeks. Bear in mind the dog's feelings; this should be the number one rule in grooming.

Once the mats are all parted into very fine tangles, return to the shoulders and with the bristle brush start brushing in a line of 45 degrees, away from your body, with your dog lying on his side with his feet towards you, head to your right, and the line starting from his shoulders down towards the top of his leg. The whole length of hair needs brushing from the root to the tip and as you brush up the hair roll your wrist into the coat, leaving the bristles behind in the coat; this action will prevent ends from cracking off, for ends are essential in a harsh textured coat. At regular intervals use your long toothed comb to remove the hair from the brush, ready for spinning (see p. 197).

On inspection this coat should be soft and fluffy with very few long guard hairs in it. If there are many of these, this means your action is too strong and you may be brushing into the body too hard, whipping the ends, or your dog could be into a heavy moult. Try to find out the reason as the last thing you need at this time is a bald dog. Assuming it *was* your grooming action and you have corrected it, continue right through one side. When this is done, let the dog have some exercise and plenty of praise. Stretch your legs and return ready to repeat the process on the other side. If you followed the instructions on the way you laid the dog down, you will have done the non-show side first, for dogs are customarily shown anti-clockwise round the outside of the ring. So the judge in the middle tends generally to view the left side of the dogs, although when each dog is handled by the judge he will look all over the dog.

The back legs are brushed out in just the same way, some dogs needing a careful combing from the hocks to the toes, as regular walks through the dew causes a tendency for the coat to clog; provided care is exercised and the wrist is rolled when using the widely spaced teeth of the comb so that the ends are not broken off, no harm will come to the leg coat even with regular combing.

It is preferable to brush out the front leg coat, using the comb infrequently, and rely on fingers to part the clogging coat. The easiest way to get the coat to stand up away from the bone is by grasping the pastern of the upper-most leg as the dog lies on its side, and start brushing away from you, just below the shoulder blade. The natural layers of the leg coat are quickly picked up by the brush, and a fairly brisk action tends to pump air between the freshly brushed hairs and hold it nicely away when the dog is standing. Work down and round in a spiral. A pleasing finish is obtained by combing out the bottom layer nearest the ground.

The head and front are areas that need careful grooming, as well as the delicate organs that could be damaged by over-vigorous action. If the dog is getting tired and restless, postpone the session. The last thing you or the dog needs is for an eye to get poked or an ear flap caught in a wrestling match. As soon as tempers start to fray, stop; grooming should be pleasurable for both of you, although this does not mean that you should give in to every one of your puppy's tantrums after a few minutes; in fact, one would expect every owner to have to prove they are 'pack leader' to every one of their dogs at some time early in their puppyhood.

The head, neck and front carry a large proportion of the marks in the show ring, so every hair on the head must be maintained. Older dogs are probably sporting a top knot, the long fall carefully brushed back on to the top of the head; a three-inch band of hair from between the eyes would be surrounded by greaseproof, tissue or polythene, and a cigar-shaped column of head coat carefully folded over twice and then gripped by a piece of stout elastic. Forget all the nonsense talked about your dog going blind if you can see his eyes; he's more likely to go blind through walking into things when his hair prevents him from seeing properly.

As soon as the precious head coat is long enough to make a 'cracker', probably not until the dog is at least ten to twelve months, you must train him not to scratch at this new decoration. We find that the use of hair grips, to get youngsters

171

used to the strange sensation, is very satisfactory, although you lose countless numbers in the process. Elastic bands placed directly on to the coat just break the hair off, as will a long period left done up in the correct manner.

Check behind the ears for mats and along the edge of the flaps; carefully comb out as already described. Then with the dog's head towards you, take the comb to the shoulder points and carefully comb out the under-coat away from you and in the manner described for the body coat, only this time reverse the role of the brush and comb, with the brush taking the coat from the comb as it is dropped into the spinning basket. The coat in this neck area will probably be white, and as you proceed, watch out for parasites or any signs of their existence i.e. black specks indicating flea droppings. A can of Nuvan Top sparingly sprayed is very handy as you groom, and is better than keeping a flea collar on a show dog. Some brands yellow the coat, some dogs absorb the chemicals through the skin and in general a collar of any sort is not too kind on the neck coat. One good spray will last the dog a few weeks, baths and rain excepting.

Once you reach the head, put aside the comb, only picking it up again to comb through the hair under the chin. These delicate regions deserve careful brushing; change your position so that the coat goes forward, away from the body, over the eyes, the aim being to emphasize the size of head and produce the famous chrysanthemum effect.

Remove the mucus that regularly gathers in the corner of each eye; the softer material will come away by using a drop of Diamond Eye, or Pretty Eyes, on a piece of cotton wool. This will remove the brown staining on the cheeks over a period of use. The brown stains around the beard may need more vigorous attention, and regular washing of the beard with a detergent seems to be the most widely used method, some exhibitors preferring biological to ordinary 'suds', some using washing-up liquids, and some, bleaches that are downright dangerous, especially so near the mouth and eyes. A regular wipe-down after meals and a ban on gravies near to the show day will ensure a fairly white chin. Shoe whitener, cornstarch, chalk and a host of show grooming powders will add that special whiteness on the day itself, although chalk is the only agent approved by the Kennel Club in the preparation of your dog, and even this must be completely removed from the coat before the dog enters the ring. This is a wise precaution anyway, for chalk is the cause of many a show coat's ruin as it does rot the coat if left in.

From under the chin right down the front, you can use the comb to remove any excess undercoat and lay the coat close to the skin by using the bristle brush; this will give a nice straight-looking front from the judge's point of view. At no time in your grooming should you use the comb to excess. Better to go through a second time if your dog looks stuffy in the neck or too full in the front, remember you can always comb away a little more, but if you overdo the grooming, you have a long wait for the coat to grow again. The wrong comb or brush in the right hands or the right comb in the wrong hands have spoilt many a dog's chances in top flight competition, so look out at the shows to see what the top winning handlers use on their dogs. Our recommendations are to be found in Chapter Four.

If you are not satisfied that every hair on your dog has been groomed, stand him up and run your hands all over his body just to check. Remove any hidden mats and then let your dog out into the garden for a good shake and a stroll; a drink of water should be available as the dog breathes in the dust as well.

A thorough brushing every week with no recourse to the comb should see the coat thicken up in the four weeks previous to the show. One week before show day trim out between the pads, using the scissors very carefully; if you do it the night before or on the day, and you nick the skin, the dog could limp and throw your chances away. Also check the nails, although they rarely need cutting if your dog has had the correct exercise on a lead on the pavements or country lanes, which will have tightened up the pads and elbows and given strength to the second thighs, pasterns and forearms. A quick gallop around the field is all right, but continual exercise on grass alone is guaranteed to produce flat feet, heavy shoulders and long nails.

Check that the dew claws, if present, are clipped back to the quick, and clean the ears as described in Chapter Four.

Teeth are often coated with tartar in the older dog, whereas the puppy's set are pearly white and need little attention. Canine toothpaste is available although descaling is best left to your vet, as you could chip the enamel if you attempt the job yourself. Giving a showdog a marrow bone to chew often results in the loss of hair around the muzzle and forelegs, where the bone is held down whilst being gnawed.

Bathing of the dog is a matter of common sense. Some owners prefer to bath their exhibits the night before the show, others, two or even more nights previously, using a whitening agent on the day. Some dogs, like some children, can be filthy again five minutes after a bath, while others keep spotless at all times. If you are the lucky owner of a stagnant-water-loving, muck-rolling ditch groveller, the niceties of the show-world and the related cosmetics are not for him. No sooner dried from the bath, he will be outside trying to get his doggy smell back again. This type of bobtail will need bathing all over to remove things like caked mud and oil from the garage which smears the coat, so naturally the coat softens up and tends to mat more easily. Among all the differing opinions on when to bath, one point all exhibitors agree on is that only the white parts of the coat should be bathed, and the blue body coat of a show dog should never be washed or wetted, if possible. Dogs wet from a walk in the rain can be dried with a heavy, terry-type towel, pat the hairs in line; a brisk rub helps the matting procedure. Some owners use a chamois leather which is kept hanging by the back door, others have a drying cabinet under the kitchen table for the dog to sit in, and in which the powerful hot-air trunk dryer employed by most exhibitors to dry the white coat is used to blow a jet of hot air into a sauna-type box with plenty of holes and a mesh door to aid ventilation. Whatever your arrangements, never let the dog out into the cold night air after a bath as he is just as liable to chills as humans are. Choose a hot sunny day for preference. An old tub in the garden containing warm water, about three inches deep, and your insecticidal shampoo, is the signal for a few hours' fun. Once washed and rinsed several times, the dog will gambol over the lawn like a newly shorn lamb, and mine enjoy a tug o' war with an old towel. I would not recommend this game to an owner with a young puppy as the teeth can get sore, but the general exercise over the grass soon dries them off without the dog getting dirty.

Before bathing your dog, a plug of cotton wool should be placed in each ear, and you should use a baby shampoo to make rinsing easier, as it will not sting the eyes if they should be splashed while the head is bathed.

After an evening bathing session, leave the dog lying on several large towels in the bathroom with the radiator on full blast, to dry the worst off, then bring him into the grooming room and systematically blow dry and brush the coat against its natural lie, with a soft bristle brush. Keep the nozzle of the dryer moving, as 2 kw. of heat can be very uncomfortable on the dog's skin. Use a small hand dryer for the head as the noise and hot air blast disturb the dog a little. The use of a restraining collar and chain either fixed on a stand on the grooming table or on a hook on the wall will leave you with both hands free for the brush and hand dryer. Work in a methodical way, blowing the coat away from you and brushing up the hair.

When completely dry the dog will probably crawl away and hide for a while, hoping that you have finished. Use this time to clear up — often a major task, as a frisky, well-coated dog can leave lots of water around the bathroom and loose coat all over the floor of the grooming area. Shake the blanket outside and run the vacuum cleaner over the floor. The smell of wet wool is known to all bobtail owners, and those exhibitors who have separate dog quarters with bathing and grooming facilities suitable for all the year round use are indeed fortunate. It is wise to put the wet towels straight into the washing machine, as this helps take away the doggy odour. Keep the dog towels separate from your own.

You are now almost ready for the show, but you will need a final check on your dog's show-bag and your own needs for a day out. I find a list drawn up beforehand saves taxing the brain at four in the morning as I stumble out of the cottage. If you are attending a Championship Show or an Open Show of more than seventy-five classes, you will have a bench (a small, open-fronted kennel) allocated to you, which is numbered according to your exhibit number which appears against your name in the show catalogue. These larger shows often send you a pass and any late information that may be relevant, such as judging times and the ring you will show in. This pass will have your exhibit's number stamped on it, and possibly your entry and exit pass and car park pass attached. This must be put in the bag with the schedule which may contain a map and directions to the showground.

A benching chain is required by show regulations. This is an ordinary chain lead with swivels at both ends, so you will need to take your dog's collar and if you have an ordinary chain leash with a leather loop handle you can thread this through the benching ring and attach the dog securely. He will settle better to this strange 'kennel' if you take his blanket. A plastic container filled with water from your own cold tap and his drinking bowl should ensure no stomach upsets from drinking water he is not used to. The only food he may need is a 'treat' to tempt him in the ring and by which you can show your praise if he puts into practice all that you have taught him.

All these items are on sale at the show from a very early hour, so a lightweight nylon show lead with a sliding metal closure could be bought on arrival, and for a few pence a show ring card clip for your exhibit number which you will either find on your bench or receive from the ring steward before the class is judged, saves trying to hook the card over a convenient button.

Your own personal items will be fewer in number but should include a towel to remove the chalk from your hands and an overall to stop it getting on your clothes. Gone are the days when a whole class of exhibitors wore white coats down past the knees, and dress is informal and understandably casual. A valuable item to include for emergencies is a kitchen roll, toilet roll or box of tissues. Young dogs can be travel sick, so be prepared.

The previous evening, when checking your car over, give some consideration to the dogs' travelling arrangements. If you take friends in the car with their dogs and everybody is cramped up, do not be surprised if the dog fails to move properly in the ring. Why spoil weeks of preparation by creating conditions that result in stiff movement? Many owners eventually buy a car to suit the dogs, and hundreds of estate cars will be seen in the show car park testify to this fact. Give your dog room to stretch out in the back behind the dog guard on his favourite blanket and he will arrive fairly fresh, especially if you stop frequently on a long journey to get some exercise, but have him on a lead at all times!

On arrival at the show ground, having parked the car and exercised the dog in the area set aside for just that purpose, make your way to the benching area for the Old English Sheepdogs. It is usually very obvious as the bobtail owners are the first arrivals and can be seen grooming their dogs on every convenient spare trestle table. Tables are provided for the exhibitor's use and later on the demand is high, so if yours is a young male dog in the first classes, find your table and an area that is acceptable and start your grooming.

Once you start grooming your dog, make sure you collect all the hair and place it in a paper bag and take it home with you. Always keep the venues clean and tidy. Unfortunately, many exhibitors lose good show sites by the indiscriminate use of chalk and leaving litter behind.

The brushing routine follows exactly the same lines as before, only this time certain show ring conventions will have to be borne in mind. Following a general brush-out which will also remove any chalk you may have used on the white parts, the dog should be made to stand up and the coat brushed into the show ring style that is recognized and accepted by all judges and exhibitors. The head coat is brushed up and forward to emphasize the width of skull, the cheek coat brushed out at right angles to the head to help with this exaggeration. The nylon slip lead should be brought up under the neck but below the throat (mind the Adam's apple or epiglottis), and round behind the ears, the fastener brought down behind the skull. All hair should be brushed down into the neck. With a friend holding the lead to keep the dog's head up and steady, the neck should be brushed as slickly as possible on to the body in order to emphasize the size of head. The coat under the neck and down the chest front should be treated in the same way. Careful use of the comb can be advantageous here and on the chin hairs. The front feet can be taken in the left hand and the coat brushed up against the lie. The area you hold can be combed out carefully, although the dog usually objects as it is ticklish and this is best left to last. The area where leg coat on the up stroke and chest coat on the down, meets, can be patted in with the hand to give a clean join. The rear legs can be generally brushed in the same way, although hock coat is fluffed out, the coat on the stifles should be brushed forward to emphasize the sweep. The body coat presentation may sound strange to the novice, but what is required is an exaggeration of the rise, which should be present on your dog, from shoulder to rump. This is how we get the phrase 'pear shaped', the dog appearing narrow at the shoulders and bulbous at the rear end.

At a point six inches from the shoulders along the dog's back start brushing the coat up and forward, work in a line down the side of the body returning to the top line and repeating until one side is completed, then tackle the other side in the same fashion. Do not whip the coat with the brush and try not to remove any of the coat. Once the other side is completed, the centre line should be fanned out by brushing from the anus with radiating strokes. Try to get as much coat forward as possible here, as visually you could shorten the dog's body length by inches with careful brushing and judicious use of the comb. But be careful of the dog's scrotum when combing through.

Most exhibitors tend to time their grooming to perfection prior to entering the ring, as the dog should not be allowed to lie on its bench once the grooming is complete. If you have a few minutes before your class is called for by the ring steward, stand with your dog at the ringside and watch an earlier class to see exactly what the judge requires of each exhibitor. Look at the way other exhibitors are handling their dogs; copy what you like and make a mental note of what to avoid. Watch where the 'new' dogs, the dogs that the judge hasn't handled, go to stand on entering the ring and if you are going into another class afterwards, where the 'seen' dogs go to stand. Classes at Championship Shows reflect the popularity of the breed and thirty or even forty entries in a class are not unusual, so be prepared for a long wait in the ring before the judge handles your dog. Some exhibitors prefer to get first in the line, some like to stand at the end in order to fluff their dogs up just a little more before the critical gaze of the judge.

When you do enter the ring, the ring steward may give you your exhibit number or sometimes it is lodged in the wire over your bench; you must display this number and this is where your ring clip will prove very useful.

Stand your dog 'four square', some say 'a leg at every corner'. Generally with a young dog it is enough to get his attention in short bursts. Ideally it is when the judge walks along the initial line-up and assesses the class as a whole that you should get your dog looking alert, and altogether proud and showing off! Try to get his back legs placed in such a way that the line from hock to pastern forms an angle of 90 degrees with the ground. Do not have his legs so far under him that he roaches his back or appears tucked up, or pulled too far back so that he loses his correct 'rise to loin'; stand him on a level surface which will also help to emphasize a good rise. The front legs are placed slightly apart and should form a right angle with the ground. With the lead in the position around the neck as already described you should be able to get the neck up without 'stringing' the dog up. Many judges do not approve of handlers pulling up on the lead, preferring to see the dog standing fairly freely. The alternative way of 'stacking' your dog is to kneel down and speak to him quietly, reassuring him all the time, and place one hand on the neck almost under the throat, the other towards the rear end, on the ham. This method is useful for a young, nervous dog that continually shuffles around in circles when on a loose lead. If the dog is a continual sitter, the left hand placed gently under the groin whilst you are kneeling will correct him.

When it is your dog's turn to come before the judge, stand him up as described but as quickly as possible. You should have had plenty of experience by now, especially if you have one of those fussy ring stewards who move you along the outside of the ring every time there is a spare inch of space. Concentrate on placing the legs correctly, getting the coat up on the rump and then holding the dog's head up, but remember that being over-fussy yourself can annoy a judge, so don't spoil your dog's chances. The judge may ask the dog's age, so prepare the answer to the nearest month, but remember that Kennel Club rules forbid you to hold a conversation with the judge, so when asked a question keep the answers short and to the point.

Once the judge has finished handling your exhibit he will ask you to move your dog up and down the ring either in a straight line or in a triangle. Keep to the side of your dog away from the judge when moving as the judge is trying to assess your dog's movement and will need to see the animal at all times.

By previously watching experienced handlers in the ring you will know at what pace the judge prefers the dog to move. Gone are the days when judges asked for a walk, trot and a gallop; large entries allow time only for a trot and, if there is any doubt, maybe a walk to reassess. It is surprising how many good 'walkers' will throw a leg out when galloped and the judge on the day will have his own preference for viewing the exhibits.

Make the most of your chance, and if the dogs starts to play up, check him and start your movement again. If the judge is satisfied with what he has seen, you will be directed back to your place around the edge of the ring. Immediately set your dog into the show pose, up on his toes and head up, and generally looking alert and trying to catch the judge's eye.

If you are lucky enough to be placed first, you must stand in the centre of the ring whilst the judge makes a few notes on your dog, and in a couple of weeks you can read what the judge thought of your exhibit in the canine newspapers. Meanwhile you are still not finished in the show ring. With the system that operates at Open and Championship Shows in our breed classes, all unbeaten dogs (i.e. class winners, provided they haven't been beaten in another class), collect in the ring after the open class and the judge will select his 'Best of Breed', if it is an Open Show, or Best of Sex and winner of the coveted Challenge Certificate if it is a Championship Show. The same procedure follows for the bitch classes and the Best Dog challenges the Best Bitch for the title 'Best of Breed'.

At our Championship Shows the Best of Breed goes into the Working Group later in the day and challenges the other members, such as the German Shepherd Dog, St Bernard, Collies and any other working group dog that may be scheduled at the show. The winner of the group then challenges the other five group winners (Toy, Utility, Hounds, Gundogs and Terriers) for the Supreme Title 'Best in Show'.

A similar procedure applies for the Open Show, the main difference being that as it will be a smaller show and hence contains fewer classes, the 'Best of Breeds' challenge each other and the 'Best in Show' is declared from the dogs that parade together in the one ring.

An added bonus at the Championship Show is that a win in a Puppy, Junior, Post-Graduate, Limit or Open Class qualifies your dog to an entry at Crufts Dog Show in London during February the following year.

Considered by most of the dog-showing fraternity to be the most prestigious of doggy occasions, it is certainly a string to your bow to say 'I have a dog qualified for Crufts', as only a very limited number of bobtails can be accommodated and judged in one day by one person, and this qualification limits the entry to the best dogs in the country.

From 1 July 1980 a new type of show, the Primary Show, can be staged by a Breed Club. The highest class will be Maiden, the maximum number of classes allowed is eight, and only members of an Association, Club or Society may compete. The level of competition falls between Match and Sanction Shows.

Chapter 9

THE OLD ENGLISH SHEEPDOG ABROAD

Despite the insular sound of its name, the Old English Sheepdog has for years been an established favourite in many countries throughout the world.

THE USA AND CANADA

Ever since its introduction to the United States in the nineteenth century the Old English Sheepdog has been a popular and flourishing breed. The Old English Sheepdog Club of America was started in 1904 by Mr H. A. Tilley, and in 1905 the club was given official recognition by the American Kennel Club. The Tilley brothers were responsible for taking many fine dogs across the Atlantic from their kennels in Shepton Mallet and showed them with a great deal of success and sold them to Americans who were eager to start their kennels with good British stock.

Regulations in the United States and Canada regarding registration of stock and making up a champion differ from those in England.

Registration of Litters in the United States

Litters are registered in America, and any dog born in the USA must come from a registered litter before it can be individually registered by the American Kennel Club. Litter registration application forms are supplied to breeders and there is a section for the owner of the sire to make a declaration of the mating, specifying time and date. As in England, both sire and dam must have been previously registered for the progeny to qualify for registration. The breeder must certify the birth of the litter, giving details of date and number and sex of puppies. Still-born pups and those who die before the form is filled in do not count. The litter is then registered by the American Kennel Club and the breeder receives a 'litter kit'. This is in two sections; the top section registers the litter and the lower half is the individual registration form, one for each puppy in the litter. When a puppy is sold, the breeder must fill in one of the forms, giving the date of sale and name of buyer. Without the buyer's name the puppy cannot be individually registered. If the first buyer sells the puppy to a second buyer, transfer forms must be obtained to register the sale.

As the American Kennel Club recognizes the English Kennel Club, it will register a dog or bitch exported from England, although the methods of registration differ, so long as the imported dog has the correct export papers and pedigree forms.

Registration of Dogs in Canada

This is similar to registration in the USA but in addition, information is required as to whether the litter was a result of natural breeding or artificial insemination. Moreover, individual dogs must be identified by a nose print or a tattoo. Nose print forms are available to breeders from the Canadian Kennel Club, or alternatively, a tattoo kit is provided. A tattoo must give the following information; the tattoo number, the year letter and the place of the tattoo, e.g. R.E. right ear; R.F. right flank and so on.

It is possible also to obtain a form to be used for dogs who are to be sold for non-breeding purposes. However many owners this dog may have, each new owner has to complete a new agreement form about the non-breeding arrangement. If the agreement is infringed, and the dog or bitch is used for breeding, the resultant litter is ineligible for registration with the Canadian Kennel Club. If, for any reason, the young dog grows into a good adult and the owner wishes to breed, a 'consent to cancellation' form can be obtained.

Making a Champion in the USA

Championships in America are awarded on a points system, fifteen points being required to make a Champion. Different shows award varying numbers of points. The lowest point rating is one and the highest five. A three points win is called a major, four points a 'four point major' and five points a 'five point major,' An aspiring Champion must win at a mimimun of two shows that have a rating of three points or more under different judges. One or more of the remaining points must be won under at least one other judge. Once a dog has been made a Champion, he can only compete against other Champions, in Championship classes.

The American points system can appear quite complicated to the newcomer, the more so because the point ratings are regularly reviewed and changed. The factors which decide the number of points to be awarded at each show and to different breeds are: the number of dogs in a given breed registered annually in the zone (the country being divided into zones for the purpose), the number of dogs which compete in the zone and the number of shows given annually in the zone. With insufficient entries no points at all can be won.

Classes leading to championship points in America are:

Puppy
Novice
Bred-by Exhibitor
American bred
Open

No dog under six months is eligible to enter licensed or Championship Shows. The Open Class is for any dog over six months of age except in Member Speciality Shows for American-bred dogs only.

The majority of dogs in the American show ring are shown by professional handlers. It is the exception to see a dog shown by the breeder or owner, which is quite unusual by British standards where the practice is for the dogs to be shown by amateurs, that is, their owners, who may or may not be professional breeders.

Canadian Championships

Canadian dogs also win points under very much the same system as American dogs. One major difference is that a dog must win ten or more points under at least three different judges. The dog must also be placed in a group in which at least five different breeds are competing, or defeat at least one dog of its own breed. The aspiring Canadian Champion, unlike the American, must compete in all the classes and groups for which it is eligible. If this regulation is ignored, all the awards won at the show are cancelled. Canada is also divided into zones, and point ratings are worked out by a similar system. Fewer dogs and fewer shows in Canada mean that the numbers of dogs required to make points is lower.

Classes at Canadian Shows

As in the USA no dog under the age of six months is allowed to enter a championship show. The classes which award points are:

Junior and Senior Puppy
Novice
Canadian bred
Bred-by-Exhibitor
Open

There are also competitions for Best Canadian-bred Puppy in Breed, and Best in Show awards for puppies and Canadian bred older dogs.

It would seem that the steady flow of bobtails from the United Kingdom to the USA and Canada is slowing down as the breed gathers in numbers from home-bred stock. The only Champions to cross the water in recent years are Rollingsea Viceroy owned and bred by Mrs Jean Gould and Tynycoed Ty Gwyn who, shortly after joining Don and Barb Roberts in Indiana attained his American and Canadian titles.

THE OLD ENGLISH SHEEPDOG IN EUROPE

The breed reached the other European countries from the United Kingdom much later than it did America, and the story of the breed in European countries really does not begin until well after the Second World War. Now, there are flourishing Breed Clubs, particularly in Holland, Belgium, Italy, Denmark and Scandinavia.

International Championships (FCI)

The Federation Cynologique Internationale was founded in 1911 by members representing the interest of dog shows in Germany, Austria, Belgium, France and Holland.

Its purposes were set out as follows:
1. The mutual acknowledgement of stud books
2. Mutual agreement on Breed Standards
3. Reciprocal agreement on prefixes and affixes
4. Reciprocal agreements on disciplinary measures applied to offending judges
5. The adoption of International Rules
6. Acceptance of the Certificate of Aptitude, Championship International Beauty (CACIB) and the Certificate of Aptitude Championship International Trials (CACIT)
7. The recognition of international judges
8. The control of the schedules of shows and working trials.

Requirements of the CACIB International Beauty Championships

The dog requires four CACIB certificates given in three countries and by three different judges, one at least of which is won in the owner's own country or in the country from which the breed originated. Outside European countries, the four CACIB certificates must be won under four different judges, one of whom comes from a different continent.

Today the FCI countries include almost all the countries of Europe including the Scandinavian countries and Holland where the breed is popular. The United Kingdom is of course excluded as the English Kennel Club controls Breed Standards, registration and showing regulations, but the Club has reciprocal agreements on such things as exchange of judges and accepts the validity of certificates issued under FCI regulations.

Ireland

Another country that runs its own canine affairs is Eire, and from its offices in Dublin the Irish Kennel Club organizes its own version of Crufts with the big St Patrick's Day show. Although Eire is classified as a European country, entry to all Irish Shows is open to United Kingdom exhibitors. So if you wish to compete in Championship Show Breed Classes under a points system similar to that which operates in the USA then a visit to Ireland can be recommended. There are no quarantine or customs restrictions between the countries and many English Champions go across to try to make their Dual Championships and win the Green Stars that are on offer.

Northern Ireland has its Championship Show at Belfast, and Old English Sheepdogs were first scheduled in 1979 without Challenge Certificates. In the same year a Breed Club was given recognition by The English Kennel Club who exercise canine authority for the province, and so hopefully interest and support for the breed will now increase.

Italy

A glance at the chart showing how many export pedigrees have been issued by the English Kennel Club will reveal Italy at the top of the list of importing countries. The breed has caught on in a very big way, and many good dogs have gone to Italian families, who in turn have joined one of the bobtail clubs who run various activities in much the same way as in this country. The President of the Italian Bobtail Club, Professor Tullio Mille, is a regular visitor to Crufts as well as an enthusiastic exhibitor back in Milan.

In the list of Italian champions and consistent winners, English imports figure heavily or are the sire or dam, or both, of the winners. Bobbingay Sugar Dumpling bred in England by Ian and Pam Morrison of Canterbury and owned by Sgn. G. Pistolini of Bergamo also won the CACIB in Yugoslavia only a week after winning the CACIB at the Italian Monza show.

Italian Beauty Champions

1976

	BREEDER	OWNER
Ionic of Kenstaff	Mr Davies	Sg. Bacchini
Shaggy Wonder Blue Sammy	Mr Mevis	Sg. Allevamento del Orceo
True Blue of Mijoho	Mr Lewis	Sg. Pistolini
Wisebeck Footlights George	Mr Cawthorne-Smith	Sg. Massobrio

1977

	BREEDER	OWNER
Bobbingay Sugar Dumpling	Mr Morrison	Sg. Pistolini
Carteris of Nijoho	Mr Drews	Sg. Giorcelli
Marry Avon Blue Prince	Mr Jump	Sg. Beccadello
Morgan dell' Equinozie	Mr Garlanda	Sg. Colmayer

West Germany

The popularity of the breed has increased due to the influence of
the American troops stationed in the country who bring their
dogs with them in Air Force flights, whilst on a tour of duty.
Therefore a mixture of American, English and Continental
imports can be found amongst the few 'home-grown' dogs. A
current consistent winner at shows is Ch. Pelajilo Pincushion
owned by Karin Seidel and bred in Wales by Jilly 'Layton'
Bennett.

Netherlands

This country can boast one of the largest breed clubs on the
continent and is certainly well supported at shows. British
judges are regularly invited to officiate and imported stock
figures in the higher placings. Well-established kennels of many
years standing such as those owned by Mrs Back Bennick, the
president of the club, regularly breed and exhibit good bobtails
that win in many countries. One such is Nederland and
International Champion Ellenglaze Ladies Choice and Champion Reeuwijks Care for Beauty.

Denmark

A title that one sees honouring some lucky bobtails on the
continent is that of World Champion. It naturally rings hollow
in this country as we have no chance to compete, for our strict
quarantine regulations make a return journey impossible. But
there is no doubting the quality of the dogs that aspire to this
title. One such is World Champion Audrey owned by Birgitte
Schjoth of the Danish Delight Kennels.

Scandinavia

The dedication of exhibitors in these countries is amazing, as a
Championship Show can mean a long, hard journey over icy
conditions, and the overall cost of entry fees and related

expenses are so much more than here in Great Britain.

A young dog can enter an age class, older dogs can go into the open classes and champions have their own class, although these are usually sex-divided. An important thing to remember if you intend to export to Norway is never to have a young puppy or even an older dog vaccinated against leptospirosis as a blood test has to be taken and results checked before an import permit is granted, and a recent vaccination affects the findings.

News of dogs winning in the show rings of France, Spain and Belgium reflect the names of well-known English kennels and the desire of those already mentioned to travel long distances in search of an international title.

The bobtail is also well known on other continents; there are thriving Breed Clubs in South Africa, Australia and New Zealand, and one hears of dogs coping well with the heat in India, Mexico, Japan and Brazil.

One very important point for all those who breed and who may be asked to send a dog abroad is to remember that the puppy you send is an ambassador for the breed. Its construction, appearance and temperament will reflect your breeding and will carry your good name. If you are trusted with the task of selecting a puppy which the recipients will not have seen until its arrival, it will also reflect your honesty.

TAKING OR SENDING A DOG ABROAD

In making bookings with the airline or shipping company, you need to allow for the time it takes to obtain certificates of origin, health and pedigree forms and export licence, all of which may take several weeks to procure. While the entry of the United Kingdom into the European Economic Community has brought a certain easing of regulations governing exports to member countries, it is wise to check on existing regulations from the relevant Embassy; sometimes requirements change at short notice as one may find to one's cost.

Outside the EEC you will also have to acquaint yourself with health regulations required by the country which is receiving the dog. Any animal destined for Australia or New Zealand will go to quarantine kennels. Most states and provinces of the United States and Canada require health certificates and rabies vaccination certificates issued in this country before dogs can be accepted. The same is true of most European countries, although if the bobtail is only a puppy of about three months it can sometimes be vaccinated with live vaccine on arrival.

Once your paper work is in order and you are sure that you have complied with all the existing regulations, you will have to contact the receiver of your dog and give details of flight number (or the name of the vessel in the case of sea travel), time of departure and estimated time of arrival at a named destination.

When exporting a dog, a travelling box must be supplied by the exporter. It is possible to buy travelling boxes for dogs, and whether you are buying them or making them for yourself, remember that air freight containers should be as light as is compatible with the dog's weight and size. Sea freight crates can be of heavier construction. Air freight charges are calculated on weight or cubic capacity, while sea freight is charged solely on the distance it is carried with no reference to weight or volume.

The British Standards Institute has a simple-to-follow recommendation about crate size for dogs. Measure the dog from his nose to the end of his back (A) and from the ground to the elbow (B). A + B = the length of the crate. The width of the dog's shoulders multiplied by two is the width of the crate. To arrive at the height, measure the height of the dog from the ground to the top of the skull and add two inches (five centimetres). Air crates should be made without protruding handles as they increase the volume and consequently the freight charge.

All boxes must have adequate ventilation in the form of holes, bars or wire mesh on at least two sides, and ideally on all four sides to permit a free passage of air. The BSI Standard should find favour with all air and shipping lines or railway services, but it is as well to check with the transporting company that the crate conforms with their regulations. The travelling boxes supplied by Pinehawk Kennels of Newmarket work out no dearer than buying the wood and metal accessories involved in making your own, and they come in a variety of sizes to suit every need.

Crates must be clearly labelled. The labels should be large and the writing large and clear. Each label should bear the name of the recipient, his address and telephone number, station or port of departure, and the destination and route. Each crate sent abroad should have labels giving precise details of feeding, watering and exercise required. It is also a good idea to add the animal's pet name (rather than the kennel name) so that those in charge of him *en route* can speak to him, using a name that he recognizes. In making your arrangements, always ensure that you and the receiver at the other end can be contacted quickly if an emergency occurs.

If the dog is travelling by rail for part of his journey, try to arrange for him to travel overnight so that he is sleeping during the journey at his normal sleeping time. His rail crate (unless he is going to be loaded on to an aeroplane for part of the journey) can be of quite heavy construction to stand up to the conditions of the usual luggage van. Rail freight boxes should be marked clearly 'Livestock — Urgent' and the consignee should be told of the time of dispatch, the route to be taken and the destination and the estimated time of arrival. A list is available from British Rail of stations equipped and able to handle livestock on its journey abroad. It is illegal to use straw in boxes intended for export so wood shavings or newspapers should be used.

BRINGING A DOG INTO THE UNITED KINGDOM

If you are living outside the United Kingdom and wish to send a dog to Britain, or if you are a resident wishing to import a dog, an import licence must be obtained. This entails having booked accommodation at a quarantine kennel approved by the Ministry of Agriculture. You will be provided with a list of these kennels from the Ministry on request. In order to get the dog from its point of arrival to the kennels, there must be an authorized carrying agent who will meet the dog on arrival and clear it through customs and deliver it to the kennels. Having obtained both a place in approved kennels and a carrying agent, send a licence application form to the Ministry of Agriculture with written confirmation about the kennels and the agent. The address to write to is:

Ministry of Agriculture, Fisheries and Food,
Government Buildings
Hook Rise South
Tolworth
Surbiton
Surrey
Telephone no. 01-337-6611

Chapter 10

WEARING YOUR DOG

In comparatively recent years, dog hair has come to be used as an alternative to sheep's wool for spinning and weaving in this country. This has been practised on a small scale by a minority of enthusiasts, including owners of Old English Sheepdogs, who have realized the marvellous potential of dog hair. There are still many weavers, on the other hand, who, while accepting goat hair and camel hair as alternatives to sheep wool, have yet to accustom themselves to the idea of the dog as a primary source for creating fabric.

Poland, Lithuania and Russia, on the other hand, use great quantities of dog hair. In Russia, thousands of yards of cloth are commercially produced every year from dog hair, and dogs also supply the material for warm felt hats and boots. In Poland the national sheepdogs produce a beautiful pure white wool from their undercoat which is made into clothing, while the outer coat is used for upholstery padding.

In other parts of the world, dog hair has been used for many years. The settlers of Smith's Sound in Canada's North West Territories used the undercoat of their huskies for wool to knit warm gloves, socks and caps, and the Karchans spun and knitted the furry undercoats of their Spitz dogs into mittens and woolly caps. It must be recorded also, that according to Parkinson in his *Treatise on Breeding and Management of Livestock*, the early nineteenth-century Dorset shepherds clipped their long-haired bobtail dogs at the time of sheep shearing and made the hair into hats.

Wearing Your Dog

The weaving of dog hair is a craft which has a very ancient origin among some of the North American Indians. Long before white men settled in Canada, the Salish Indians who lived on Vancouver Island and on the mainland between the Fraser and Columbia Rivers wove ceremonial blankets using the hair of dogs or mountain goats. In order to make the dog wool go further, they used to incorporate milkweed fibre. The Salish Indians actually bred dogs for wool production; according to tradition, these dogs were mainly white in colour, although there were some brown and black varieties, and they were sheared two or three times a year. Captain George Vancouver, who discovered the island named after him recorded meeting a group of about 200 Indians, most of whom were in canoes on the water, but a few walked on land with a herd of about forty dogs sheared close to the skin like sheep. These dogs were kept on tiny rocky islands in the Straits of Juan de Fuca, the channel of water between the south coast of Vancouver Island and America. It was the women of the tribe who were responsible for looking after these dogs, and in fact in those days a woman's wealth was judged by the number of wool dogs she had.

During the time of shearing, the hair was either pulled out or, more usually, hacked off with mussel shells. It was spun on a primitive spindle, and blankets and other garments were woven from it. Dog and goat hair was used for many years for the making of blankets until the coming of the white traders to the west. When three Hudson Bay trading posts were established in Salish territory during the first half of the nineteenth century, at Forts Langley, Yale and Hope, the Indians discovered that, in return for sixty fresh salmon, they could buy a ready-made Hudson blanket. It was quicker to catch sixty fish, which were very plentiful, than to weave one blanket, so the art of blanket making died out and with it, the breeding of dogs for wool.

One has to rely mainly on traditional verbal descriptions to get an exact idea of what these dogs looked like. Salish dogs appear to have been a Pomeranian type, while the neighbouring Chilliwack tribe used a wool dog more nearly resembling a coyote, which had a soft, woolly undercoat covered by a coarser outer coat. In 1846 Paul Crane painted a picture of the interior of a tepee where a Salish woman is seated on the floor at a loom weaving a blanket. In the background another woman is spinning wool while a wool dog, recently shorn, sits beside the weaver. The weaver's baby, in its papoose, is swinging from a support built on to the frame of the loom. The picture was presumably painted while some wool dogs were still in use, or at least while they could still be remembered. The dog on the floor of the tepee looks very much like a shorn poodle.

The modern North American Indians have recently revived their ancient arts of spinning and weaving to which they have added knitting which they were taught by white settlers only after their wool dogs ceased to be bred. Although the Indians have not, so far, taken up weaving dog wool again, the use of dog hair has become increasingly popular among other Canadian and American weavers. Modern spinners have found that dog hair knits up into a warm, durable fabric, rather like good-quality mohair.

Many Canadian and American dog owners have been encouraged to learn to spin and use their dogs' hair, and many more regularly collect the combings from their dogs' coats until they have a reasonable supply to take to a weaver to have it spun for them. The wool is then woven professionally or returned to the owner to use as knitting yarn. Weavers are always ready to try new breeds for their wool; some dog hair is too short to do anything with, however, and they all agree that the best hair comes from dogs with a profuse woolly undercoat. In other words, although one talks of hair, wool is a better description because, with the exception of some silky outer hair from breeds like Afghans which is used along with other fibres, it is the soft, woolly undercoat which is the material the spinner uses to produce the yarn for knitting or weaving. Because of this, brushings and combings are preferable to clippings, as brushing takes out the undercoat in such a way that it more closely resembles other types of raw wool which have no clipped-off ends and so is easier to put through the spindle. Among the list of suitable breeds for producing spinnable wool, the Old

English Sheepdog always stands near the top. Other good wool producers are the Samoyed, Husky, St Bernard, Pyrenean Mountain Dog, Keeshond, Elkhound, Golden Retriever and Collie.

COLLECTING YOUR DOG'S HAIR

Using your brush, groom your dog in the normal way (see Chapter Four, p. 69) and take the soft undercoat gently from the bristles. During the process of grooming, many owners tend to twist the undercoat round their fingers as they take it from the brush, in order to make a small, compact ball which is easy to throw away. Never do this when grooming for spinning; the wool needs to be soft with plenty of air among the fibres; like this it is light and easy to handle during the carding and spinning process.

Having finished grooming your dog, you may decide to separate grey wool from white. Work in a good light while you are doing this because the white undercoat is really off-white and some of the grey undercoat is so light in colour that the two shades may be mixed, in which case you will end up with a woven or knitted article spoiled by unwanted grey streaks.

For general purposes, however, the wool works up best if the various gradations of shades of off-white and grey are left mixed in together. The end result is an attractive grey material of different shades merging into one another in an interesting manner. If you have gone to the trouble of sorting the wool, you can try making off-white articles, or experiment with the effect of using a two-ply wool composed of one ply of white and one ply of grey.

Collect the wool in plastic or brown paper bags, placing it loosely inside; do not press the wool down into a small space. If you need a lot of wool which is going to take several months to collect, store it in an airtight container or containers, like glass jars or plastic ice-cream boxes.

If you have no time or inclination to learn to spin or weave yourself, but would like to wear some garments made from your dog's coat, begin collecting the wool and seek out a spinner who will prepare it for you. Weavers who are interested in using dog hair are always pleased to meet owners of various breeds so that they can try out and test the properties of different types of hair; it is only with the co-operation of individual dog owners that they are able to do this, so you may find your tentative offers of bags of bobtail wool welcomed with open arms. You may make arrangements with the weaver for the yarn to be returned to you after the spinning process for use as knitting wool, or you may ask for it to be made up into a woven fabric. If you are going to make a knitted garment, you will find that two ply knits very well. Dog wool is very durable and warm. Experienced knitters suggest that the yarn obtained from dog wool should be knitted on fine needles if an extra warm and tough material is required, but fabric knitted on larger needles will also wash again and again without wearing out.

Many owners who are collecting dog wool feel tentative about offering the results of their grooming from a dog which has not just recently been bathed. They may console themselves in the knowledge that dog wool cannot be spun effectively unless there is a fair proportion of oil or grease in the wool. Bathing takes the natural oils from the coat and the wool is too soft and fly-away to be spun successfully. Of course, spinners and weavers always prefer hair from a dog which has been groomed frequently, fed sensibly and exercised well. In other words, a healthy dog with a healthy skin produces the best hair.

WASHING THE HAIR

Always consult the person who is going to do the spinning before washing any dog wool. Many weavers feel that washing before spinning is a waste of time because, just as in bathing the dog, the soap and water remove the natural grease from the hair and the washed wool has to be oiled with olive oil, lanolin, mineral oil, or some commercially produced baby oil or spinning oil before it is to be spun. Unless the natural odour of the dog hair is really repellent, washing at this point does seem to be unnecessary.

If, however, you are asked to provide *washed* wool for spinning and weaving, there are one or two hints about washing the wool which are worth noting.

The masses of soft undercoat must somehow be contained before you place them in the sink, if you want to avoid blocking up your entire drainage system. Put the wool into muslin bags or even old nylon stockings and secure the ends so that no wool can escape. Wash the wool in pure soap flakes, like Lux, or use a shampoo, but not a detergent. (Detergent is recommended if the wool is going to be dyed, but this applies more to white dogs like Samoyeds than to the grey bobtail.) About half a pound of wool can be washed in four gallons of tepid water to which you have added two to three tablespoonfuls of Lux soapflakes. In order to get the soap to dissolve thoroughly, you will probably have to start with less water, but make sure it is hot to start with, and top up to the required amount with cold water once the soap has dissolved. Always treat the wool very gently. Pat, but do not squeeze it. After soaking it in the soapy water, move it to and fro very gently and then give it four or five rinses to make sure of getting the soap out. Again, treat it gently; do not rub or wring. After the final rinse, press the water out carefully. It is possible to enclose the wool in a pillowcase with the ends stitched up, and spin it dry for a few seconds. However, the washing process itself must always be done by hand, never in a machine at whichever stage it is washed, and this includes the finished garment.

It is impossible to provide in a single chapter complete instructions for owners who want to try spinning their dog's hair. For one thing, such a practical art as spinning requires expert practical tuition and guidance. You need to enrol in a spinning class or take a weaving course. Ideally, you should find a teacher who is interested in working with dog hair, although knowledge of using sheep wool is an adequate basis for going on to experiment with other materials, including dog hair, which are suitable for spinning and weaving. Most learners will find themselves using sheep wool anyway, because it is generally easier to spin, and the novice who is trying to spin dog hair for the first time is usually encouraged to mix a little sheep wool with the dog hair in order to make his early attempts at producing an even yarn more successful.

However, each practical spinning session can only be of a limited duration, and it is very helpful to consolidate what you have learnt by following it up by reading a helpful manual. One of the best is *Putting on the Dog* by Carol Knoll, obtainable from P.O. Box 266, Jefferson, W.I. 53549 USA. Mrs Knoll's book is full of helpful, practical advice accompanied throughout by diagrams.

Another useful book, also from across the Atlantic, is Susan Wallace's *Hair of the Dog*. This book is obtainable from the author, Route 4, Box 4851, Bainbridge Island, Washington 98110 USA. Both books deal specifically with spinning dog hair, but do not include instructions for weaving. If the art of making yarn and fabric from dog hair becomes more popular in England, it is to be hoped that similar publications will appear over here.

In England, an expert who prefers to wash her wool once it has been spun is Mrs Zoë Wyatt, the Honary Secretary of the South Western Old English Sheepdog Club. From her home outside Bath where she lives with her family of bobtails, comes a steady output of articles knitted from Old English Sheepdog wool. Mrs Wyatt was taught to spin when a very young child by her grandmother, and although she gave it up during her later schooldays, she never lost the art and took it up again after she was married, but with a difference; she began using bobtail hair instead of sheep wool. She is now one of our best-known Old English Sheepdog spinners, finding time to give talks and demonstrations, and she has appeared on television with her dogs and her spinning wheel.

All manner of articles, wearable and otherwise, can be made from dog hair. There is no end to the garments which can be knitted, crocheted or woven from the yarn, and one can also weave wall hangings and rugs and make up cushion covers, purses and bags. If you like the idea of toy-making, try a bobtail knitted from bobtail hair. If you have a limited supply of dog hair, confine yourself to smaller articles, like caps, hats, mittens and earwarmers or a pair of slippers. However large or limited your supply, there are certainly endless ways of wearing your dog!

Chapter 11

THE WORKING OLD ENGLISH
SHEEPDOG

The Old English Sheepdog is now probably best known as a show dog or a family pet, but it is of course a working breed. The story of the Old English Sheepdog and its emergence from working stock to the show ring is told in Chapter One. In the early years of showing, many of the best dogs in the show ring were also working dogs, and when the Breed Standard was first published, it included under the rubric on teeth, these words: 'Teeth . . . strong and firm and should be evenly placed in the jaw. Working dogs often have their incisors broken off. This is in no way detrimental.'

The reference to broken incisors alludes to the practice shepherds adopted at that time to teach their dogs to pin a sheep down by the ear, holding it with its teeth so that it could be examined. Parkinson, in his *Treatise on Breeding and Management of Livestock*, describes this practice and remarks that '. . . when the teeth are broken in the proper manner' no harm is done to the sheep. This method of singling out a sheep for inspection seems to have died out; at least one no longer hears of the deliberate cutting of dogs' teeth.

Another practice working Old English Sheepdogs are reputed to have been taught in the past was to climb over the backs of the sheep in their charge. In this way, a compact mass of 300 sheep or more could be made to move through or around an obstacle. Gossett and Parkinson both refer to this and suggest that it was a special trick of the bobtail's, but Rawdon Lee, in his *History of the Collie or Sheepdog*, maintains that collies were taught to do it as well. It is difficult to find an instance of Old English Sheepdogs who do this today, but a hundred years ago it was standard practice in many parts of the country.

About this time there were also certain bye-laws which effectively hampered a sheepdog's performance on occasion. Gossett recalls a story of a shepherd attempting to bring sheep into Chichester with the help of his Old English Sheepdog. The sheep were out of hand, the shepherd was old and the sheepdog tired, added to which, he was muzzled in order to conform with a local bye-law. Fearful of losing his sheep, the old man removed the dog's muzzle and the dog at once rounded the sheep up and had them under control. A policeman appeared and fined the shepherd eleven shillings, quite a large sum in those days.

Throughout his history as a working sheepdog, the bobtail has often been the subject of controversy among farmers as to whether he is best suited to sheep or cattle. Obviously the ideal sheepdog for the small farmer is a dog who can cope with both. Farmers who have used Old English Sheepdogs for work with sheep usually swear by them, praising them for their sagacity and speed in herding flocks. Despite his size, the Old English Sheepdog is surprisingly swift of foot, and his gallop is extremely fast. Working bobtails who are used for sheep are very often clipped so that they do not get over-heated. If the Old English Sheepdog gets hot, he tends to be an unwilling worker, so a clipped coat, often cut once a year when the sheep are clipped, is the answer. George Ewart Evans recalls a Suffolk shepherd, working during the first half of this century who had tried out many kinds of dog. 'One of the best was a bobtailed dog, an Old English Sheepdog. He was a "rare good dog", very quick and intelligent and as gentle as a maid'. His master owned that he had one fault. Because of his thick coat, the dog used to be too exhausted to work during the hot weather, unless he could find a pond or ditch in which to cool himself. Emerging from this '. . . he came out refreshed and worked the sheep with vigour.' (*Ask the Fellows Who Cut the Hay*, Faber and Faber, 1956).

It seems, however, that the majority of Old English Sheepdogs of the past as well as those who work today, were used as cattle dogs. Their size is an obvious advantage in dealing with larger animals, and generally, the dog is not required to move so quickly when working with cattle. One elderly Mendip farmer still recalls how his father bought an Old English Sheepdog puppy for the cattle on their Priddy farm because a large dog was thought to be better than a small one and other farmers who were using these dogs in the area seemed to be doing very well with them. The puppy in question grew to be enormous and fulfilled his promise as an excellent cattle dog, but unfortunately he became too big for the house. His favourite trick was to stand underneath the kitchen table and as he moved forward, so did the table. So he was sold to Mr Henry Tilley of the Shepton Mallet kennels who was always ready, as a working farmer and President of the Old English Sheepdog Club, to purchase a good dog for working and breeding purposes.

This story illustrates the humane qualities of the family who were willing to take the dog into their home when its working hours were over. All too many working dogs, both bobtail and collie, are treated very badly by their owners who chain them to small, inadequate kennels and leave them there in all weathers after a hard day's work. Any criticism from an outsider is likely to be countered by the reply that the Old English Sheepdog has an all-weather coat. This may be; the coat is waterproof (provided the undercoat is thick), but its very thickness and texture make it particularly vulnerable to matting. It also conceals infestations of flies' eggs, fleas, lice and ticks. Without proper maintenance, the working Old English Sheepdog's coat can get into such an unhygienic tangle that the working qualities of the dog are seriously impaired.

In the search for 'pure-bred' examples of the breed which are working today, one comes across many dogs whose owners claim to be partly Old English Sheepdog and partly some other breed. Farmers whose prime interest is in a working dog are rarely bothered about Breed Standards. They want a dog which will do the work required of it, and if it has a manageable coat, so much the better. The old shepherd to whom George Ewart Evans referred resolved the difficulty of the Old English Sheepdog's coat by cross-breeding and reported, ' "The best dog ever I had was the first cross of an Old English Sheepdog and a red collie" '.

On the other hand, some farmers do own pedigree dogs who work sheep and cattle, and they are usually clipped to save the coat from tangling and to keep the dogs cool while they work. Both sexes are used for working and breeding and it is generally from these strains that other working sheepdogs are obtained. This is not always is not always the case, however, and some of working dogs go on to have successful showing careers. Nowadays, the standards of grooming and presentation in the show ring tend to rule out the presence of the full-time working dog, so farmers with an interest in showing the breed have to keep their working dogs and show dogs separate. One wonders what some of the early pioneers would say to the position today; many of them saw the bobtail as essentially a working breed even while introducing it to a position of importance in canine shows at home and abroad. The success of the breed as a show dog and later as a family pet appears to have seriously affected its use as a working dog.

Nowadays, in fact, the term 'working' as applied to the Old English Sheepdog tends to have a quite different meaning — the dog is probably in show business as a film or television star, or in advertising. Just as Basset Hounds are generally known, outside the breed at least, as 'Hush Puppies', so the bobtail is recognized everywhere as 'the Dulux dog'. He achieved another sort of recognition early in 1979 by having his portrait on the 9p stamp. Four different breeds of dog were chosen to represent the four countries which make up the United Kingdom, and the Old English Sheepdog had the honour of representing his country of origin.

As a breed, the bobtail has become something of a prestige

dog; he is expensive to buy and can count among his owners, film stars, pop stars, celebrities from all walks of life, and a former President of the United States. But however we humans tend to invest him with the temporal glory of some of his better-known owners and however well-known he becomes through starring in the media, he remains at heart the same good-natured, simple-hearted creature he always was. It is to be hoped that the temptation of money-making will not cause his type and temperament to suffer at the hands of unscrupulous breeders.

Appendix 1

USEFUL ADDRESSES

The Kennel Club, 1 Clarges Street, London W1Y 8AB.

Breed Clubs (*titles registered at the Kennel Club*)

The Old English Sheepdog Club (founded 1888)
Secretary: Mrs I. Lapwood, 9 Highfield Road, Northwood, Middlesex

North Western Old English Sheepdog Club (founded 1922)
Secretary: Mrs D. Brocklesby-Evans, 85A Bentley Road,
    Doncaster, Yorkshire

Old English Sheepdog Club of Scotland (founded 1932)
Secretary: Mr L. McWilliam, 19 Kirkhill Road, Gartcosh, Glasgow,
    Scotland

South Eastern Old English Sheepdog Club (founded 1946)
Secretary: Mrs C. Masterson, 43 The Avenue, Gravesend, Kent

Old English Sheepdog Club of Wales (founded 1965)
Secretary: Mrs G. Mogford, Upper Maendy Farm, Lower Machen,
    Nr Newport, Gwent, Wales

South Western Old English Sheepdog Club (founded 1974)
Secretary: Mrs Z. Wyatt, Vale View, Longsplatt, Kingsdown, Box,
    Wilts

Midlands Old English Sheepdog Club (founded 1976)
Secretary: Mrs P. Guest, The Eaves, Long Common, Nr Swindon,
    Dudley, West Midlands DY3 4PY

Appendices

North Eastern Old English Sheepdog Club (founded 1977)
Secretary: Mrs C. Marshall, 16 Fourstones Close.
  Kenton Bar Estate, Newcastle-upon-Tyne

Old English Sheepdog Club of Northern Ireland (founded 1979)
Secretary: Mr D. Manton, 7 Hendersons Avenue, Belfast 15,
  N. Ireland

Breed Clubs (*titles not registered at the Kennel Club at November
  1979*)
East Anglian Old English Sheepdog Club (founded 1979)
Secretary: Mrs K. Eburne, Bleauville Cottage, Greenbank, Shepeau
  Stow, Whaplode Drove, Nr. Spalding, Lincs

Wirral Bobtail Supporters Club (founded 1977)
Secretary: Mrs A. Cleverley, 4 Belford Drive, Moreton, Wirral

Central Old English Sheepdog Society (founded 1974)
Secretary: Mrs C. Sinclair-Day, Boston Lane, Evesham, Worcs WR11
  6RD

Lancashire Old English Sheepdog Club (founded 1979)
Secretary: Mr D. Kilpatrick, Last Penny Cottage, Gill Lane,
  Longton, Preston, Lancs

The Old English Sheepdog Rescue Scheme
Hon Secretary: Jill Harwood, The Old Farmhouse,
  High Hameringham, Horncastle, Lincs. Tel. Winceby (06585) 644

PRO Dogs
Founder and Secretary: Mrs L. Scott-Ordish, Arden House,
  Holtwood, Aylesford, Kent

Ministry of Agriculture, Fisheries and Food, Government Buildings,
  Hook Rise South, Tolworth, Surbiton, Surrey. Tel. 01-337-6611

APPENDIX 2
TABLE OF CHAMPIONS

Year	Name	Sex	Date of Birth	Sire	Dam	Breeder	OWNER
1887	Sir Guy	D	?–6–80	Bob	Nell	A. Ling	1. Dr Edwardes-Ker 2. D. Parry-Thomas
1888	nil						
1889	Gwen (late Mrs Weldon)	B	?–6–83	Mayor of Cardiff	Mayoress of Cardiff	Mr Rees	Mrs L. Mayhew
1890	nil						
1891	Sir Cavendish	D	29–5–87	Sir Caradoc	Dame Ruth	Owner	Dr Edwardes-Ker
1892	Grizzle Bob	D	?–5–86	details unknown			1. J. Fernaby 2. W. G. Weager
	Dairymaid	B		details unknown			1. P. W. Knight 2. W. G. Weager
1893	Mayor of Newport (late Davonas Druid)	D	29–5–87	Sir Caradoc	Dame Ruth		1. Dr Edwardes-Ker 2. W. Ratcliffe 3. B. S. Freeguard
1894	nil						
1895	Masterpiece	D	14–8–93	Mayor of Newport	Cotts Bess	Owner 1.	1. B. S. Freeguard 2. A. Megson

Year	Name	Sex	Date of Birth	Sire	Dam	Breeder	Owner
1896	nil						
1897	Bouncer	D	1–7–90	Bouncing Bob	Nellie II	Abbot Bros.	G. Childs
	Lady Scaramouche	B	14–4–93	Watch Boy	Lady Cavendish	Owner	Dr J. Lock
	Watchboy	D	1–7–90	Stracathro	Nellie II	R. Abbot	1. T. Woodhouse
				Bouncing Bob			2. Dr McGill
1898	Dame Barbara	B		details unknown			Sir Humphrey de Trafford
	Merle Princess	B		details unknown			W. G. Weager
	Sir Ethelwolf	D	12–3–96	Sir Staverton	Dame Jessie	Owner	Dr Edwardes-Ker
1899	Thundercloud	D	21–9–96	Sir James	Birthday	Owner	Mrs Fare Fosse
	Kirkdale Bango (late Bango)	B	23–2–92	Middleton Bob	Duchess	G. H. Gosling	1. B. S. Freeguard
							2. F. Travis
	Fairweather	B	10–5–98	Sir James	Birthday	Owner	Mrs Fare Fosse
	Cupid's Dart	D	27–11–95	Harkaway	Psyche	Owner	F. W. Wilmot
1900	Victor Cavendish	D	1–1–97	Young Watch	Grey Queen	Mssrs Tricket & Shaw	W. F. Clayton
1901	Wilberforce	D	22–6–97	Washington	May Blossom	S. Woodiwiss	W. F. Clayton
1902	Bouncing Lass	B	18–6–99	Young Watch	Peggy Primrose	E. Y. Butterworth	C. W. MacBeth
1903	Baden Powell	D	Unknown	Ch. Bouncer	Wall-eyed Flo	T. R. Jones	W. H. Rees

	Dolly Gray	B	26-4-01	Stylish Boy	Dolly Daydream	F. H. Travis	Tilley Bros.
1904	Robert The Bobby	D	15-4-99	Ch. Cupids Dart	Watchwork	Abbot Bros	F. W. Wilmot
	Rough Weather	D	27-8-00	Sir James	Daphne	Owner	Mrs Fare Fosse
1905	Handsome Boy	D	21-7-02	Stylish Boy	Dolly Daydream	Owner 1.	1. Mrs F. H. Travis 2. H. Dickson
	King Edward	D	?-4-00	Ch. Victor Cavendish	Queen of Gipsys	Mr Clements	1. Lund Bros 2. C. W. King
	Ragged Man (late Mr Joplin)	D	Unknown	Ch. Cupid's Dart	Ch. Fairweather	Mrs Fare Fosse	A. Hopwood
	Brentwood Country Girl	B	3-9-02	Roseberry	Queen Maisie	H. Dickson	Mrs S. Charter
1906	Beat the Band	D	24-7-02	Stylish Boy	Dolly Daydream	Mrs F. Travis	Mrs P. Runciman
	Dame Doris (late Florodora)	B	?-4-02	Ch. Bouncer	Wall-eyed Flo	Mrs Jones	H. Dickson
1907	Shepton Hero	D	24-3-05	Lord Cedric	Avalon Lass	Tilley Bros	1. Mrs P. Runciman 2. Mrs S. Charter
1908	Mimi	B	Unknown	Ch. Victor Cavendish	Lady Alice	Unknown	Tilley Bros
1909	Rough Rider	D	16-2-04	Captain Rough Weather	Primrose Dame	Owner	Miss J. Edwards
	Home Farm Country Lass	B	27-7-05	Roseberry	Home Farm Lassie	Owner 1.	1. R. Carr 2. H. Dickson

Year	Name	Sex	Date of Birth	Sire	Dam	Breeder	Owner
1910	Brentwood Hero	D	22–4–08	Ch. Shepton Hero	Ch. Brentwood Country Girl	Owner	Mrs S. Charter
	Ominous	B	20–3–06	Storm Cloud	Goneaway	Owner 1.	1. A. Over 2. Tilley Bros
1911	Doverdale Dignity	B	28–3–07	Seymour Hicks	Doverdale Queen	Owner	G. Dovey
	Home Farm Britannia	B	27–2–08	Union Jack	Ch. Home Farm Country Lass	Owner 1.	1. R. Carr 2. F. Birch
	Home Farm Shepherdess	B	7–7–04	Primrose Knight	Home Farm Lassie	Owner 1.	1. R. Carr 2. Mrs A. Phillips
	Shepton Perfection	B	9–4–08	Shepton Brilliant	Shepton Sincere	W. Badgery	Tilley Bros
1912	Barkis	D	23–3–09	Falcon Valentine	Country Lass	Owner	Mrs E. Goodricke
	Shepton Laddie	D	14–8–08	Shepton Matchless	Shepton Violet	Owner 1.	1. Tilley Bros 2. Mrs J. Oakman
1913	Falcon Laddie	D	1–1–09	Falcon Valentine	Arklow Marguerite	Owner	W. Burgoyne
	March Storm	D	23–3–09	Falcon Valentine	Country Lass	Owner	Mrs E. Goodricke
	Brentwood Merry Widow	B	22–4–08	Ch. Shepton Hero	Ch. Brentwood Country Girl	Owner	Mrs S. Charter

Year	Name	B/D	Date	Sire		Dam	Breeder
	The Duchess	B	22-4-08	Ch. Shepton Hero	Mrs S. Charter	Ch. Brentwood Country Girl	A. S. Scott
	Shepton Gem	B	17-7-08	Shepton Matchless	Owners	Shepton Dainty	Tilley Bros
1914	Tip Top Weather	D	31-8-12	Typical Weather	Miss McTurk	Clara	Mrs Fare Fosse
	Lady Bountiful	B	29-5-10	Ch. Brentwood Hero	Dr Stork	Bettina	Dr Stork & Miss Collins
	Lady Rider	B	19-1-09	Ch. Rough Rider	Mrs G. B. Allen	Clatford Nella	Mr E. C. Young
	Miss Starlight	B	17-6-07	Tom O'Bills	Owner	Lady Starlight	Mr H. Wolstenholme
1915	Hallaton Country Lad (late Brentwood Country Lad)	D	14-2-10	Brentwood Pete	Mrs S. Charter	Ch. Brentwood Country Girl	Miss McTurk
	Falcon Bessie	B	24-5-10	Typical Weather	Owner	Calm Weather	W. Burgoyne
1916	Nil						
1917	Midsummer Weather (late Bethnal Green Daisy)	B	1-4-12	Dennis	W. Harris	Melbourne Daisy	Mrs Fare Fosse
1918	Nil						
1919	Nil						
1920	Bully The Tramp	D	1-5-17	Peter the Tramp	Owner	Wayward Tramp	B. Breakspear

Year	Name	Sex	Date of Birth	Sire	Dam	Breeder	Owner
	Night Raider	D	20-6-17	Tiptoes	Lucy	Owner	Miss M. McTurk
	Lady Golightly	B	13-8-13	Night Rider	Lady Lightfoot	Owners	Misses Stork & Collins
	May Morn	B	19-5-15	Ch. Tip Top Weather	Betsy Day	Mrs G. B. Allen	Mrs F. Gatehouse
1921	Claude Duval	D	13-8-13	Night Rider	Lady Lightfoot	Owners	Misses Stork & Collins
	Elusive Tramp	B	27-6-19	Shepton Moonshine	Comic	T. Coombes	Mrs E. Breakspear
	Moonlight	B	30-8-17	Wall-eyed Victor	Betsy Day	Owner	Mrs Gatehouse
1922	Old Bill	D	20-4-19	Tip Toes	Milkmaid	A. Over	Miss M. McTurk
	Sunlight	D	30-8-17	Wall-eyed Victor	Betsy Day	Owner	F. Gatehouse
	Whimsical Weather	B	1-12-20	Ch. Night Raider	Juno	Mr Wilkinson	Mrs Fare Fosse
1923	Matchless Weather (late Storm Maid)	B	7-6-20	The Bearer of Hallaton	Kennington Floss	F. A. Grundy	Mrs Fare Fosse
	Miss March Storm	B	11-2-22	Ch. Old Bill	Montford Judy	G. F. Wilkinson	A. M. Tingey
1924	Blue Blossom	B	30-5-22	Snowstorm	Snowy Lass	J. G. Weeks	Mrs M. Sheffield
	Blue Lady	B	25-3-20	Gerrards Hero	Gerrards Mary	Mrs Dobbin	Mrs M. Sheffield
	Darkest of All	B	26-11-22	Penzance Wall	Bubbles	W. E. Roberts	W. N. Tod

	Name		Date	Sire	Dam		
	Daylight Patrol	D	14-6-20	Ch. Night Raider	Thimbleby Queen	G. F. Wilkinson	Miss F. A. White
	Elkington Squire	D	?-12-21	Ch. Old Bill	Montford Girlie	G. F. Wilkinson	Mrs K. M. Beard
	Faithful Tramp	D	17-7-22	Shepton Moonshine	Peaceful Tramp	Owner	Mrs E. Breakspear
	Peggy Wallflower	B	26-7-22	Penzance Wallflower	Colleen	T. Coombes	Mrs K. Beard
1925	Blue Knight	D	22-4-23	Shepton Moonshine	Blue Lady	Owner	Mrs M. Sheffield
	Glorious Weather	D	17-7-22	Shepton Moonshine	Peaceful Tramp	Mrs Breakspear	1. Mrs Fare Fosse & Dr King Brown 2. Lady Dunbar of Hempriggs
1926	Captain Bill	D	4-2-22	Ch. Old Bill	Montford Judy	G. Wilkinson	F. J. Sanders
	Lucky Prince	D	16-10-22	Shepton Moonshine	Sea Mist	F. J. Sanders	Mrs F. E. Sanders
	Mistress Sylvia	B	29-6-24	Ch. Faithful Tramp	Waysgreen Peggy	Miss H. Hickson	Miss Tireman
	New Moon	B	21-12-21	Good Morn	Colleen	T. Coombes	Mrs F. Gatehouse
1927	Blue Coat	D	22-4-23	Shepton Moonshine	Blue Lady	Owner	Mrs M. Sheffield
	Bridal Gown (late Bluefields Pride)	B	26-7-22	Penzance Wallflower	Colleen	T. Coombes	Mrs F. Gatehouse
	Moonshine Weather	D	30-7-25	Ch. Glorious Weather	Whimsical Weather	Mrs Fare Fosse & Dr King Brown	Mrs Fare Fosse
	Spare a Penny (late Wall-Eyed Robbery)	B	14-12-24	Ch. Faithful Tramp	Dulverton Danegeld	Miss V. Croft	W. N. Tod

Year	Name	Sex	Date of Birth	Sire	Dam	Breeder	Owner
1928	Stella Maris	B	11–11–23	Shepton Moonshine	Ranee	Owners	Miss M. Johns & Mrs A. Beard
	Beara Leader	D	9–7–24	Ch. Daylight Patrol	Dearest Peggy	Owner	C. M. Whitehead
	Bridget	B	1–10–25	Old Henry	Brightlight	R. Cook	W. N. Tod
	Happy Go Lucky	D	19–6–25	Old Henry	Penpol Peggy	W. E. Roberts	W. N. Tod
	Hillgarth Blue Princess	B	6–8–25	Ch. Blue Knight	Ch. Blue Blossom	Owner	Mrs M. Sheffield
	Pastorale Bo Peep (late Montford Lucy)	B	4–11–26	Careful Jim	Lady Morna	O. J. Stupple	Miss A. Tireman
1929	Armistice Sunshine	D	11–11–23	Shepton Moonshine	Ranee	Owner 1.	1. Miss M. Johns 2. Mrs A. Beard
	Beara Dame	B	9–7–24	Ch. Daylight Patrol	Dearest Peggy	Owner 1.	1. C. M. Whitehead 2. Miss A. Tireman
	Downderry Enchantress	B	1–6–26	Ch. Elkington Squire	Ch. Peggy Wallflower	Owner 1.	1. Mrs A. Beard 2. Mrs W. Durham-Waite
	Downderry Vanity	B	27–6–26	Shepton Guardsman	Shepton Grey Mist	H. A. Tilley	Mrs W. Durham-Waite
	Hillgarth Blue Boy	D	7–3–27	Ch. Blue Knight	Ch. Blue Blossom	Owner	Mrs M. Sheffield
	Moonshine Girl	B	11–11–23	Shepton Moonshine	Ranee	Owner	Miss M. Johns

Year	Name	Sex	Date	Sire	Dam		
	Wall-eyed Bill	D	26–2–25	Shepton Moonshine	Old-Fashioned Weather	Mrs J. Russell	1. H. W. Bishop 2. W. N. Tod
1930	Aristocrat	D	26–4–26	Sergeant Murphy	White Blossom	Owners	Mr & Mrs Sanders
	Newcote Blossom	B	22–5–24	Ch. Blue Coat	Ch. Blue Blossom	Mrs M. Sheffield	Miss E. M. Flint
	Pastorale Blue Stocking	B	27–8–27	Ch. Lucky Prince	Alice of Barnego	Miss A. Tireman	A. Howell
	Thamara	B	30–9–29	Ch. Wall-eyed Bill	Glittering Cascade	W. N. Tod	Mrs I. Tod
	Tommy Tittlemouse of Pastorale	D	19–3–28	Ch. Faithful Tramp	River Girl	Owner	Miss A. Tireman
1931	Highroad Robbery	D	10–10–26	Ch. Faithful Tramp	Dulverton Danegeld	Owner	Miss V. Croft
	Southridge Ida	B	2–3–29	Hammerwood Jolly Roger	Nancy	Owners 1.	1. Messrs G. Sim & R. Cornelius 2. Miss C. Ashford
	Southridge Roger	D	2–3–29	Hammerwood Jolly Roger	Nancy	Owners 1.	Messrs G. Sim & R. Cornelius 2. H. A. Tilley
	Trumpeter Trundle	D	2–1–28	Brisk Weather	Old Raggy	Owner	D. J. Bowyer
1932	Courtesy	D	16–9–29	Ch. Aristocrat	Mary Ann	Owners	Mr & Mrs Sanders
	Mistress Petticoats of Pastorale	B	5–3–30	Ch. Beara Leader	Biddy the Tramp	Miss C. Ashford & Owner	Flt. Lt. H. B. Pett

Year	Name	Sex	Date of Birth	Sire	Dam	Breeder	Owner
1933	Stoney Broke	D	7–10–29	Ch. Happy Go Lucky	Ch. Spare a Penny	Mrs I. Tod	Mrs M. Keith-Gibson
	Mistress Flash of Pastorale	B	15–12–30	Ch. Beara Leader	Pastorale Pride of the Morning	Misses Tireman & Taylor	Capt. S. E. Bower
	Pensford Autocrat (late Autocrat)	D	16–9–29	Ch. Aristocrat	Mary Ann	Owners	Mr & Mrs F. Sanders
1934	Colin	D	16–1–28	Careful Jim	Margaret	Owner	Mrs M. Bradford
	Hammerwood Honeybee	B	17–10–29	Hammerwood Jolly Roger	Hammerwood Honeysuckle	Owner 2.	1. Miss M. Tucker 2. Miss C. Ashford
	Lady Flirt of Pickhurst	B	16–10–31	Wadhurst Bobby of Pastorale	Peggy Ann of Pickhurst	Owner	T. E. T. Shanks
	Pride of Pickhurst	D	16–10–31	Wadhurst Bobby of Pastorale	Peggy Ann of Pickhurst	T. E. T. Shanks	H. A. Williams Jnr
	Rag Tag of Pickhurst	D	16–10–31	Wadhurst Bobby of Pastorale	Peggy Ann of Pickhurst	Owner	T. E. T. Shanks
	Sally of Pickhurst	B	16–7–30	Ch. Beara Leader	Lady Peg of Pastorale	Miss F. White	T. E. T. Shanks
1935	Bobs Son of Pickhurst	D	17–5–33	Wadhurst Bobby of Pastorale	Peggy Ann of Pickhurst	Owner	T. E. T. Shanks

						Owners	
Chieftain of Bewkes		D	1–5–28	Hammerwood Jolly Roger	Rani of Bewkes	Owners	Misses H. Smailes & H. Knight-Bruce
Hammerwood Hurly Burly		D	30–8–32	Ch. Tommy Tittlemouse of Pastorale	Ch. Hammerwood Honeybee	Owner	Miss C. Ashford
Khydel Lassie		B	12–3–31	Tenet Hengist	Noonday Bess	Owner	Mrs M. Bradford
Saucy Girl of Pickhurst		B	16–10–31	Wadhurst Bobby of Pastorale	Peggy Ann of Pickhurst	Owner	T. E. T. Shanks
Sweetheart		B	1–1–32	Ch. Courtesy	Hayes Lady	Miss N. Brooks	Mrs F. Gatehouse
Dolly Dimple of Pickhurst	1936	B	16–10–31	Wadhurst Bobby of Pastorale	Peggy Ann of Pickhurst	Owner	T. E. T. Shanks
Mistress Flounce of Pastorale		B	19–7–33	Ch. Tommy Tittlemouse of Pastorale	Ch. Mistress Petticoats of Pastorale	Flt. Lt. H. B. Pett	Capt. S. Bower
Pastorale Mistress of Fullson		B	19–7–33	Ch. Tommy Tittlemouse of Pastorale	Ch. Mistress Petticoats of Pastorale	Flt. Lt. H. B. Pett	Mrs W. Harcourt-Brigden
Piccolo Pete of Pickhurst		D	28–7–33	Ch. Rag Tag of Pickhurst	Pat of Pickhurst	owner	Mrs H. Shanks
Plucky Peter		D	4–12–32	Ch. Hillgarth Blue Boy	Esmeralda	Owner	F. Lord

Year	Name	Sex	Date of Birth	Sire	Dam	Breeder	Owner
	Wake of Bewkes	B	17–7–32	Celandine of Pastorale	Mistress Jennifer of Pastorale	W. C. Clacksfield	Misses H. Smailes and H. Knight-Bruce
1937	Bouncer of Pickhurst	D	17–5–33	Wadhurst Bobby of Pastorale	Peggy Ann of Pickhurst	T. E. T. Shanks	Mrs A. D'Arcy Thompson
	Shepton Dolly Grey	B	14–1–35	Ch. Southridge Roger	Pensford Blue Mist	Mr & Mrs Sanders	H. A. Tilley
	Thyrza	B	10–9–32	Samson of Eskgrove	Jess Sanstail	D. N. Ure	Miss B. Davidson
	Watchers Watermark	D	1–5–35	Ch. Hammerwood Hurly Burly	Beara Shepherdess	Owner	Miss M. Tucker
1938	Hammerwood Halcyon (late Pastorale Grey Shadow)	B	7–7–36	Ch. Hammerwood Hurly Burly	Mistress	Miss A. Tireman	Miss C. Ashford
	Imitation	D	2–4–35	Ch. Wall-eyed Bill	Penny Halfpenny	F. Chapman	J. Ramsay
	Perfect Lady	B	9–7–36	Ch. Hammerwood Hurly Burly	Ch. Mistress Flash of Pastorale	Owner	Capt. S. Bower
	Sally Ann	B	16–1–35	Shaggy Shoes of Pastorale	Mistress Alison of Pastorale	Owner	A. C. Brown
	Sir John Marksman	D	26–2–35	Tit Willow of Pastorale	Blue Coquette	Owner	Miss I. Webster

Year	Name	Sex	Date	Sire	Dam		
1939	Tom Noddy of Pastorale	D	7-7-36	Ch. Hammerwood Burly Burly	Mistress Prudence of Pastorale	Owner	Miss A. Tireman
	Dinah of Woodburn	B	24-11-34	Ch. Southridge Roger	Lady Pamela	Rev. W. Buchanan	Miss I. Nichol
	The Ladye of Fullson	B	4-12-37	Ch. Tom Noddy of Pastorale	Ch. Pastorale Mistress of Fullson	Owner	Mrs W. Harcourt-Brigden
	Pastorale Dame of Fullson	B	7-7-36	Ch. Hammerwood Hurly Burly	Mistress Prudence of Pastorale	Miss A. Tireman	Mrs W. Harcourt-Brigden
	Silent Leader	D	30-1-37	Ch. Plucky Peter	Miranda	Owner	F. Lord
1940	Nil						
1941	Nil						
1942	Nil						
1943	Nil						
1944	Nil						
1945	Nil						
1946	Nil						
1947	Shepton Home Guard	D	11-10-43	Nosey Parker of Pickhurst	Snowwhite of Pickhurst	Mrs Shanks	H. Tilley
	Bashurst Sally Ann of Pickhurst	B	6-5-44	Nosey Parker of Pickhurst	Snowwhite of Pickhurst	Mrs Shanks	Mrs P. V. Maidment

Year	Name	Sex	Date of Birth	Sire	Dam	Breeder	Owner
1948	Shepton Surf King	D	4-8-46	Boldwood Bombardier	Boldwood Bustle	Mrs Grillett	H. A. & H. A. F. Tilley
	Watchers Bobs Son	D	11-1-46	Watchers Warrant	Watchers Grey Dawn	Owner	Miss M. Tucker
	Watchers Boulgehall Toby	D	11-1-46	Watchers Warrant	Watchers Grey Dawn	Owner	Miss M. Tucker
	Dreamer of Northmarsh	B	6-8-45	Don of Northmarsh	Lady Butcher	Owners	Mr & Mrs Hartland
	Shepton Perfect Picture	B	11-10-43	Nosey Parker of Pickhurst	Snowwhite of Pickhurst	Mrs Shanks	H. A. & H. A. F. Tilley
1949	Shepton Sonny Boy of Marlay (formerly Marlay Top Dog)	D	20-9-46	Beau Brigand of Marlay	Comedy Starlight	Mrs H. Booth	1. Miss Tilley 2. Mrs L. Jones
	Bashurst Polly Flinders	B	28-6-46	Ch. Sir John Marksman	Lady Audrey of Warridge	Owner	Mrs P. V. Maidment
1950	Hillgarth Blue Commander	D	7-6-47	Saffwalden Eskgrove Bushy	Pastelblue Top Notcher	Miss Davidson	Mrs Sheffield, later Mr Brocklesby
	Shepton Indomitable	D	5-8-48	Ch. Shepton Surf King	Ch. Shepton Perfect Picture	H. A. & H. A. F. Tilley	Mr & Mrs Howells

	Name		Date	Sire	Dam	Breeder	Owner
	Perrywood Blue Charm	B	8–8–48	Ch. Shepton Sonny Boy of Marlay	Perrywood Lady Linda of Yasabel	Mrs L. M. Jones	Mrs W. Randell
	Shepton Peggy's Pet	B	18–9–47	Ch. Shepton Home Guard	Monarch Sunshine	F. C. Padfield	C. Abbott
	Shepton Sincerity	B	4–8–46	Boldwood Bombardier	Boldwood Bustle	Mrs W. Grillett	A. Uttley & Miss E. Hulme
	Watchers Shepherdess	B	11–1–46	Watchers Warrant	Watchers Grey Dawn	Owner	Miss Tucker
1951	Perrywood Shepherd Boy	D	8–6–48	Ch. Shepton Sonny Boy of Marlay	Lady Diamond of Warridge	Miss C. F. Workman	Mrs McLellan
	Gordale Blue Lady	B	10–11–48	Watchers Grey Monarch	Jill of the Hills	Mrs P. Davies	C. J. Stacey
	Shepton Lovely Memory	B	5–8–48	Ch. Shepton Surf King	Ch. Shepton Perfect Picture	H. A. & H. A. F. Tilley	Mrs W. Randell
	Boldwood Berengaria	B	18–3–47	The Sword of Pastorale	Boldwood Blossom	R. F. Matthews	Mrs W. Grillett
1952	Kentish Man	D	4–4–49	Gay Lad of Pickhurst	Pastelblue Showlady	Owner	Mrs S. Talbot
	Paul of Squarefour	D	9–11–48	Shepton Brave Boy	Prudence of Squarefour	Owner	Mrs I. C. Nicol
	Shepton Prince Charles	D	5–8–48	Ch. Shepton Surf King	Ch. Shepton Perfect Picture	Owners	H. A. & H. A. F. Tilley

Year	Name	Sex	Date of Birth	Sire	Dam	Breeder	Owner
	Drybrook Forerunner	B	12–9–50	Drybrook Danny Boy	Duchess of Drybrook	Mr & Mrs Elston	G. Self
1953	Shepton Pearlstone Precious Gem	B	12–4–50	Ch. Watchers Bobs Son	Shepton Precious Pearleen	Miss P. M. Peart	H. A. & H. A. F. Tilley
1954	Bridewell Major	D	20–10–51	Ch. Shepton Sonny Boy of Marlay	Ch. Shepton Lovely Memory	Owner	Mrs W. Randell
	Bridewell Likeable Miss	B	20–10–51	Ch. Shepton Sonny Boy of Marlay	Ch. Shepton Lovely Memory	Owner	Mrs W. Randell
	Pastelblue Carol Ann	B	14–1–50	Pastelblue Sir John	Cobbydale Periwinkle	Miss I. Webster	Mr & Mrs A. G. Wilkinson
	Perrywood Maid Marion	B	15–6–50	Ch. Shepton Sonny Boy of Marlay	Daybreak of Shirehall	Miss D. Castello	Mrs W. Edsforth
	Watchers Butterfly	B	15–5–51	Gay Lad of Pickhurst	Watchers Sweetbriar	Miss M. Tucker	Mrs S. Talbot
1955	Beckington Tom Tod	D	13–7–52	Shepton Celebrity	Shepton Charming	Owner	Mrs M. Keith Gibson
	Roderick of Squarefour	D	22–11–52	Gordale Grey Guardsman	Priscilla of Squarefour	Owner	Mrs I. Nicol
	Reculver Sally Ann	B	22–12–52	Pastelblue Sir John	Fridays Beautiful Dream	Mr & Mrs A. G. Wilkinson	Mrs W. T. Rickards

Year	Name	Sex	Date	Sire	Dam	Breeder	Owner
1956	Shepton Grey Monk	D	27–6–49	Saffwalden Eskgrove Bushy	Pride of Yeldhams	H. Lindsell Clark	A. V. Sharpe
	Lady Blue of Grendonfell	B	30–3–51	Sir Milo of Grendonfell	Newlodge Lassie	A. R. King	Mrs I. Cooke
	Linnifold Mischief	B	30–9–51	Ch. Watchers Bobs Son	Shepton Lovely Souvenir	Mr & Mrs J. S. Mason	Mrs J. R. Gould
	Shepton Rowena of Squarefour	B	22–11–52	Gordale Grey Guardsman	Priscilla of Squarefour	Mrs I. C. Nicol	H. A. & H. A. F. Tilley
1957	Perrywood Old Faithful	D	6–9–51	Ch. Shepton Sonny Boy of Marlay	Perrywood Lady Mary	Mrs L. M. Jones	Mrs J. McLellan
	Perrywood Sonny Boy	D	18–1–52	Prince Willow of Lyneal	Perrywood Sun Bonnet	Mrs L. M. Jones	Mr F. Brocklesby
	Reculver Sugar Bush	B	20–12–54	Julian of Bewkes	Ch. Pastelblue Carol Ann	Owners	Mr & Mrs A. G. Wilkinson
	Talmoras Mary Tudor	B	25–4–55	Ch. Kentish Man	Ch. Watchers Butterfly	Owner	Mrs S. Talbot
1958	Oberon of Grendonfell	D	23–7–53	Ch. Kentish Man	Ch. Lady Blue of Grendonfell	Mrs I. F. Cooke	A. E. Mason
	Perrywood Bonny Boy	D	6–9–51	Ch. Shepton Sonny Boy of Marlay	Perrywood Lady Mary	Mrs L. M. Jones	Mrs E. D. Hallett
	Shepton Field Marshall	D	6–11–55	Shepton Wonder	Pastelblue Pantallettes	Mrs E. Storey	Miss K. Roussell

Year	Name	Sex	Date of Birth	Sire	Dam	Breeder	Owner
	Beckington Lady of Welbyhouse	B	22–8–55	Shepton Bridewell Brave Brigadier	Shepton Butterfly	H. & R. Houghton	Mrs M. Keith Gibson
1959	Nil						
1960	Fairacres Bosun	D	27–12–55	Fairacres Commander	Ingestre Tiptoes	Mrs E. M. Bloor	Mr A. B. Little
	Fernville Fernando	D	14–1–58	Nero of Hardwickings	Shepton Silver Wendy	Mrs B. A. Fox	N. W. R. Harrison
	Rosalinda of Squarefour	B	22–11–52	Gordale Grey Guardsman	Priscilla of Squarefour	Owner	Mrs I. C. Nicol
1961	Beanville Silver Count	D	13–10–57	Ch. Roderick of Squarefour	Amberford Aclea	Miss V. Keeling	Mrs M. Mottram
	Thor of Dalcroy	D	6–9–56	Fairacres Commander	Weirwood Shepherds Joy	Owner	Mrs A. McGill (née Lloyd)
	Reculver Penelope Jane	B	6–8–58	Julian of Bewkes	Ch. Pastelblue Carol Ann	Mr & Mrs A. G. Wilkinson	Mrs K. A. Hudson
1962	Beanville Silver King	D	13–10–57	Ch. Roderick of Squarefour	Amberford Aclea	Miss V. Keeling	Mrs I. C. Nicol
	Blue Brigand of Tansley	D	9–3–58	Daphnis Fearless	Silver Bell of Tansley	Mrs E. Goodwin	1. F. Brocklesby 2. J. F. Boleyn

	Name	Sex	Date	Sire	Dam	Breeder	Owner
	Jane of Knockanlyn	B	10–12–56	Ch. Roderick of Squarefour	Pastelblue Silver Jewel	Owner	Mrs J. A. Muirhead
1963	Reculver Christopher Robin	D	22–6–61	Nicefella of Danehurst	Ch. Reculver Sugar Bush	Owners	Mr & Mrs A. G. Wilkinson
	Fernville Fantasy	B	1–4–61	Ch. Fernville Fernando	Fernville Flora	Mrs B. A. Fox	N. W. R. Harrison
	Rollingsea Starlight	B	11–6–58	Greystoke Gem	Broadwell Rosy Dawn	J. Wasley	Mrs J. R. Gould
1964	Beckington Fernville Flamingo	D	6–1–62	Ch. Fernville Fernando	Fernville Fiona	N. W. R. Harrison	Mrs M. Keith Gibson
	Fernville Flanagan	D	12–5–61	Ch. Fernville Fernando	Fernville Fascination	N. W. R. Harrison	Mr & Mrs M. Smith
	Rollingsea Ringleader	D	9–2–60	Rollingsea Surfrider	Ch. Rollingsea Starlight	Mrs J. R. Gould	Mr & Mrs S. E. Fisher
	Teddy Boy of Tansley	D	7–8–59	Daphnis Fearless	Miss Pam of Tansley	Mrs E. Goodwin	J. F. Boleyn
	Blue Glamour Girl	B	23–6–58	Newcote William	Sally Blue Mist	Owner	Mrs I. Lawson
	Rayvil Rosalinda	B	16–6–59	Nero of Hardwickings	Shepton Silver Wendy	Mrs B. Fox	Mr & Mrs M. Smith
1965	Bevere Proud Monarch	D	15–8–63	Baucottblues Boy	Blue Chiffon	Owner	Mrs E. M. Foster
	Prospectblue Bulk	D	8–8–63	Eng. & Scand. Ch. Prospect Shaggy Boy	Farleydene Peggotty	Mrs I. Lawson	1. J. R. Andrews 2. Mrs D. Sly

Year	Name	Sex	Date of Birth	Sire	Dam	Breeder	Owner
	Bess of Coldharbour	B	25–10–59	Reculver Son of Carol	Sally Blue Mist	Mrs I. Lawson	Mrs B. Tidley
	Reculver Little Rascal	B	22–6–61	Nicefella of Danehurst	Ch. Reculver Sugar Bush	Mr & Mrs A. G. Wilkinson	1. Mr P. Gardner 2. Mrs Ann Davis
	Wrightways Glorious Day	B	22–6–61	Ch. Rollingsea Ringleader	Amberford Cwoen	Owner	Mrs M. E. Fisher
1966	Bevere Stalwart	D	29–10–64	Baucottblues Boy	Blue Chiffon	Mrs E. M. Foster	R. J. MacKinnon
	Prospect Shaggy Boy	D	10–5–61	Ch. Blue Brigand of Tansley	Ch. Blue Glamour Girl	Mrs Lawson	1. Mrs Lawson 2. Caj Haakansson
	Bluecrest Carousel	B	22–8–61	Reculver Hurley Burly	Shepton Katrina	Owner	Miss G. Scribbins
	Bumblebarn Holloways Homespun	B	28–12–63	Farleydene Reculver King Pin	Holloways Penny Dreadful	Mrs J. Innocent	Mrs C. W. Pearce
	Boss of Duroya	D	6–3–63	Holloways Royalist of Duroya	Azure Queen of Duroya	Mrs A. Woodiwiss	W. Howarth
1967	Prospectblue Rodger	D	26–10–64	Eng. & Scand. Ch. Prospect shaggy Boy	Farleydene Peggotty	Mrs I. Lawson	1. Mrs I. Lawson 2. Mrs Berkowitz
	Rollingsea Snowboots	D	15–5–65	Rollingsea Surfrider	Ch. Rollingsea Starlight	Owner	Mrs J. R. Gould

	Name	Sex	Date	Sire	Dam	Breeder	Owner
	Barkaway Ambition	B	28-3-66	Ch. Bevere Proud Monarch	Fairacres Fair Exchange	Mrs E. M. Bloor	Mr & Mrs R. MacKinnon
	Bumblebarn Bluejeans	B	29-10-64	Shepton Holloways Benjamin	Faithful Tramp	Mrs A. Maidment	Mrs C. W. Pearce
1968	Oakhill Peter Pan	D	11-1-66	Ch. Bevere Proud Monarch	Beth of Oakhill	Mrs M. Hargreaves	Mr & Mrs R. Ashcroft
	Sukray Statesman	D	6-12-64	Ch. Fernville Fernando	Prospectblue Haze	R. Stretton	Mr & Mrs Westwell
	Prospectblue Cindy	B	26-10-64	Ch. Prospect Shaggy Boy	Farleydene Peggotty	Mrs I. Lawson	M. Garnett
	Shepton Pick of the Bunch	B	15-2-65	Rusherman	Gittisham Minx	F. Bussell	J. Featherstone
	Viento Sceaphirde Rhapsody in Blue	B	17-5-65	Baucottblues Boy	Knotting Silver Rippel	Mrs B. John	Mr & Mrs Wallis
1969	Pendlefold Prince Hal	D	1-8-67	Ch. Oakhill Peter Pan	Smokey Jane of Nelson	C. Riddiough	Mr & Mrs C. Riddiough
	Wrightway Blue Mantle	D	18-5-66	Eng. & Am. Ch. Prospectblue Rodger	Ch. Wrightways Glorious Day	Mr & Mrs S. Fisher	I. Morrison
	Bumblebarn Paddys Pride	B	21-8-66	Ch. Rollingsea	Ch. Bumblebarn Holloways Snowboots Homespun	Mrs C. W. Pearce	G. Cherry
	Farleydene Fezziwig	B	23-12-66	Farleydene Dombey	Fernville Francesca	G. Gooch	Mesdames Tingle & Masterson

Year	Name	Sex	Date of Birth	Sire	Dam	Breeder	Owner
	Hyal Pennys Pride	B	20–11–65	Baucottblues Boy	Roycroft Penny	Owner	Mrs M. E. Ince
	Prospectblue Twotrees Arrabella	B	23–11–66	Ch. Rollingsea Snowboots	Prospectblue Louise	Mrs G. Little	Mrs I. Lawson
1970	Shepton Happy Go Lucky	D	18–8–66	Baucottblues Boy	Faithful Tramp	Mrs Maidment	Mrs J. M. Shuard
	Wrightways Char-maine	B	18–5–66	Eng. & Am. Ch. Prospectblue Rodger	Ch. Wrightways Glorious Day	Owners	Mr & Mrs S. Fisher
	Gwehelog Welsh Maid	B	2–9–67	Gwehelog Welsh Tammie	Gwehelog Welsh Melody	Owner	Mrs B. Tidley
1971	Twotrees Break O'Day	B	14–5–67	Am. & Eng. Ch. Prospectblue Rodger	Rollingsea Sunbeam	A. W. Little	James Lynn
	Rollingsea Twotrees Aurora	B	23–11–66	Ch. Rollingsea Snowboots	Prospectblue Louise	Mrs G. Little	Mrs J. Gould
	Barnolby Mr. Barrymore	D	20–9–68	Ch. Oakhill Peter Pan	Barnolby Eastertide	Owners	Mr & Mrs R. Ashcroft
	Bumblebarn Ragamuffin	B	25–3–69	Somerstreet Chieftain	Ch. Bumblebarn Holloways Homespun	Owner	Mrs C. W. Pearce
	Pendlefold Sweet Charity of Cinderwood	B	18–7–69	Ch. Oakhill Peter Pan	Smokey Jane of Nelson	Mr C. Riddiough	Messrs M. Banks & H. Bentley

1972	Lameda Pandora Blossom	B	18–10–67	Bruce Faithful Master	Amanda Faithful Lady	K. Rallison	Messrs J. P. Smith & S. J. Mallard
	Tynycoed Ty Gwyn	D	18–1–70	Wenallt Masked Man	Beckington Blue Rhapsody	Mrs J. Real	Mr W. S. Real
	Nan of the Embages	B	14–7–65	Ch. Reculver Christopher Robin	Bess of the Embages	Owner	Miss D. E. A. Malins
	Hyal Pastimes Panspal	D	12–6–70	Ch. Oakhill Peter Pan	Hyal Pennys Pastime	Owner	Mrs M. E. Ince
1972	Shaggyshire Bumblebarn Caesar	D	25–3–69	Somerstreet	Ch. Bumblebarn Holloways Chieftain Homespun	Mrs C. W. Pearce	Mrs M. B. Fisher
	Cornelia of Trimtora	B	25–9–69	Fairacres Rollalong	Tina of Trimtora	Mr & Mrs R. Marriott	Mrs R. Wilkinson
	Mosscarr River Girl	B	21–12–67	Ch. Boss of Duroya	Sheba of Mosscarr	Mrs L. Ingham	Mr & Miss D. Brocklesby
	Barkaway Tattie Bogal	D	27–11–67	Ch. Bevere Stalwart	Brownswall Annabella	Mr King	Mr & Mrs K. L. E. Davis
	Fernville Lord Digby	D	1–7–70	Fernville Raydor Blue Boy	Fernville Merry Widow	Owner	N. W. R. Harrison
	Barnolby Snowdrift	B	9–3–69	Ch. Cakhill Peter Pan	Marlay Shepherds Song	Mr & Mrs R. Ashcroft	Mrs G. Chambers

Year	Name	Sex	Date of Birth	Sire	Dam	Breeder	Owner
1973	Snowserf Lancer of Barnolby	D	20-7-69	Ch. Oakhill Peter Pan	Miss Bruin of Halsall	Mr & Mrs R. Ashcroft	Mr & Mrs D. C. Bloomfield
	Lameda Lucy Locket	B	10-9-70	Ch. Wrightway Blue Mantle	Lena of Lingar	Mr T. Pettitt	Messrs J. P. Smith & S. J. Mallard
	Silverstone of Abbeywood	D	12-1-70	Oakhill Thundercloud	Old Tyme of Halsall	Miss M. E. Dawson	Mr & Mrs H. Smellie
	Twotrees Loakespark Tosca	B	19-8-68	Somerstreet Chieftain	Fernville Debutante	Mrs A. Davis	Mrs G. E. Little
	Rollingsea Viceroy	D	4-8-69	Rollingsea Hawthorn Pride	Ch. Rollingsea Twotrees Aurora	Owner	Mrs J. Gould
	Lomax of Lingar	D	17-11-69	Ch. Barnolby Mr Barrymore	Blue Mist of Ramnee	Mr G. P. Mitchell	Miss N. Fielding
	Barnolby Wendy Bruin	B	17-8-70	Ch. Oakhill Peter Pan	Miss Bruin of Halsall	Owners	Mr & Mrs R. Ashcroft
	Rollingsea Venus	B	4-8-69	Rollingsea Hawthorn Pride	Ch. Rollingsea Twotrees Aurora	Owner	Mrs J. Gould
	Summers Grace of Dalcroy	B	29-7-70	Raydor Bundle	Pandora of Dalcroy	Owner	Mrs A. McGill
	Lameda Pearly Princess	B	14-10-70	Ch. Pendlefold Prince Hal	Lameda Pearly Queen	Owners	Messrs J. P. Smith & S. J. Mallard

1974	Paddington Bear of Gower	D	13–10–71	Gwehelog Welsh Tammie	Mistyblue Lady	Mrs C. A. Walkey	Mrs G. Chambers
	Roncott Blue Belle	B	9–2–71	Dougal Cosy Corner	Jolliver Prudence	Miss R. L. Norcott	Miss S. McCartney
	Bluwalder Lady Syringa	B	10–9–71	Champion Wrightway Blue Mantle	Tzandora Easter Bee	Owner	Mrs W. Farrer
	Wenallt Trooper	D	5–6–69	Wenallt Farmers Boy	Arabella of the Embages	Owner	Mrs P. M. Jones
	Aberfells Georgey Porgey	D	3–5–72	Barnolby Midwinter	Aberfells Cindy Lou	Mrs J. McCunnall	Mrs S. Curd
	Whitevale Christmas Knight	D	16–12–71	Master of Chadsley	Blumark Bluelens	Mr & Mrs W. H. Chadwick	Mr & Mrs D. Kilpatrick
	Lameda Perfect Pal	D	4–8–69	Somerstreet Chieftain	Bobbycroft Majestic Moonbeam	G. Maidment	Messrs J. P. Smith & S. J. Mallard
1975	Meadowblue Homeward Bound	D	5–7–71	Barnolby Present Hope	Meadowblue Nancy	Mrs M. Meades	Mesdames White & Evans
	Lameda Midnight Rebel	B	9–7–72	Lameda Mr. Kipps	Andrews Delight	Messrs J. P. Smith & S. J. Mallard	Messrs J. P. Smith & S. J. Mallard & Mr & Mrs D. J. Moir
	Pockethall New Shoes	D	31–10–72	Ch. Shaggyshire Bumblebarn Caesar	Ch. Cornelia of Trimtora	Owner	Mrs R. Wilkinson
	Beowulf Silver Fizz	B	21–6–71	Barnolby Present Hope	Mosscarrs Morning Mist	Mr & Mrs P. Cooper	Mrs M. C. Hodgson

Year	Name	Sex	Date of Birth	Sire	Dam	Breeder	Owner
	Tynycoed Pen-y-Bryn of Southview	D	18–12–72	Ch. Pendlefold Prince Hal	Tynycoed Merch Dda	Mrs J. Real	Mr & Mrs R. A. R. Cowie
	Follyfoot of Shepton and Longdorham	B	4–12–72	Wonder Boy of Shepton	Arabella of The Embages	Mrs P. M. Jones	Mrs M. & Miss S. Duffin
	Fernville Special Style of Trushayp	D	22–5–73	Ch. Fernville Lord Digby	Fernville Gypsy Madonna	N. W. R. Harrison	Mr & Mrs M. Lewis
	Little Princess Pearl	B	3–9–72	Shepton Martini	Oborne Silver Lace	J. Ham	Mrs L. Cross
	Bumblebarn New Penny	B	2–4–71	Ch. Lameda Perfect Pal	Ch. Bumblebarn Blue Jeans	Mrs C. Pearce	Mr & Mrs P. Cooper
1976	Dorianblue Shepherd Boy	D	8–1–71	Gwehelog Bess's Nosdda	Blue Rapture	Mrs Cousins	1. P. A. Instone 2. Mrs & Miss Duffin
	Ginnsdale Stargazer Blue of Barnolby	D	19–10–72	Jason Marcos Ginn Junior	Saucy Paw Sheba	Mr & Mrs Ginns	Mr & Mrs Ashcroft
	Mr Bluedan of the Embages	D	28–9–73	Foxtwist Mr Jumbo	Blueberry of the Embages	Miss D. Malins	Mr & Mrs Hartland
	Arlils Cilla of Southview	B	2–9–72	Ch. Meadowblue Homeward Bound	Arlils May Blossom	Mrs White & Evans	Mr & Mrs Cowie
	Tynycoed Merch Lisi Fisi	B	9–10–73	Ch. Dorianblue Shepherd Boy	Baucott Blues Busy Lizzie	Owner	Mrs J. Real

	Name	Sex	Date	Sire	Dam	Breeder	Owner
	Wenallt Emerald	B	29–12–72	Ch. Wenallt Trooper	Twotrees Esmeralda	Mrs Jones	Mr & Mrs Underwood
	Sincerity of Barnolby	B	21–4–73	Barnolby Midwinter	Barnolby My Honey	Mr & Mrs J. Hammersley	Mr & Mrs Ashcroft
	Rollingsea Christobelle	B	18–12–73	Ch. Rollingsea Viceroy	Ch. Rollingsea Venus	Owner	Mrs J. Gould
1977	Bartines Most Happy Fella of Jenards	D	12–10–74	Ch. Fernville Lord Digby	Bartines Precious Holly	Mrs C. Siddall	Mr & Mrs Baker
	Sensation of Shepton	D	27–8–73	Kinlockmore Buster	Shepton Miss Rascal	Mrs H. Jones	Miss F. Tilley
	Wenallt Andrew	D	13–8–73	Ch. Oakhill Peter Pan	Wenallt Wensday	Owner	Mrs P. M. Jones
	Cinderwood by Jupiter of Craigsea	D	22–9–73	Ch. Lomax of Lingar	Barnolby Cinderella	Messrs Banks & Bentley	Mrs E. Horner
	Cinderwood Great Gatsby of Bartines	D	16–8–74	Ch. Aberfells Georgey Porgey	Ch. Pendleford Sweet Charity of Cinderwood	Messrs Banks & Bentley	Mrs C. Siddall
	Morgans Lady of Amethyst	B	3–10–73	Bobbingay Plainsman of Amblegait	Mosscars Silver Lace	Mrs P. Kelsey	Mrs Tomes
	Krisina Magic Moments in Jedforest	B	5–11–74	Ch. Barkaway Tattie Bogal	Krisina Miss Jessie	Mr & Mrs Underwood	Mrs Collins
	Pockethall Shoeshine of Southview	B	6–11–74	Ch. Pendlefold Prince Hal	Ch. Cornelia of Trimtora	Mrs R. Wilkinson	Mr & Mrs Cowie

Year	Name	Sex	Date of Birth	Sire	Dam	Breeder	Owner
	Pockethall Silver Shoes	B	6–11–74	Ch. Pendlefold Prince Hal	Ch. Cornelia of Trimtora	Owner	Mrs R. Wilkinson
	Tynycoed Bor-O-Waunwyn	B	8–4–74	Ch. Tynycoed Ty Gwyn	Tynycoed Mair Fach	Mrs Parker	Mr & Mrs G. Swanson
1978	Monoval Legion Knight	D	14–11–71	Ch. Tynycoed Ty Gwyn	Somerstreet Charmer	Owners	Mrs & Miss Rampton
	Pockethall Blue Cloud	D	6–11–74	Ch. Pendlefold Prince Hal	Ch. Cornelia of Trimtora	Mrs Wilkinson	Mr & Mrs Wilkinson
	Brithdirs Lady Burry	B	11–12–72	Lynces Blue Monarch	Peggotty of the Embages	D. Little	1. Mrs J. Woodford 2. Mrs G. Mogford
	Melody of Fairacres	B	14–1–76	Ch. Pockethall New Shoes	Fairacres Blue Belle	Mrs P. Guest	Mrs E. Bloor
	Southview Society Miss	B	6–5–75	Ch. Tynycoed Pen Y Bryn of Southview	Tynycoed Llygad Y Dydd	Owners	Mr & Mrs Cowie
	Tagalong Overshadowin	B	22–9–75	Wildahar Lynces Blue Diamond	Hightop Misty	Owner	Mrs Eade
	Wishful of Pockethall	B	21–7–74	Pockethall Shanandoah	Fell Gay Lady	F. Austen	Mrs Wilkinson
	Winstonholme Memorys of Oldoak	B	17–8–74	Ch. Lomax of Lingar	Drakeshead Redscare Lady Jayne	Miss N. Fielding	Mrs D. Oakes

1979	Barnolby White Bear	B	27-2-74	Ch. Aberfells Georgey Porgey	Ch. Barnolby Wendy Bruin	Owners	Mr & Mrs Ashcroft
	Branduin Cotton Picker	D	28-5-76	Ch. Aberfells Georgey Porgey	Sireva Blue Beauty of Branduin	Owners	Mr & Mrs Hodgson
	Jemsue Just Jessica	B	5-4-76	Ch. Pockethall New Shoes	Arjems Lady Molly	Owners	Mr & Mrs Swatkins
	Keyingham Double Daisy	B	20-3-77	Ch. Ginnsdale Stargazer Blue of Barnolby	Halsall Brooklyn at Keyingham	Owner	Mrs M. Park
	Lady Milly of Lamacres	B	29-7-75	Ch. Snowserf Lancer of Barnolby	Venator Elixir	Mrs P. Birkett	Mrs P. Guest
	Snowfall Gentle Ben of Marleigh	D	27-7-75	Ch. Aberfells Georgey Porgey	Waterhead Lady Sarah	Mrs Freeman	Mrs M. Fraser
	Splendael Sunday Best	B	23-11-75	Ch. Pockethall New Shoes	Underhill Lady Jane	Owners	Mr & Mrs Fletcher
	Tinkerbelle of Prospectblue	B	12-5-76	Danum Blue Commander	Blue Morn	S. Jackson	Mrs I. Lawson
	Trushayp Special Edition	D	21-1-76	Ch. Fernville Special Style of Trushayp	Lady Amber	Owner	Mr & Mrs M. Lewis

Index

Index

Index